# ROMMEL

# ROMMEL

*A Reappraisal*

*Edited by*
IAN F.W. BECKETT

Pen & Sword
MILITARY

First published in Great Britain in 2013 by
Pen & Sword Military
an imprint of
Pen & Sword Books Ltd
47 Church Street
Barnsley
South Yorkshire
S70 2AS

Copyright © Ian F.W. Beckett and contributors, 2013

ISBN 978 1 78159 359 2

The right of Ian F.W. Beckett and contributors to be identified as the authors of this work has been asserted by them in accordance with the Copyright, Designs and Patents Act 1988.

A CIP catalogue record for this book is available from the British Library.

All rights reserved. No part of this book may be reproduced or transmitted in any form or by any means, electronic or mechanical including photocopying, recording or by any information storage and retrieval system, without permission from the Publisher in writing.

Typeset in Ehrhardt by Chic Graphics

Printed and bound in England
by CPI Group (UK) Ltd, Croydon, CR0 4YY

*Pen & Sword Books Ltd incorporates the imprints of*
Pen & Sword Aviation, Pen & Sword Maritime,
Pen & Sword Military, Pen & Sword Family History,
Wharncliffe Local History, Wharncliffe True Crime,
Wharncliffe Transport, Pen & Sword Discovery, Pen & Sword Select,
Pen & Sword Military Classics, Leo Cooper, Remember When,
The Praetorian Press, Seaforth Publishing and Frontline Publishing.

*For a complete list of Pen & Sword titles please contact*
PEN & SWORD BOOKS LIMITED
47 Church Street, Barnsley, South Yorkshire, S70 2AS, England
E-mail: enquiries@pen-and-sword.co.uk
Website: www.pen-and-sword.co.uk

# Contents

*List of Contributors* . . . . . . . . . . . . . . . . . . . . . . . . . . . . . . . . . . . vii

*Introduction – Ian F.W. Beckett*. . . . . . . . . . . . . . . . . . . . . . . . . . . 1

| | | |
|---|---|---|
| Chapter One | Rommel and the Rise of the Nazis<br>*Alaric Searle*. . . . . . . . . . . . . . . . . . . . . . . . . . . . 7 | |
| Chapter Two | Rommel and 1940<br>*Claus Telp* . . . . . . . . . . . . . . . . . . . . . . . . . . . 30 | |
| Chapter Three | Rommel in the Desert, 1941<br>*Niall Barr* . . . . . . . . . . . . . . . . . . . . . . . . . . . 60 | |
| Chapter Four | Rommel in the Desert, 1942<br>*Niall Barr* . . . . . . . . . . . . . . . . . . . . . . . . . . . 81 | |
| Chapter Five | Rommel in Normandy –<br>*Peter Lieb*. . . . . . . . . . . . . . . . . . . . . . . . . . . 113 | |
| Chapter Six | Rommel and the 20 July 1944 Bomb Plot<br>*Russell A. Hart*. . . . . . . . . . . . . . . . . . . . . . . 137 | |
| Chapter Seven | Rommel as Icon<br>*Mark Connelly* . . . . . . . . . . . . . . . . . . . . . . . 157 | |

*Bibliography* . . . . . . . . . . . . . . . . . . . . . . . . . . . . . . . . . . . . . . . . 179

*Index*. . . . . . . . . . . . . . . . . . . . . . . . . . . . . . . . . . . . . . . . . . . . . 180

# List of Contributors

Dr NIALL BARR is Senior Lecturer in Defence Studies at the Defence Studies Department, King's College, London, based at the Joint Services Command and Staff College, Watchfield. He has published widely on British military history including (with J.P. Harris), *Amiens to the Armistice* (Brasseys, 1998); *Pendulum of War: The Three Battles of El Alamein* (Cape, 2004) and *The Lion and the Poppy: British Veterans, Politics and Society 1921–1939* (Praeger, 2005).

Professor IAN BECKETT is Professor of Military History at the University of Kent. A Fellow of the Royal Historical Society, he is also Chairman of the Council of the Army Records Society. He has published widely on the First World War, British auxiliary forces, and the late Victorian Army. His most recent book is *The Making of the First World War* (Yale University Press, 2012).

Professor MARK CONNELLY is Professor of Modern British Military History at the University of Kent. He has published on both world wars, and on war and the media including *Steady the Buffs! A Regiment, A Region and the Great War* (Oxford University Press, 2006), *We Can Take It: Britain and the Memory of the Second World War* (Pearson/Longman, 2004) and, most recently (with Tim Bowman) *The Edwardian Army* (Oxford University Press, 2012).

Dr RUSSELL A. HART is Associate Professor of History and Chair of the Department of History at Hawai'i Pacific University, Honolulu. He has published widely on the Second World War, including *Clash of Arms: How the Allies Won in Normandy* (Lynne Rienner, 2001), and *Guderian: Panzer Pioneer or Mythmaker?* (Potomac, 2006).

Dr PETER LIEB is Senior Lecturer in War Studies at the Royal Military Academy, Sandhurst. He has particular interests in the

German Army on the Eastern Front in both world wars. His publications include *Konventioneller Krieg oder NS-Weltanschauungskrieg? Kriegführung und Partisanenbekämpfung in Frankreich 1943/44* (Oldenbourg Verlag, 2007); and (with Christian Hartmann et al.) *Der deutsche Krieg im Osten 1941–1944. Facetten einer Grenzüberschreitung* (Oldenbourg Verlag, 2009).

Dr ALARIC SEARLE is Reader in Military History and Director of the Centre for European Security at the University of Salford. A Fellow of the Royal Historical Society, he is also a member of the Executive Committee of the *ArbeitskreisMilitärgeschichte*, the leading scholarly military history society for German-speaking central Europe. As well as numerous journal articles and contributions to edited works, he is the author of *Wehrmacht Generals, West German Society, and the Debate on Rearmament, 1949–1959* (Praeger, 2003).

Dr CLAUS TELP is Senior Lecturer in War Studies at the Royal Military Academy, Sandhurst. He has interests in eighteenth-century warfare as well as the Second World War. He is the author of *The Evolution of Operational Art from Frederick the Great to Napoleon, 1740–1813* (Cass, 2005), and the commemorative booklet, *The Advance from the Seine to Antwerp* (MOD, 2005).

# Introduction

## Ian F.W. Beckett

Seventy years after the second battle of Alamein, the name of Erwin Rommel is still recognized in a Britain in which the popular knowledge of the events and personalities of the Second World War has steadily decreased among younger generations. 'Our friend Rommel', as the British commander-in-chief in the Middle East, Sir Claude Auchinleck, characterized him on one occasion, continues to enjoy a substantial military reputation. While he achieved much with often scant resources through dint of charismatic leadership, Rommel was not the military genius popularly portrayed and could be utterly reckless. As one German historian put it on the occasion of the twenty-fifth anniversary of Alamein, compared to a consummate director of large-scale operations such as Erich von Manstein, Rommel 'was just a commander with an impressive manner and a capacity to carry his troops with him by dramatic personal example'.[1]

In part, of course, much of Rommel's reputation also rests on the manner of his death, compelled to take poison on 14 October 1944 after being implicated in the unsuccessful 20 July 1944 bomb plot against Hitler. It elevated Rommel as a suitable model of soldierly honour for the reformed West German *Bundeswehr* after 1955, when those directly involved in the conspiracy were less satisfactory exemplars of military virtues in having attempted to kill their commander-in-chief. Paradoxically, Rommel's rise to higher command had been eased by his close identification with the Nazis. Cinema, too, added to Rommel's laurels with his sympathetic portrayal by James Mason in *The Desert Fox* in 1951, contrasting markedly with his wartime portrayal by Erich von Stroheim as a stock Nazi villain in *Five Graves to Cairo* in 1943.

Not surprisingly, Rommel has been the subject of many biographers with varying perspectives, beginning with the generally laudatory *Rommel* by Desmond Young in 1950, through to the more critical recent works by German authors, such as Maurice Remy's *Mythos Rommel* in 2002, and Ralf Georg Reuth's *Rommel: Das Ende einer Legende* in 2004. In part, they reflect the increasing amount of material that has become available to historians unearthing the story of an intriguing and complex figure worthy of deeper analysis. Accordingly, the essays in this volume seek to illuminate the real Rommel and his place in history.

Born in Heidenheim in Württemberg on 15 November 1891, Rommel was the son of a Swabian schoolmaster who died in 1913. Württemberg was one of the four constituent kingdoms of Imperial Germany with Bavaria, Saxony and Prussia. Technically, there was no single unified German Army until the creation of the *Reichsheer* in 1919 and, on 19 July 1910, Rommel joined the 124th Württemberg Infantry Regiment as a cadet. Passing on to the Imperial War School in Danzig in November 1911, he was commissioned as Second Lieutenant in the 124th Infantry Regiment in January 1912. Briefly posted to a field artillery regiment between March and July 1914, Rommel was back with his Württemberg unit when war broke out in August 1914. Initially serving in the Argonne, Rommel was badly wounded in the left thigh on 24 September 1914, being decorated with the Iron Cross (2nd Class). He returned to regimental duty in January 1915, being awarded the Iron Cross (1st Class) for a successful trench raid later that month. Promoted first lieutenant, Rommel joined the Württemberg *Gebirgsbataillon* (Mountain Battalion) at the end of September 1915 under the command of Major Theodore Sproesser. The Germany army was noted for its tactical innovation during the course of the war as a whole and, as suggested by its title, the Mountain Battalion was intended for specialist duties as a larger than usual battalion with its own integrated machine-gun companies, various detachments being capable of fighting as battle groups separated from the battalion as necessity dictated.

Deployed first in the Vosges and then in Romania, the battalion moved to the Italian front in September 1917. Rommel had again been wounded in August 1917 and rejoined the battalion in October, just in time for the German offensive at Caporetto that shattered the Italian Army. Commanding one of the battalion's battle groups, Rommel played a significant part in seizing the key Kolovrat Ridge on 25 October. To Rommel's chagrin much of the credit went to a Bavarian lieutenant,

Ferdinand Schoerner, who was rewarded with the Pour Le Mérite. Rommel next helped seize Monte Matajur on 26 October, though once more the credit was given to another officer. Rommel's relentless pursuit of the Italians across the River Tagliamento, however, culminating in the capture of over 8,000 Italian troops at Longarone on 9 November 1917, saw him finally rewarded with the much coveted Pour Le Mérite.[2] Rommel saw out the war attached to various staffs on the Western Front between January and December 1918.

Rommel's experiences were to form the basis of his 1937 book, *Infanterie greift an* (first translated into English in the United States as *Infantry Attacks* in 1944), which went through some twelve editions in the next seven years, earning Rommel substantial royalties and a high profile. It arose from Rommel's highly popular lectures following his appointment as an instructor to the Infantry School at Dresden in October 1929. Rommel had spent the intervening years on regimental duties at Stuttgart and, following his time at Dresden, took command of the 3rd/17th Infantry Battalion, a Jäger formation, at Goslar in October 1933. *Infanterie greift an* was a masterly tactical manual and was published during Rommel's subsequent tenure in the rank of lieutenant colonel as an instructor at the Potsdam *Kriegsschule*. By the time of its publication, moreover, Rommel had become known to the Nazis, meeting Hitler for the first time while still at Goslar. Rommel's links with the Nazis are examined by Alaric Searle, starting with those aspects of his early career which may have predisposed Rommel to view the movement with favour. Searle concludes that Rommel had already developed an aptitude for self-publicity, as demonstrated by the general tone of *Infanterie greift an*, and was somewhat in thrall to Hitler. In turn, Rommel became one of Hitler's favoured soldiers, his career effectively sponsored by him.

Having been appointed commandant of the Kriegsschule at Wiener Neustadt in November 1939, the now Major General Rommel was posted to command Hitler's personal bodyguard in August 1939. As shown by Claus Telp, although an infantryman Rommel was able to use his position to persuade Hitler to give him command of 7th Panzer Division in February 1940. Telp argues that Rommel proved a tactically competent divisional commander in the battle for France, not least in securing the surrender of the 51st Highland Division at Cherbourg on 12 June 1940. Only the British counter-attack at Arras on 21 May had caught him unawares. But Rommel's grasp of logistics was poor and his generally good judgement of risk was outweighed by his penchant for glory hunting.

On 15 February 1941 Rommel left 7th Panzer Division to assume command of German forces in Libya. The most celebrated phase of his career, extending to 1943, is examined in two chapters by Niall Barr. Rommel gained an extraordinary success in his first offensive in March 1941, the British forces having been weakened by the diversion of troops and resources to what was to become an ill-fated campaign in Greece. Rommel, however, had disobeyed the orders of the chief of the general staff in Berlin, Franz Halder, who was far from enamoured with his field commander. As in the 1940 campaign, Rommel displayed a low opinion of trained staff officers and was again disdainful of logistic realities. As Barr suggests, Rommel's first desert campaign failed to alter the strategic balance in the Middle East and his touch was distinctly lacking in his conduct of the defence against the British Eighth Army's Operation Crusader in November 1941. As Barr demonstrates, Rommel reached the peak of his success with the fall of Tobruk on 21 June 1942, his second desert offensive again having significant early success. By July 1942, however, further success for the Afrika Korps was unlikely, Auchinleck having blunted its efforts in the first battle of Alamein. Rommel was to lose his intelligence sources in the course of the next few months and Allied intelligence was increasing through the progressive breaking of German codes by Ultra. While a significant build-up of resources now assisted the Eighth Army under Montgomery in its preparations for the Alamein offensive, Berlin had ceased to treat North Africa as a serious theatre of operations. Once more Rommel had not grasped logistic realities. Rommel's own health was failing and he was absent in Germany when the Alamein offensive commenced on 23 October 1942. Ordered back to the Middle East, Rommel was hampered by Hitler's refusal to accept retreat, extracting but a shadow of his army.

Barr ends with the British re-entry into Tripoli on 23 January 1943, but this was not the end of Rommel's North African service, for Hitler poured reinforcements under the command of General von Arnim into Tunisia in response to both the advance of the Eighth Army westwards and the Anglo-American landings in Morocco and Algeria – Operation Torch – that had commenced in November 1942. Von Arnim, whom Rommel disliked, commanded what was designated Fifth Panzer Army, and Rommel's *Panzerarmee* was bizarrely renamed First Italian Army, with Rommel under deferred orders to hand it over to Italian command and the clear intention that von Arnim would take overall command. Since the ever-cautious Montgomery would not attack Rommel's Mareth Line for some time, Rommel was able to contemplate a blow against the Anglo-American First Army. He chose to attack the American II Corps between Gafsa and Fondouk, behind which American defensive positions at the Kasserine Pass were particularly weak. The US 1st Armoured Division was overrun on 14 February 1943, opening up the whole Allied front, though Rommel then called off the attack as American resistance hardened and time was not on his side given Montgomery's build-up at Mareth. Now once more given overall command, Rommel then turned to attack Montgomery at Medenine on 5 March, the attack being an utter failure given the superiority of British forces. Again ill, Rommel then flew back to Rome and on to Hitler's headquarters to urge Hitler to send more reinforcements. The German Sixth Army had just surrendered to the Russians at Stalingrad and it was no longer possible to supply Tunisia due to superior Allied naval and air strength. Von Arnim, indeed, surrendered on 12 May 1943.[3]

As Peter Lieb shows, Rommel was in something of a military limbo after his return from Tunisia until he was appointed supreme commander in the Balkans in July 1943. Rommel lost out to Albert Kesselring, however, who received the command of the Italian front following the Allied invasion of Italy in September 1943. Rommel's Army Group B, a shadow formation since the summer, then became more of a reality with his appointment to examine the defences in the west in November 1943. Lieb recounts the serious disagreements on how to defend France against an Allied invasion between Rommel, the commander-in-chief in the west, Field Marshal Gerd von Rundstedt, and the commander of *Panzergruppe West*, Leo Geyr von Schweppenburg. In the event, Rommel was at home in Germany celebrating his wife's birthday when the Allies landed in Normandy on 6 June 1944. Lieb judges that little of the battle for Normandy was fought according to Rommel's intentions but, in any case, it is unlikely that he could have prevented Allied victory. Rommel was kept in post when Rundstedt and Geyr were dismissed, but he was increasingly regarded as a pessimist. On 17 July he was badly wounded when his staff car was attacked by RAF aircraft.

6   *Rommel: A Reappraisal*

While Rommel remained in hospital, Hitler survived the bomb plot against his life on 20 July 1944. As Russell Hart explains, there is no credible evidence that Rommel had more than limited and superficial knowledge of the plot. He abhorred the suggestion of assassination, and would not have moved against Hitler on 20 July even had he been fully fit. Ironically, Rommel was implicated primarily by association with Field Marshal Gunther von Kluge, Rundstedt's successor as commander-in-chief in the west, who was himself only peripherally involved but who committed suicide on 15 August when recalled to Berlin. Ironically, Rommel disliked von Kluge. Rommel was also implicated by the confessions of the military governor of Paris, General Carl-Heinrich von Stülpnagel, and his adjutant, Lieutenant Colonel Caesar von Hofacker. In the fevered atmosphere following the plot, the Gestapo believed what they were told. As Hart demonstrates, Rommel's supposed part in the plot was subsequently played up by Lieutenant General Hans Speidel, Rommel's chief-of-staff, who managed to persuade the Gestapo that he was not involved himself. Speidel played a considerable role in establishing Rommel's post-war reputation and it is appropriate that the volume ends with Mark Connelly's analysis of Rommel's iconic status. As Connelly concludes, Rommel's myth and the power and popularity of his image has proved remarkably resilient, resisting academic attempts to contextualize and explain his strengths and weaknesses. It is hoped that these essays will contribute to that process.

### Notes

1. Hans-Adolf Jacobsen and Antony Terry, 'The Enemy: Rommel Reassessed', in Derek Jewell (ed.), *Alamein and the Desert War* (London: Sphere Books, 1967), pp. 120-25, at p. 123.
2. For Rommel in Italy, see John Wilks and Eileen Wilks, *Rommel and Caporetto* (Barnsley: Leo Cooper, 2001).
3. For Rommel in Tunisia, see Bruce Allen Watson, *Exit Rommel: The Tunisian Campaign, 1942-43* (Westport, CT: Praeger, 1999).

CHAPTER ONE

# Rommel and the Rise of the Nazis

*Alaric Searle*

The obsessive praise which Erwin Rommel has attracted in Britain and America is, in many ways, a peculiar phenomenon: after all, Rommel failed in his two major campaigns in the Second World War. In the Western Desert, he was drawn into attritional battles, sacrificing the main body of his tanks, which laid the basis for the defeat of the *Afrika Korps*. In Normandy he was absent from the front at the crucial moment, so that the response to the Allied landing was too slow to achieve anything other than local successes. This has not prevented, however, a string of effusive and often uncritical biographies appearing in English, extolling the virtues of Rommel as a commander and master of manoeuvre – and, at least between the lines, a man less tainted with Nazism than many of his fellow generals.[1] Memoirs written by German generals in the 1950s, which provided sketches of Rommel's command style and abilities, appeared to provide evidence to support the image of him which had already begun to take root in the British public's mind.[2]

Yet, after the war, one German general offered – in private at least – a very different perspective on the capabilities of the 'people's general'. According to *General der Panzertruppe* Leo Freiherr Geyr von Schweppenburg, commander of *Panzergruppe West* in Normandy on D-Day, Guderian was intellectually superior to Rommel.[3] Moreover, writing to a fellow tank general in 1960, he argued that Rommel had been glorified by the British in order to cover up for their own poor military performance in the opening years of the war. In fact, he considered the

Field-Marshal's operational understanding of the defence of Normandy to have been patently wrong.[4] These were fundamental points of critique. Setting aside the question marks about Rommel's abilities at the operational and strategic levels of war, the accusation that the British artificially built up Rommel's reputation has a core element of truth. It was, undoubtedly, convenient in Britain in the 1950s to explain away some indifferent battlefield performances in the Western Desert in 1941 and 1942 with glowing references to the 'Desert Fox'. But there was another 'strategic element' to the Rommel myth.

In Britain, at the latest by early 1950, Conservative political circles, military officers and intelligence officials had come to the conclusion that a West German defence contribution would be required in order to counter-balance the numerical superiority of the Soviet Army in central Europe. But knowledge of the culpability of German generals in the crimes of the Third Reich was still being added to, not least through the British war crimes trial in Hamburg of Field-Marshal Erich von Manstein, which had just concluded in December 1949.[5] German generals needed their image boosting if there was to be any hope of German rearmament. One of the first individuals to contribute to the call for the foundation of West German armed forces, and who also lent his support for a revision of the conviction of Manstein, was the journalist and historian Basil Liddell Hart.[6] He had published, in 1948, the first book explaining the war and the rise of the Nazism from the perspective of German generals, entitled *The Other Side of the Hill*. This book had devoted a chapter to Rommel, who was portrayed as an outsider due to his lack of General Staff training. Additions to this chapter in the second edition, published in 1951, show that Liddell Hart, too, played his part in the creation of the myth surrounding Rommel.[7]

The 'Rommel myth' came to be cemented through mutual self-interest and cooperation between former German generals and the British. One of the results was the Rommel biography by Desmond Young, first published in 1950. Young collaborated with several individuals who had been close to Rommel, among them Hans Speidel, who had written his own memoir of the Normandy campaign, Vice-Admiral Friedrich Ruge, and Stuttgart's wartime mayor, Karl Strölin. Likewise, British generals, such as Field Marshal Sir Claude Auchinleck, Field-Marshal Earl Wavell and Sir Richard O'Connor supported the project, as did the pro-rearmament military writers Basil Liddell Hart and Major-General J.F.C. Fuller.[8] Creating a myth surrounding Rommel was no difficult task in the newly-founded Federal Republic of Germany, since the general had been turned into a propaganda icon of the Third Reich during the war. Indeed, according once again to the private correspondence of Geyr von Schweppenburg, Hans Speidel had announced his intention in early 1946 to turn Rommel into 'the hero of the German people'.[9]

What made Rommel so appealing in the post-war world was that his forced suicide, due to his implication in the July 1944 bomb plot, turned him into a 'victim' of Hitler, leading to the assumption that he had not been a supporter of the Third Reich. The brief chapter on the interwar period provided by Young suggested that Rommel had had little interest in politics, that he had had no desire to see another war, had no real connections with the Nazis, and was generally apolitical. It was noted that he had met both Heinrich Himmler and Joseph Goebbels in 1935; Himmler he disliked, but Goebbels made a good impression on him. It was not until late in 1938 that Rommel came into closer contact with Hitler. Throughout this chapter there is an underlying message: Rommel served the National Socialist regime, but was not of them, he did not support them; if he had a human failing, then it was his political naivety.[10] Since most writers on Rommel concentrate on his wartime exploits, paying only cursory attention to his interwar career, this generous view of Rommel's attitude to the Third Reich has remained virtually unchallenged in the English language works since Young's biography, with the exception of David Irving's 1977 biography.

Hence, in order to provide any serious reappraisal of the man, the commander and the myth, there is an urgent need to devote closer attention to his reactions to the rise of the National Socialists. One of the reasons why the long-standing image of Rommel as 'the good German general' – a necessary image manufactured to serve German rearmament – has rested for so long in spirit on the interpretation provided by Young[11] has been the lack of source material relating to Rommel in the interwar years. Nonetheless, by considering his interwar career in proper historical perspective, and utilising some of the latest research by German historians, a fuller and more revealing interpretation than the one provided by Desmond Young can now be offered.

## A Predisposition to Nazism? Rommel's Early Career, 1910–21

For any reappraisal of Erwin Rommel's reactions to the rise of Hitler and the Nazi Party (NSDAP), the problem has to be considered from a number of angles, the first of which is his early military background. Naturally, this must begin with the army he belonged to before the Imperial German Army disappeared to be replaced by the army of the Weimar Republic, the *Reichsheer*, as this might provide a first indication of any potential disposition towards supporting, or rejecting, the Nazi movement. His experience of the First World War, which fronts he fought on, and how he experienced the collapse of the German Empire and its armed forces, and the period of revolution and uprisings, may also provide further clues as to his later reactions to the Nazi state.

The basic details of his early career are well known. Born on 15 November 1891 at Heidenheim, in Württemberg, Rommel joined the 124th Infantry Regiment of the Imperial Württemberg Army on 19 July 1910, and took the oath to the monarch on 25 July 1910. In March 1911 he was sent to the *Königliche Kriegsschule* in Danzig, then, on 27 January 1912, he was promoted to *Leutnant*, the equivalent of First-Lieutenant.[12] If any significance can be attached to this early introduction to the military profession, then it is that Rommel joined the army when he was already a young man, and was not sent from a military family to Cadet School as a boy. He had had, in other words, plenty of time to absorb the values of civilian life. Moreover, although he was posted relatively quickly to Danzig, he had joined the Royal Army of Württemberg, which followed rather different military policies to the other armies in Imperial Germany. While there was a certain creeping encroachment of Prussian military methods and procedures before 1914, the Württemberg Army had, for example, a much more enlightened attitude towards conscientious objectors and Jewish conscripts.[13] In other words, Rommel does not seem to have been exposed to especially militaristic influences, either in terms of the region in which he grew up, the military culture of the army he joined, or the family he was born into (his father was a school headmaster).

What about his experiences during the First World War? Are there clues here to understanding his later reactions, thoughts and motives? In an important article on the attitude of officers towards National

Socialism, the German historian Johannes Hürter has identified four characteristics which desensitised military leaders towards brutality and suffering in the Second World War, tracing this back to the influence of the First World War on their outlook and military thinking: first, their anti-Semitic, anti-Slav, and anti-Socialist tendencies; second, their sense that military operations had become radicalised, which made them susceptible to the belief that total war was necessary; third, the final phase of the Great War had encouraged them to think that a totalitarian state was necessary; and, fourth, the consequences of defeat in 1918 led them to be impressed by Hitler's early foreign policy successes.[14] There is a possible pointer here to what Rommel's experience in the First World War might have meant for his subsequent willingness to accept at least some aspects of National Socialism. While it is obvious that his later emphasis on troops digging in, and his aggressive use of counter-attacks, had their roots in his experience on the Western and Italian fronts, little has been said by historians about his time in Romania.

Certainly, Rommel experienced the carnage of the Western Front exactly as other officers did, serving in the Verdun area in 1914, in the Argonne region in 1915, and from late December 1915 to October 1916 at Hilsen Ridge, in the Vosges, with a mountain battalion. From November 1916 to early July 1917 he was sent to Romania, before returning to the Hilsen Ridge, then spending another brief period at the Mount Cosna Front in Romania from August to October 1917. It could be argued that the time Rommel spent in Romania was too short to have had any lasting impact upon him. What may, however, be significant is that Rommel was present on that front precisely at the moment when the Germans achieved two important successes: shortly after his first arrival, Bucharest fell on 6 December 1916; during his second posting, Mount Cosna was captured on 19 August 1917.[15] Thus, these successes may have helped reinforce any existing feelings of superiority over the Slavs he already had, or at least made him more open to some of Hitler's goals in Eastern Europe.

Another key element in the outlook of German officers towards the NSDAP was the collapse in November 1918 of the German front in the West.[16] Interesting here is that Rommel spent most of 1918, 11 January to 20 December, as an *Ordnanzoffizier* at the Württemberg General Headquarters z.b.V. 64 in Friedrichshafen; in other words, he was engaged in staff work. Rommel's experience of the collapse was unlikely to have belonged to the more dramatic episodes of his career. He returned to the 7th Company of the 124th Infantry Regiment in his home town of Weingarten around Christmas 1918, having been promoted to captain on 18 October 1918. By March 1919 Rommel was commanding the Württemberg Security Company 32 in Friedrichshafen; he then became a company commander in the Württemberg *Schützenregiment* No. 25 on 25 June 1919. His regimental commander then recommended on 1 August 1919 that he remain in the army.

What is significant about the years 1919 and 1920 is not only that he swore the oath to the Weimar Constitution on 18 October 1919 (meaning he had successfully survived the dramatic cull in personnel which the *Reichswehr* was required to undertake), but also that he was involved in fighting against Communist rebels in Lindau, Münsterland and Westphalia. One of the key biographical elements for early supporters of National Socialism was often their participation in the semi-legal activities of the *Freikorps* (Free Corps) units, which operated at times in conjunction with the *Reichswehr*. But Rommel experienced both the collapse and the early period of Weimar instability mainly in the quieter western part of the country, does not seem to have fought as a member of a *Freikorps*, and was not involved in border fighting in the eastern territories of Germany. Despite this, it seems likely he would have been exposed to the widely held series of clichés about the 'stab-in-the-back' and the betrayal of Imperial Germany and its army by Jews, Communists and Social Democrats.[17]

On 1 January 1921, as part of the agreements contained in the Versailles Treaty, the process of the reduction in the size of the Weimar Republic's army had been completed. Of the 100,000 men, only 4,000 were officers. What this meant in practice was that the most competent General Staff officers, those who came from the nobility, those with the best social connections, and those who were regarded as exceptional war heroes, were the ones who managed to 'make the cut'. Rommel was fortunate in that, first, he was a holder of Germany's highest military decoration, the *Pour le Mérite*, and, second, he had gained staff experience at the Württemberg Army's General Headquarters in 1918. These two 'qualifications' helped him squeeze through the extremely rigorous selection process.

The basis upon which the *Reichsheer* was founded was something new for those 4,000 officers who were accepted into its ranks. As a result of a law passed on 21 August 1919, conscription was abolished. The final military law of 21 March 1921 defined the *Reichswehr* as 'the armed forces of the German Republic', which meant for the first time in its history that Germany now possessed a single, unified army, rather than a force which consisted of armies from different regions. Although soldiers swore to be loyal to the constitution on the basis of the version of the oath of 14 August 1919, according to the new version of 2 March 1922 the reference to the constitution of the Republic had disappeared and the oath was sworn to the Fatherland. It was not until a further version of 9 May 1930 that soldiers were required to swear to be loyal to the constitution once again.[18] The changes to the oath tell their own story about the uneasy relationship between the Weimar Republic and its army. While some officers may have felt a degree of loyalty to the Republic,[19] on the whole the Officer Corps was a caste in which anti-democratic views had the best possible potential to be preserved.

**Service in the *Reichsheer* (1921–33)**
With the dust slowly settling on the turmoil of the immediate post-war period, Rommel settled down into a period of mundane, military routine.[20] Although part of an organisation which saw itself as threatened by the new Republic, and by all types of enemies, Rommel had been spared some of the more extreme experiences of fighting in the East in 1919/20. In December 1921 he became commander of a machine-gun company in Stuttgart. In 1924 he joined the staff of the 2nd Battalion of the 13th Infantry Regiment, serving from 1925 to 1929 as commander of the 4th Machine-Gun Company of this regiment. Little is known about this period of his peacetime career. All that can be said about it is that Rommel remained in provincial south-west Germany, engaged in training activities, while the *Reichswehr* leadership reflected on questions of future war in Berlin, far from this military backwater.

But at this point it is important to consider some of the claims made by Desmond Young on Rommel's attitudes during the Weimar Republic. According to him, 'Until Hitler became Chancellor on January 31st, 1933, Rommel had taken little interest in politics.'

Allegedly, the tradition of the German officer class was to remain aloof from political parties. Rommel's wife only remembered one mildly negative comment by her husband on the Nazi movement when he had remarked that it was a pity that Hitler surrounded himself with such undesirables. Rommel had apparently had little contact with the Nazi movement.[21] These claims of a disinterested stance towards politics recall countless statements made by German officers after the war. One of the most popular arguments which they made was that they did not have the right to vote as a professional soldier (this had been laid down in law) and the *Reichswehr* was in fact completely apolitical. Yet this is no longer the historical wisdom on the army's Officer Corps during the Weimar Republic.

In many ways, the apolitical front had been a necessary compromise, since officers had found it extremely difficult to accept the loss of the old system. In fact, loyalty to the new Republic was by no means a prerequisite for re-enlistment in the army. From among the higher army leadership during the Second World War, those few letters which have survived from the Weimar period show that these officers were anything but apolitical. Lack of party membership did not mean a lack of interest in politics, particularly since what characterised the Republic was the high number of parties all vying for attention. Rejection of the 'Weimar system' was, in itself, a clear political position, and one which small, right-wing parties adopted very quickly. Even looking back after 1945, officers still regarded the period 1919–33 as one of civil war and instability. But while older officers reminisced fondly about the era of the monarchy, younger men were in search of leaders who would put an end to the hated Weimar experiment.[22]

Indeed, it seems clear that officers in the 1920s were highly susceptible to the conservative and nationalistic messages which were being propagated about Germany's need for 'living space'. Even if they had not read Hitler's *Mein Kampf*, there were other more respectable works propagating similar ideas. Hans Grimm's *Volk ohne Raum*, first published in 1926, was one such work, which became a bestseller in the Weimar Republic. Written in the form of a novel, Grimm advocated the securing of 'living space' as a solution to the economic and political problems of Weimar. Although Grimm conceived of 'living space' within the context of Imperial Germany's search for colonies, he became one of Hitler's favourite authors; and, very quickly, the NSDAP was to reformulate his idea into the concept of 'living space in the East'.[23] Even an officer who was critical of the regime before the outbreak of war in 1939, and a supporter of the 20th July bomb plotters after the war, regarded Grimm's work as 'a wonderful book', even if he did not agree with his views.[24]

Trapped in garrison duty in Württemberg, Rommel's first real break came when he was selected in 1929 to become an instructor of officer cadets at the Infantry School in Dresden. He took up his duties in October; and, according to later recollections, Rommel was respected by his fellow officers, admired by the cadets, but came across as very straightforward. One of his fellow officers in Dresden considered him to be 'no great thinker'. This posting was, though, an important moment in Rommel's career. Having spent time consigned to an unimportant and routine role, he had gained a modest opportunity to kick-start his career. An appointment of this nature carried with it the opportunity for promotion and he was duly elevated to major on 1 April 1932. His duties also motivated him to publish a small instructional manual on the teaching of tactical tasks for the platoon and company.[25] Moreover, the posting, which lasted until September 1933, placed him in a large city during the period when the National Socialists seized power.

The time Rommel spent in Dresden was actually a crucial period in the development of the attitude of officers towards the NSDAP.[26] Until September 1930, when the party rose to be the second largest group in the *Reichstag*, the Officer Corps of the *Reichsheer* had regarded it more with disinterested curiosity. It was just one among many small parties, one which could only consider itself to have serious support among officers in Munich. But the sudden rise of the NSDAP to a political force which was to be taken seriously awakened among army officers the hope that here was a movement which offered a chance to achieve two goals which lay at the heart of their political outlook: first, they promised to unite the working class behind a strong state, thereby removing the Communist danger; second, they were the party which promised to undertake a revision of the Versailles Treaty. Still, even if ordinary soldiers were becoming enthusiastic about the NSDAP, at this stage their officers remained cautious.[27]

When Adolf Hitler finally became Chancellor on 30 January 1933, the reaction among officers was one of relief. The final two years of the

Weimar Republic had been plagued by political violence, offering up 'martyrs', principally to the Nazi and Communist causes. For some, the accession of Hitler to power appeared to offer not a one-party dictatorship, but a unification of conservative forces. Crucial in the development of officers' reactions to the new government was 'Potsdam Day' on 21 March 1933, which demonstrated Hitler's genius for psychology. As Hitler and the *Reichspräsident* Paul von Hindenburg walked together, in a deeply symbolic gesture, it appeared as if the old military traditions had been revived and the NSDAP had created a unification of Nazi and national-conservative ideas. Even in 1937, an official army yearbook carried a photograph of Hitler, with Hindenburg in full uniform in the foreground, under the heading 'Four Years of National Socialist Military Politics'.[28]

Rommel's thoughts when Hitler became Chancellor are not difficult to gauge. Despite later protestations by German generals of their reserve towards the Nazi Party and its leader, it is obvious from the comments made at the time that, at least after the 'Tag von Potsdam', the Officer Corps had been won over. One indication of the positive reaction in the *Reichsheer* can be seen in a front-page editorial published in April 1933 in the main army newspaper, the *Militär-Wochenblatt*, simply entitled 'Hitler'. According to the article, although the new leader had been born outside the borders of the German Reich, he was destined for the rescue and reforming of the German Fatherland. Hitler's sense of duty was held up as that of an 'unknown frontline soldier'. His rise had been filled with incessant battles, but now he enjoyed the trust of President Hindenburg and the enthusiasm of the entire people. The article concluded with the loud cry that: 'We soldiers have first and foremost one burning desire: Military Freedom!' This was expressed as the 'freedom and the right to defend ourselves with all our strength against oppression and rape from outside'. The belief was expressed that 'our Chancellor' would find the right way to achieve this and that 'we declare our willingness to cooperate and follow.'[29] There seems little doubt that the majority of army officers now shared these sentiments.

**Peace-time Service in the Third Reich (1933–1938/9)**
On 1 October 1933 Rommel took up his next post as commander of the 3rd Battalion *GolsarerJäger*, part of Infantry Regiment No.17.[30] He

occupied this post until mid-January 1935. Given the emphasis upon leadership of soldiers which was placed in the *Reichsheer*, this was a positive career development, demonstrated by the fact that he was promoted to lieutenant-colonel on 1 January 1935. Goslar was also an old, medieval town with strong military traditions. The time in Goslar was also significant for the way in which it contributed to Rommel's attitude to the National Socialists. According to Young in his biography, Rommel was disgusted by the SA ruffians and, thus, was not horrified by the Night of the Long Knives on 30 June 1934, when elements of the *Sturmabteilung* (SA) leadership were murdered by the SS.[31] The latest research by German historians has shown that this statement was correct for very specific reasons.

In late 1933 and early 1934, Rommel's unit came into conflict with the brown-shirted paramilitary forces of the SA, who repeatedly provoked fights with soldiers stationed in Rommel's battalion. Worse still, a retired general, Ernst von Oven, was verbally abused and threatened after he continued to make purchases in Jewish shops. According to a post-war account (which cannot be verified), Rommel posted a machine-gun unit in the staircase of the general's house and threatened to respond with force to any further attacks. Whether this anecdote is true or not, his distaste for the SA was almost certainly genuine and conformed to the general reaction of the Officer Corps as a whole. The removal of any possibility that the SA might present a threat to the army through the action of the 'Night of the Long Knives' won the army back into the National Socialist camp. Many officers, probably like Rommel, chose to ignore the murder of one of their own, Kurt von Schleicher, in probably the first significant example of quiet acquiescence in the murderous acts of the new regime.

Following the death of Field-Marshal Paul von Hindenburg on 2 August 1934, the new oath of the armed forces to Hitler came into effect. But the wearing of party emblems on uniforms, helmets and caps had already been instituted on 11 February 1934. On 30 September 1934, Rommel also came face-to-face with Hitler for the first time in Goslar. The Chancellor reviewed the regiment and Rommel can be seen in a photograph marching together with five other officers behind him as he salutes the troops standing to attention. The meeting was brief and of a purely formal character. But by 30 September 1934, the Officer Corps appeared already to be marching behind the regime. The National Socialists had not only promised to 'tear up' the Treaty of Versailles, they seemed to offer the prospect of the restoration of the old status of officers. All the various resentments which had built up in the conservative, nationalist camp were now being taken seriously. The new leader promised to restore Germany's former position, assert her rights on the world stage, and build up the country's armed forces. For the 4,000-strong Officer Corps, expansion of the armed forces meant career opportunities which had previously not been dreamt of. For a man of Rommel's impulsive and impatient character this must have been an opportunity which seemed too good to miss. Until Hitler's accession to power, those officers without the best social connections, who had spent the 1920s in remote garrisons, with promotion effectively frozen, seemed to be facing a bleak – indeed almost humiliating – future.

With the two military laws of 16 March and 21 May 1935, a series of measures were introduced which marked not only the reintroduction of conscription, but the replacement of the term *Reichswehr* with *Wehrmacht*, the final binding of the armed services to the Nazi state and the beginning of a rearmament programme. It was against this background that, in mid-October 1935, Rommel received another boost to his career. He was appointed *Lehrgangsleiter* of the new War School in Potsdam, an appointment which put him in charge of cadet training. As is often the case with officers posted to military academies, service at a training establishment can offer the opportunity to write books based on lectures. Rommel, too, took this opportunity, penning a work on infantry tactics. At the beginning of October 1937 he was promoted to colonel. Finally, and parallel to his post at the War School in Potsdam, from 21 February 1937 to 31 August 1938 he was the *Wehrmacht* liaison officer to the leader of the Hitler Youth, Baldur von Schirach. Rommel was to remain in Potsdam until November 1938: it was a decisive phase in the development of his positive attitudes to the National Socialist regime and, thus, one which requires close analysis.

Let us first consider his book on infantry tactics, which drew on his lectures at the War School.[32] Sales were slow until his popularity rocketed in 1941, once he became an icon of Goebbels's wartime propaganda; reputedly, by 1945, it had sold some 400,000 copies. So what, if anything, does the book tell us about its author? There are, in fact, two points of significance. The first is that, while the intention was clearly to communicate to its military audience a series of lessons related to Rommel's personal experience as a junior infantry officer, at the same time the main figure in the book is the author. Unlike many tactical handbooks produced in the interwar years, Rommel departs from the dry, General Staff-style language,[33] thrusting himself into the centre of every engagement which is described. From the General Staff point of view, a work such as this was a clear departure from the typical conventions of military instructional writing. Second, while there was an obvious element of self-publicity, there is also a clear military-propagandistic message delivered in Rommel's foreword. Here he wrote: 'The following examples are proof of the tremendous power of the German infantry, even when faced with superior odds in men and equipment; and these sketches are again proof of the superiority of the junior German commander to his enemy counterpart.'[34]

What is the relevance of these two points for our consideration of Rommel's attitude to the National Socialist regime? The first observation is that he had clearly developed a desire for self-publicity, and was quite prepared to depart from military convention in order to promote his own interests. The second point is that his comments about superior odds in men and equipment of Germany's opponents recalls much of the propaganda during the Great War which portrayed Germany as battling heroically against superior numbers. This underpinned a broadly held view within the German Army that superior forces could be overcome by energetic leadership, ruthlessness, self-sacrifice and heroism. It was the new regime which had now created the conditions under which these qualities would be both valued and encouraged. When viewed in historical context, there are hints in this book that Rommel was already, by 1937, prepared to accept the new regime for what it could offer both him and the armed forces.

When it came to Rommel's liaison duties between the *Wehrmacht* and the Hitler Youth leader, the Rommel apologists were faced with a problem after the Second World War. How could they possibly explain away this apparent connection, indeed approval, offered up by the leaders of the Third Reich? Young achieved this by passing off this unsightly detail by sleight of hand. First, he noted that Rommel heard in 1935 – 'with no great enthusiasm' – that he had been suggested as the commander of the SA, in order that the Army take charge of the organisation. But nothing came of this. He continued, however, that 'Rommel was not to escape contact with the Nazis', as he was selected to train the Hitler Youth in military ways. Moreover, he explains that von Schirach and Rommel fell out because the latter objected to an over-emphasis on sport and military training. These objections are explained by reference to the fact that Rommel's father had been a school teacher. His account of this episode concludes with the assertion that von Schirach portrayed Rommel as not ideologically sound enough to be entrusted with the education of the Hitler Youth.[35] Is this an accurate description of what occurred?

Rommel was appointed on 21 February 1937 as the Wehrmacht's liaison officer to the Hitler Youth[36] – shortly after he had attended a 'National Socialist Training Course for the Wehrmacht' from 15-23 January, at which such individuals as Wilhelm Frick, Joseph Goebbels, Rudolf Hess, Alfred Rosenberg and Heinrich Himmler spoke. In early 1937, he met with the leader of the Hitler Youth, Baldur von Schirach, at his home overlooking Lake Kochel in southern Bavaria. The wife of von Schirach sought to break the ice by pointing out how beautiful the Bavarian Alps were, which provided Rommel with the perfect opportunity to launch into a two-hour long lecture on his storming of Mount Matajur in the Great War. This incident points also to an obvious clash of personalities: Rommel, the gruff, 'simple solider', had been given the task of persuading the suave, cosmopolitan, half-American, Nazi careerist von Schirach, to allow the *Wehrmacht* to take over the Hitler Youth for the purposes of pre-military training. An unsuccessful attempt had already been made two years before and had got nowhere.

Matters came to a head in May 1938 when Colonel Rommel presented the draft version of a written agreement to the deputy-leader of the Hitler Youth, Hartmann Lauterbacher, in an effort to enable the *Wehrmacht* to conduct pre-military training in the Hitler Youth. His reaction was one of outrage, since it must have been clear that the Hitler Youth would have ceased to be an organisation of the NSDAP if the military leadership had their way. Although a revised version of the document was produced, Rommel then handed the original contract to von Schirach for his signature, which only succeeded in aggravating him completely. The Hitler Youth leader appealed directly to Hitler and Rommel was quietly removed from his post in August 1938. The Hitler Youth was thus to remain an organisation of the party; Baldur von Schirach even commented privately to Martin Bormann that Rommel could not be regarded as a Nazi. Was this high-ranking servant of the regime correct in his judgment?

It is at this point that caution needs to be exercised. In particular, it would be a mistake to attach any great weight to Baldur von Schirach's claim that Rommel was somehow not a Nazi. Rommel showed himself to be a straight-forward soldier, lacking in diplomatic skills, interested only in securing access to the Hitler Youth for the purposes of pre-military training. Certainly, there had been a clash of personalities between him and von Schirach, but this cannot be taken as evidence at this stage of any rejection of the broad military and foreign policy goals of the regime. Like many other front-line officers, with little awareness of the military planning underway, Rommel was simply trying to carry out his orders, with a minimal mastery of negotiation skills, as it turned out. For the majority of army officers, the state leadership had now accepted that the army was the 'school of the nation': Hitler had said so in *Mein Kampf*, and they regarded the SA, SS and Hitler Youth as important instruments for the improvement of military training.[37]

The Potsdam phase of Rommel's pre-war career was concluded on 9 November 1938, the fifteenth anniversary of the Beer Hall Putsch in Munich. But not before a further form of semi-political task was accorded to him: he was seconded from the War School in Potsdam to the temporary role of commander of a force tasked with securing the personal safety of Hitler, constituted as the *Kommando 'Führerreise'* in June 1938.[38] This secondment was made so that he could command the unit during the march into the Sudetenland from 1-9 October 1938. According to Young, Hitler had personally sought out Rommel for the task because he had read *Infanterie greift an* and was anxious to meet its author.[39] This may have some truth to it, but the fact that Rommel had already been a Wehrmacht liaison officer to the Hitler Youth hardly suggests any form of distance from the regime. Moreover, Young omits to mention the previous occasion on which Rommel had fulfilled this duty during the *Anschluss* with Austria in March 1938. It is at this point that that the account provided by Young starts to become questionable. The claim by him that Rommel was brought in October 1938 into close proximity to Hitler 'for the first time', on the initiative of Hitler because the dictator had read *Infanterie greift an*, is patently untrue. Of course, we do not know what documents Young had at his disposal, but this failure to mention a crucial part of Rommel's interwar biography – whether unintentional or not – raises questions about just how close the Swabian was at this point to the regime.

The day after his appointment at the War School in Potsdam ended, Rommel was called to serve as the commander of the old Maria Theresia Military Academy in Wiener Neustadt, located in a mountainous area south-west of the Austrian capital. This appointment ran from 10 November 1938 to 22 August 1939. What is significant here is that to take over the command of a military academy in a country which Germany had annexed only a few months before, was a task unlikely to be entrusted to anyone not regarded as sufficiently 'on side' with the regime. While a majority of Austrians welcomed the *Anschluss* with Germany, it was nonetheless a mission which held potential dangers. Almost certainly Rommel's Swabian background, and his distinctive southern German accent, played a part in the appointment, since Austrian soldiers were unlikely to have taken to the harsher tones of a northern German or Prussian. At any rate, Rommel was now enjoying the benefits of having come to Hitler's attention.

### Hitler's Follower: From the Eve of War to the French Campaign (1938/9–1940)

Shortly after taking up his appointment at the former Maria Theresia Military Academy, Rommel attended his third 'National Socialist Training Course' between 29 November and 2 December, this time for senior officers. Attendance at such a course, which was unlikely to have been voluntary, did not in itself, of course, mean that the attendees believed every word spoken. What is significant in this case, however, is Rommel's own reaction to a speech given by Hitler on 1 December. He wrote to his wife on the following day: 'The Führer spoke yesterday: the soldier today must be political because he must always be ready to go into action for the new politics. The German Wehrmacht is the sword of the new German world view.'[40] Although he did not make any statements in favour of particular Nazi policies, there is in these words a clear sign of his drift towards uncritical support for the Nazi regime.

Shortly after this course, towards the end of the year, he delivered a series of lectures in Switzerland based on his book, *Infanterie greift an*, which had been used by the Swiss Army in the teaching of their cadets. However, as a result of a complaint by the Italian military attaché in Switzerland, who accused Rommel of speaking in a derogatory fashion about the Italian troops in the First World War, he was required to provide an explanation. In a two-page letter to the Army High Command, he denied the charge and, presumably to create a good impression, noted that younger Swiss officers had expressed their sympathy for 'the new Germany'. Individual officers had also showed some understanding towards the 'Jewish question'. Although the statement he made in this letter was rather ambiguous, the 'Crystal Night' of 9 November 1938 can hardly have passed Rommel by. There is no evidence earlier or subsequently in his career that he showed any support or sympathy for the anti-Semitism of the Nazi movement. But he was clearly aware of what the official stance of the regime was.[41]

In March 1939 Rommel spent, once again, two weeks in charge of the *Kommando 'Führerreise'* during the German occupation of the rump Czechoslovak state and Memmelland. Rommel confided later to a friend that he had persuaded Hitler to drive into Prague in an open car, right up to the imposing Hradschin Castle. According to Rommel, Hitler never forgot what he regarded as excellent advice. Perhaps this was just a boast. If it was, then it was a further indication that he was now under the spell of the dictator. For his part, Hitler was obviously impressed with Rommel. When his appointment at the military academy in Wiener Neustadt ended on 23 August 1939, he was promoted to *Generalmajor*. He returned as the commanding officer in charge of Hitler's Headquarters, in effect the successor organisation to the *Kommando 'Führerreise'*, renamed, also on 23 August, as the *Frontgruppe der FHQu. Truppen*. Hitler's promotion of Rommel to major-general was backdated to 1 June 1939, which would have been a happy surprise for Rommel when he received his next pay cheque.[42]

Thus, on the eve of the Second World War, Rommel had already achieved the rank of *Generalmajor*, before he had had any opportunity to distinguish himself as a higher commander in combat. It is obvious that his career had already been heavily sponsored by Hitler. In the letters which he wrote to his wife during and after the Polish campaign, it emerges that Rommel was by this point completely under the spell of the Nazi dictator. Referring to Hitler's infamous speech on 1 September

1939, in which he declared war on Poland, he wrote to his wife on 2 September: 'What do you say to the events of 1st [September]? Isn't it wonderful that we have this man?'[43] The following evening, 3 September, the Führer's special train left Berlin, together with the security detachment, the *Frontgruppe der FHQu.*, commanded by Rommel. His promotion to general was without doubt the result of Hitler's desire to see him command this unit in wartime.

The task of protecting the dictator during the Polish Campaign was a challenging one, as Hitler travelled extensively throughout areas very close to the front line. When he travelled, there were two groups of cars, consisting of aides, party figures, armed SS guards and others. These groups of cars were, in turn, surrounded by various motorcycle detachments of troops under Rommel's command, including two armed reconnaissance vehicles. At this stage in the war, the level of security was quite lax, which motivated Rommel to fly to Berlin to try and persuade the military authorities that the existing security arrangements were inadequate and that a larger escort battalion would be necessary. This led, subsequently, to the establishment of the *Führer-Begleit-Battalion* in November 1939.[44]

The close proximity to Hitler Rommel experienced during the rapid victory over Poland caused him to fall wholly under the dictator's spell. Writing to his wife on 10 September he reported that he had been allowed to attend some of the evening situation conferences and was 'even allowed to speak a word'. Writing again to his wife on 19 September, he noted enthusiastically how he appeared to have risen in the Führer's estimation: 'Was allowed to chat for almost two hours with him about military problems yesterday. He is extraordinarily friendly towards me.' These private remarks to his wife not only show that Rommel had found favour with the Nazi regime, but also that he was delighted with the preferential treatment he was receiving. This clearly coloured his view of the events going on around him. On 22 October 1939 he wrote to his wife from Warsaw describing the devastation, the fact that every tenth house had been destroyed, and that there had been no water, no light, no gas and no food for the previous two days. His final remark gives an indication of the extent to which he had become intoxicated by the first battlefield success of the *Wehrmacht* and lost touch with reality: 'The inhabitants draw a breath of relief that we have arrived and rescued them.'[45]

A privileged view of the Polish Campaign as the commander of Hitler's headquarters, complete with a uniform with a cuff band carrying the title *Führerhauptquartier*, completed what had been a gradual process of drawing ever closer to the regime and profiting from the benefits of Hitler's patronage. Not surprisingly, Rommel was horrified by the assassination attempt on Hitler made by Georg Elser on 8 November 1939 in Munich, writing to his wife on 9 November that it did not bear thinking about what would have happened had it succeeded. A few weeks later, on 24 November, he wrote again to his wife about a speech made to military commanders and their superiors: 'The Führer spoke very bluntly. But then this seems necessary, as when one speaks with a group of comrades there is seldom a single one who participates with wholehearted conviction.' Rommel was, in other words, by this point fully behind the regime and, presumably, its military and foreign policy goals – at least as they had been enunciated in public.[46]

By the end of 1939 Rommel had achieved the status of one of Hitler's most favoured generals. This was to benefit his career once again – and this time decisively. He had made a request for a transfer to a panzer division, which had been turned down by the head of army personnel, who had recommended instead that Rommel take over command of a mountain division. He had served with a mountain division in the First World War and, after all, had no experience with tanks. But as a result of Hitler's personal intervention, Rommel's wish to take over the command of a division equipped with tanks was fulfilled on 15 February 1940 when he was appointed commander of the 7th Panzer Division. He greeted his new divisional staff in mid-February with a barked 'Heil Hitler', his arm raised in the Nazi salute. On 17 February 1940, he wrote to his wife that for some in the army National Socialism was still a strange idea, there being more than a hint of disapproval. On the occasion of his departure from the *Führerhauptquartier*, the dictator presented Rommel with a copy of *Mein Kampf*, complete with a hand-written dedication 'To General Rommel – with friendly memories', dated 13 February 1940.[47] The admiration was mutual.

## Conclusion

Erwin Rommel, the modest Swabian, had made a complete journey by the eve of the French Campaign, from a typical *Reichswehr* officer to an enthusiastic and blindly naïve supporter of Hitler. He had appealed to the Führer because of his southern German, very un-Prussian origins, and the fact he was a soldier without General Staff training. His military philosophy was one which rejected aristocratic values and adulated bravery on the battlefield and leadership from the front. Like many others of his generation, he chose to acquiesce in the military policies of the National Socialist regime during the mid-1930s, concentrating on the profession of arms rather than what was going on around him. The foreign policy successes scored by Hitler, and the bloodless territorial expansion before war came, blinded him as to the true nature of his beloved Führer. Disillusionment only set in towards the end of his North African campaign.

In his reactions to the establishment of the National Socialist state, Erwin Rommel was representative of senior officers of his generation who had fought in the Great War. The rise of the Nazi Party promised the removal of the 'shackles' of the Versailles Treaty, career opportunities and, later, the prospect of military action against Germany's traditional enemies in the East. A distinction was made between the party and the leader in an effort to still troubled consciences. The problem for Rommel, the 'people's general' in the Third Reich, was that his lack of General Staff training meant he was uninformed on strategy and blind to the military catastrophe which war was likely to mean for Germany. His failure to recognise the true nature of the Third Reich makes Rommel a tragic figure in the history of military command. His downfall was the regime which had propelled him to fame, but he was as much a victim of his own myopic and narrowly military view of the world around him.

In wartime, the 'Desert Fox' was a dashing, creative and energetic commander – but his rise to fame was made possible by his enthusiastic and uncritical adulation of Adolf Hitler. The real Erwin Rommel was not the same man that Desmond Young created back in 1950.

### Notes

1. Among the most prominent are: Ronald Lewin, *Rommel as Military Commander* (London: Batsford, 1971); David Irving, *On the Trail of the Fox: The Life of Field Marshal Erwin Rommel* (London: Macmillan, 1977); David Fraser, *Knight's Cross: A Life of Field Marshal Erwin Rommel* (London: Harper Collins, 1993);

and Kenneth Macksey, *Rommel: Battles and Campaigns* (London: Arms & Armour Press, 1979). Typical of the numerous shorter biographical sketches is Martin Blumenson, 'Rommel', in Correlli Barnett (ed.), *Hitler's Generals* (London: Weidenfeld & Nicolson, 1989), pp. 293-316.
2. To give just a few examples: Hans Speidel, *We Defended Normandy* (London: Herbert Jenkins, 1951); Siegfried Westphal, *The German Army in the West* (London: Cassell, 1951), pp. 98-134; F.W. von Mellenthin, *Panzer Battles. A Study of the Employment of Armour in the Second World War* (London: Cassell, 1955), esp. pp. 51-65.
3. Institut für Zeitgeschichte, Munich (hereafter IfZ), Nachlass Leo Freiherr Geyr von Schweppenburg, ED91/11, Geyr von Schweppenburg to Hellmut Stöber, 15 December 1960.
4. IfZ, ED91/12, Geyr von Schweppenburg to Oskar Munzel, 4 July 1960.
5. On the Manstein trial, Oliver von Wrochem, *Erich von Manstein: Vernichtungs politik und Geschichtspolitik* (Paderborn: Schoeningh, 2006), pp. 107-211.
6. On this whole question, Alaric Searle, 'A Very Special Relationship: Basil Liddell Hart, Wehrmacht Generals and the Debate on West German Rearmament, 1945-1953', *War in History*, 5 (July 1998), pp. 327-57. See also Kerstin von Lingen, *Kesselring's Last Battle: War Crimes Trials and Cold War Politics, 1945-1960* (Lawrence, KS: University Press of Kansas, 2009), pp. 128-225.
7. B.H. Liddell Hart, *The Other Side of the Hill* (London: Cassell, 1948), pp. 52-61. In the 1951 edition of the book, Liddell Hart adds the claim that Rommel had studied books on tank warfare, and that 'in his African notes he speaks of "the outstanding way" in which the theory had been expounded by English writers'. The chapter concludes with a statement that shows Liddell Hart was involved in the creation of the Rommel myth: 'The more deeply his record is examined the clearer it becomes that his gifts and performance, in a theatre of independent command, qualified him for a place in the role of the "Great Captains" of history.' B.H. Liddell Hart, *The Other Side of the Hill* 2nd edn., (London: Cassell, 1951), pp. 78, 85.
8. Desmond Young, *Rommel* (London: Collins, 1950), pp. 5-6.
9. IfZ, ED91/12, Geyr von Schweppenburg to Hoesch, 11 June 1964.
10. Young, *Rommel*, 'Between Two Wars', pp. 46-68.
11. As late as 1995, John Keegan could still speak of Young's biography as if there were little reason to doubt its veracity. According to him, 'Young had unpicked the mystery and, in doing so, made Rommel all the more attractive.' John Keegan, *The Battle for History: Re-Fighting World War II* (London: Hutchinson, 1995), p. 57.
12. Hauptstaatsarchiv Stuttgart (hereafter HStAS), M660/200 Bü 1, fol. 1, Personal bogen., Akten Nr. 3862.
13. On the pre-war Württemberg Army, see Daniel Kirn, *Soldatenleben in Württemberg 1871-1914. Zur Sozialgeschichte des deutschen Militärs* (Paderborn Schoeningh, 2008).

14. Johannes Hürter, '"Es herrschen Sitten und Gebräuche, genauso wie im 30-jährigen Krieg." Das erste Jahr des deutsch-sowjetischen Krieges in Dokumenten des Generals Gotthard Heinrici', *Vierteljahrshefte für Zeitgeschichte*, 48 (2000), pp. 329-403.
15. For Rommel's Great War service record, HStAS, M660/200, Bü 1, fol. 6, Gefechtskalender; and, for his service on the Romanian Front, Erwin Rommel, *Infantry Attacks* (London & Mechanicsburg, PA: Fall River Press, 1990), pp. 82-167.
16. Biographical material on Rommel for the period 1918-19 is drawn from HStAS, M436/2, Kriegsranglisten-Auszüge, M660/200 Bü 1, Lebensdaten Rommel.
17. On attitudes to the Revolution among officers, see Johannes Hürter, *Hitlers Heerführer. Die deutsche Oberbefehlshaber im Krieg gegen die Sowjetunion 1941/42* (Munich: Oldenbourg, 2007), pp. 86-96.
18. Jürgen Förster, *Die Wehrmacht im NS-Staat. Eine strukturgeschichtliche Analyse* (Munich: Oldenbourg, 2007), pp. 4-6.
19. Even a rare article, which attempted to deal with democracy even-handedly, displays considerable reserve towards the new form of government. See Generalleutnant a.D. v. Wetsch, 'Bemerkungen über Heer und Demokratie', *Wissen und Wehr*, 10 (May 1929), pp. 264-78.
20. Unless otherwise stated, biographical details for this section draw from: Fraser, *Knight's Cross*, 81-99, 563; Maurice Philip Remy, *Mythos Rommel* (Munich: List, 2004), pp. 27-31.
21. Young, *Rommel*, pp. 55-56.
22. Hürter, *Hitlers Heerführer*, pp. 96-111.
23. Hans Grimm, *Volk ohne Raum* (Munich: Albert Langen, one vol. ed., 1932). Among several works on this subject, see Heike Wolter, *Volk ohne Raum. Lebensraumvorstellungen im geopolitischen, literarischen und politischen Diskurs der Weimarer Republik* (Münster: Lit, 2003).
24. IfZ, ED91/8, Geyr von Schweppenburg to Graf Bjoenstjerna, 22 November 1961.
25. Erwin Rommel, *Gefechts-Aufgaben für Zug und Kompanie: Ein Handbuch für den Offizierunterricht* (Berlin: E.S. Mittler, 1934).
26. It is also likely to have had some impact upon Rommel's political outlook because the final phase in the history of the Weimar Republic was marked by an upsurge in political violence. The Nazi dead from the street battles were celebrated by the party once it had taken power. One such 'martyr' was Heinrich Gutsche, who was shot by Communists on 7 June 1931 in Chemnitz, the next large city to the west of Dresden. A unit of the *Reichsarbeitsdienst* (RAD) was named after him. The biographical sketch in an official RAD publication described the SS man as 'a fanatical fighter for a better Germany', who was able to 'look the Führer in the eyes once more before his German soul breathed its last'. [Artur] Helff (ed.), *Grenzland Baden Spaten zur Hand! Vom Werden und Schaffen des Arbeitsgaues XXVII Baden* (Karlsruhe: E.F. Müller, 7th ed., 1939), p. 138. Given the strong

anti-Communist outlook of the Officer Corps, it seems likely that their sympathies will have been with the Nazi dead in clashes with Communists. On political violence in the Weimar Republic, see Dirk Schumann, *Political Violence in the Weimar Republic, 1918–1933: Fight for the Streets and Fear of Civil War* (New York/Oxford: Berghahn, 2012).
27. Hürter, *Hitlers Heerführer*, pp. 123-26.
28. Photograph under the caption 'Vier Jahre nationalsozialistischer Wehrpolitik', in Major Walter Jost (ed.), *Jahrbuch des deutschen Heeres 1937* (Leipzig: Breitkopf, 1937), p. 8.
29. 'Hitler', *Militär-Wochenblatt*, 117(23 April 1933), col. 1313-16.
30. Unless otherwise stated, biographical and other historical details in this section draw from: Remy, *Mythos Rommel*, pp. 32-41; Ralf Georg Reuth, *Rommel: The End of a Legend* (London: Haus Books, 2005), pp. 24-34; Förster, *Die Wehrmacht im NS-Staat*, pp. 19-53.
31. Young, *Rommel*, p. 56.
32. The German edition appeared as Erwin Rommel, *Infanterie greift an. Erlebnisse und Erfahrungen* (Potsdam: Voggenreiter, 1937).
33. Typical of this type of military manual is Oberstleutnant [Friedrich] von Cochenhausen, *Die kriegswissenschaftliche Fortbildung des Truppenoffiziers. Ein Handbuch für Lehrer und Lernenden mit praktischen Beispielen* (Berlin: E.S. Mittler, 1926).
34. Rommel, *Infantry Attacks*, p. xv.
35. Young, *Rommel*, pp. 59-62.
36. For background on the emergence of the Hitler Youth as a party organisation, see H.W. Koch, *The Hitler Youth: Origins and Development 1922-45* (London: Macdonald & Jane's, 1975), pp. 57-203, and also Baldur von Schirach, *Ich glaubte an Hitler* (Hamburg: Mosaik Verlag, 1967), with a short account of the clash with Rommel, pp. 233-34.
37. See, for example, Oberstleutnant [Hermann] Foertsch, 'Der Führer und seine Wehrmacht', in Oberstleutnant Walter Jost (ed.), *Jahrbuch des deutschen Heeres 1938* (Leipzig: Breitkopf & Härtel, 1938), pp. 13-18.
38. Peter Hoffmann, *Hitler's Personal Security* (London: Macmillan, 1979), p. 59.
39. Young, *Rommel*, p. 62.
40. Cited in Remy, *Mythos Rommel*, p. 41.
41. Ibid., pp. 41-42.
42. Hoffmann, *Hitler's Personal Security*, p. 59; Remy, *Mythos Rommel*, pp. 42-43.
43. Cited in Remy, *Mythos Rommel*, p. 44.
44. Hoffmann, *Hitler's Personal Security*, pp. 59, 134-36, 138.
45. Letters cited in Reuth, *Rommel*, pp. 37-39.
46. Ibid., pp. 31, 37.
47. Remy, *Mythos Rommel*, pp. 46-48.

CHAPTER TWO

# Rommel and 1940

## Claus Telp

*'This is the age of Seydlitz and Ziethen all over again. We've got to look at this war like a cavalry action – we've got to throw in tank divisions like cavalry squadrons, and that means issuing orders from a moving tank just as generals once used to from the saddle.'*[1]

On 12 February 1940, Major-General Erwin Rommel took command of 7th Panzer Division in Bad Godesberg. At that time, the division was deployed in the Eiffel mountains close to the Belgian border in anticipation of the campaign against France.

The division had originally been established in 1938 as 2nd Light Division, a light armoured division intended for pursuit operations. After the end of the Poland Campaign, the division became a full-blown panzer division and was renamed 7th Panzer Division. The organisation and equipment of panzer divisions was not standardised. On 10 May, 7th Panzer Division's major units were Panzer Regiment 25, Rifle Regiments 6 and 7, and Artillery Regiment 78. Panzer Regiment 25 had three battalions with a combined strength of 225 panzers. The rifle regiments had two battalions each, and the artillery regiment had two motorised battalions with a total of twenty-four 105mm howitzers.[2] Other divisional units included Motor-Cycle Battalion 7, Panzer Reconnaissance Battalion 37, Anti-Tank Battalion 42, Engineer Battalion 58, Supply Battalion 58, Signals Battalion 83, and Light Flak Battalion 59. In addition, Flak Battalion 86, 1st Battery Flak Battalion 23, and a flight of Henschel 126 tactical reconnaissance aircraft were attached.[3] The most numerous panzer type in the division was the 38t, a Czech design which was neither particularly well armoured nor armed, but had a satisfactory speed and operational radius.

Rommel had no previous experience with tanks, but having seen them in action in Poland, he used his political connections to achieve his appointment. What he lacked in personal experience with armour, he could compensate for with a combination of his ample experience in daring schemes and swift movement gained in his days as a light infantryman, his natural tactical instinct, and his study of the theory and technology of armoured warfare.

The officers of the division were initially sceptical about the new commander, who was a political appointee. The doubts of the more conservative officers must have deepened due to Rommel's open commitment to the Nazi regime. His enthusiasm went so far that he often used the Nazi salute instead of the traditional military salute and he even ended his private letters with 'Heil Hitler'.[4]

Rommel used the time available to train his division, a learning experience as much for him as for his men. Deficiencies identified during the Poland campaign were addressed; live firing and combined arms training were conducted, but weather conditions, the mountainous nature of the Eiffel, the scattered deployment, delays in panzer deliveries and false alarms impaired training.[5]

Manstein's Sickle Cut plan aimed to fix the Allied left wing in Belgium by an advance of Bock's Army Group B through the Netherlands and Belgium, and the Allied right wing at the Maginot Line by feints of Leeb's Army Group C, whilst the main effort was the advance of Rundstedt's Army Group A through the wooded and hilly Ardennes region against the weak Allied centre behind the Meuse. Five out of ten German panzer divisions and three motorised infantry divisions were concentrated in Army Group A's Panzer Group Kleist. This powerful formation, closely supported by the Luftwaffe, would cross the Meuse and then dash to the coast in order to cut off the Allied 1st Army Group in Belgium and north-eastern France.[6] The Allies, who believed that the Germans would attempt a second Schlieffen Plan, intended to swing their First Army Group forward into Belgium to meet the German onslaught head-on. The wooded and hilly Ardennes area in the Allied centre was only weakly covered.[7]

Seventh Panzer Division, together with 5th Panzer Division, was part of General Hoth's XV Corps. The corps' task was to advance through the Ardennes parallel with Panzer Group Kleist to cover its right flank. This merely supporting role was confirmed by the subordination of XV Corps under Kluge's 4th Army.

In the early hours of 10 May 1940, Rommel's division, with 5th Panzer Division as right neighbour, began its move through the Ardennes. Belgian road obstructions and demolitions slowed the division's advance. The division fired the first shots in anger when encountering *Chasseurs Ardennais* at Chabrehez.[8] Rommel was well forward and personally directed the engagement, which resulted in the quick rout of the greatly outnumbered enemy. On 11 and 12 May, French cavalry of French 1st Light Mechanised Division rendered more serious resistance at the River Ourthe, but finally had to concede defeat and conduct a fighting withdrawal towards the Meuse. The forward elements of the division reached the Meuse at Dinant in the afternoon of 12 May. The bridges had been blown, but motorcyclists of 5th Panzer Division succeeded in establishing a shallow bridgehead opposite the island of Houx.[9]

On 13 May, with artillery in position on the heights on the right bank, the rifle regiments attempted to cross the river in two places between Dinant and Houx. French 18th Infantry Division, only recently arrived and not yet properly settled into defensive positions, fired from the wooded heights on the left bank of the Meuse, and subjected the infantry in their inflatables to withering small arms and well-directed artillery fire. When the crossing stalled in the face of this fire, Rommel quickly ordered houses to be set alight in order to create a smoke screen. He also ordered panzers down to the water's edge in order to suppress the enemy by direct fire. Throughout the crossing operation, he darted back and forth between the two crossing points, paying little heed to enemy fire even after his adjutant had been wounded by his side.

In spite of enemy resistance and the difficult terrain, the crossing succeeded due to French mistakes, but also Rommel's hands-on approach to command. When a French counter-attack threatened the shallow bridgehead, Rommel crossed and took direct command of the rifle battalion in the lodgement.[10]

On Hoth's orders, Rommel then dispatched Rifle Regiment 7 to Onhaye and quickly ferried panzer and armoured cars across the river in order to exploit the success. Rommel's subsequent exploitation was greatly aided by Hoth's decision to put the corps bridging train at his disposal, and thus condemned 5th Panzer Division to playing catch-up.[11]

During the night from 13 to 14 May, Rifle Regiment 7 continued its advance to the edge of Onhaye. Due to a garbled radio message, Rommel wrongly believed Rifle Regiment 7 was encircled. He immediately jumped into a panzer and rushed off with all panzer and armoured cars available to save the unit. When the situation had been clarified, Rommel led a panzer attack to outflank Onhaye. During this outflanking move, which had not been preceded by reconnaissance, Rommel's panzer suddenly encountered two French field batteries, which opened fire, disabled his panzer, and wounded him.

In the evening of 14 May, Rommel pushed further west, even though he was well aware that his left and right neighbours were still far back. He also knew that strong armoured forces, French 1st Heavy Armoured Division as it turned out, were in his right flank. Nevertheless, he took the risk to advance further west towards Rosée with his panzer regiment and one rifle regiment, forming a narrow and vulnerable salient in the process. Taking this risk paid off, since his advance had pierced the French second line. This forced French 1st Light Mechanised Division and 18th Infantry Division to withdraw further in disorder. Rommel's bold exploitation thus created the conditions for a further advance in depth.[12]

On 15 May, the division received the order to continue the advance in the direction of Philippeville-Cerfontaine. Rommel set off with the panzer regiment and soon clashed with elements of French 1st Heavy Armoured Division in the Flavion area. After a short encounter, Rommel decided to bypass this formation and continued his advance, securing the flank with artillery and anti-tank guns as well as a brief flank attack by a panzer battalion. He was also confident that his flank protection, combined with Stuka attacks and the advance of 5th Panzer Division on his right, would be able to contain the threat. Leading with the panzer regiment, Rommel then bypassed the town of Philippeville, which was held by elements of 4th North African Division. During the rapid advance, Rommel had failed to notice that Rifle Regiment 7 could not keep pace because remaining enemy machine-gun nests continued to offer resistance. This was not to be the last time that Rommel overestimated the ability of the soft-skin vehicles of his division to follow in the wake of the panzers. Rommel was forced to double back to bring up the infantry. By evening, Cerfontaine was reached.[13] The fifteenth of May was the day when the Meuse line finally collapsed due to the breakout of Guderian's XIX Corps at Sedan, 6th Panzer Division's advance to Montcornet, and 7th Panzer Division's advance to Cerfontaine. The way to the coast was now open for Panzer Group Kleist. Rommel's exploitation hence contributed to, but did not create, a very favourable operational situation.

On 16 May, Panzer Gruppe Kleist could be unleashed as envisaged in the Manstein Plan. Rundstedt and Hitler, however, became concerned that the panzer divisions might become isolated, since the infantry divisions had been unable to keep pace. The 'Halt Order of Montcornet' was the result of these fears. Aggressive panzer commanders, however, found ways to creatively interpret this order without directly violating it.[14] Rommel must have sensed that higher command echelons might put him on a tighter leash. When a preliminary corps order arrived that directed him to breach the Maginot Line extension at Sivry and advance all the way to Avesnes, Rommel did not wait for a confirmatory order, but immediately set off. Frieser shows convincingly that Rommel merely pretended not to have radio contact with his divisional headquarters, thus preventing higher headquarters transmitting a stop order.[15] Rommel thus used a variation of Nelson's Copenhagen ploy to have his own way without directly disobeying orders. This precaution turned out to be necessary as a halt order did indeed arrive in divisional headquarters later on.

In the late afternoon and evening, the lead elements of 7th Panzer Division reached the Maginot Line extension. After a short reconnaissance, Rommel quickly organised a combined arms attack with artillery, flak, panzer, engineers, and infantry, which overwhelmed French 84th Fortress Regiment of 101st Fortress Division and created a breach through the fortified lines.[16] With the breakthrough achieved, Rommel dashed down the Avesnes road with the reinforced panzer regiment. En route, during the dusk and night, his force encountered columns of French 5th Motorised Division, 4th Light Cavalry Division, 9th Motorised Division, 18th Infantry Division, and 1st Heavy Armoured Division, which were resting by the side of the road. Rather than stopping

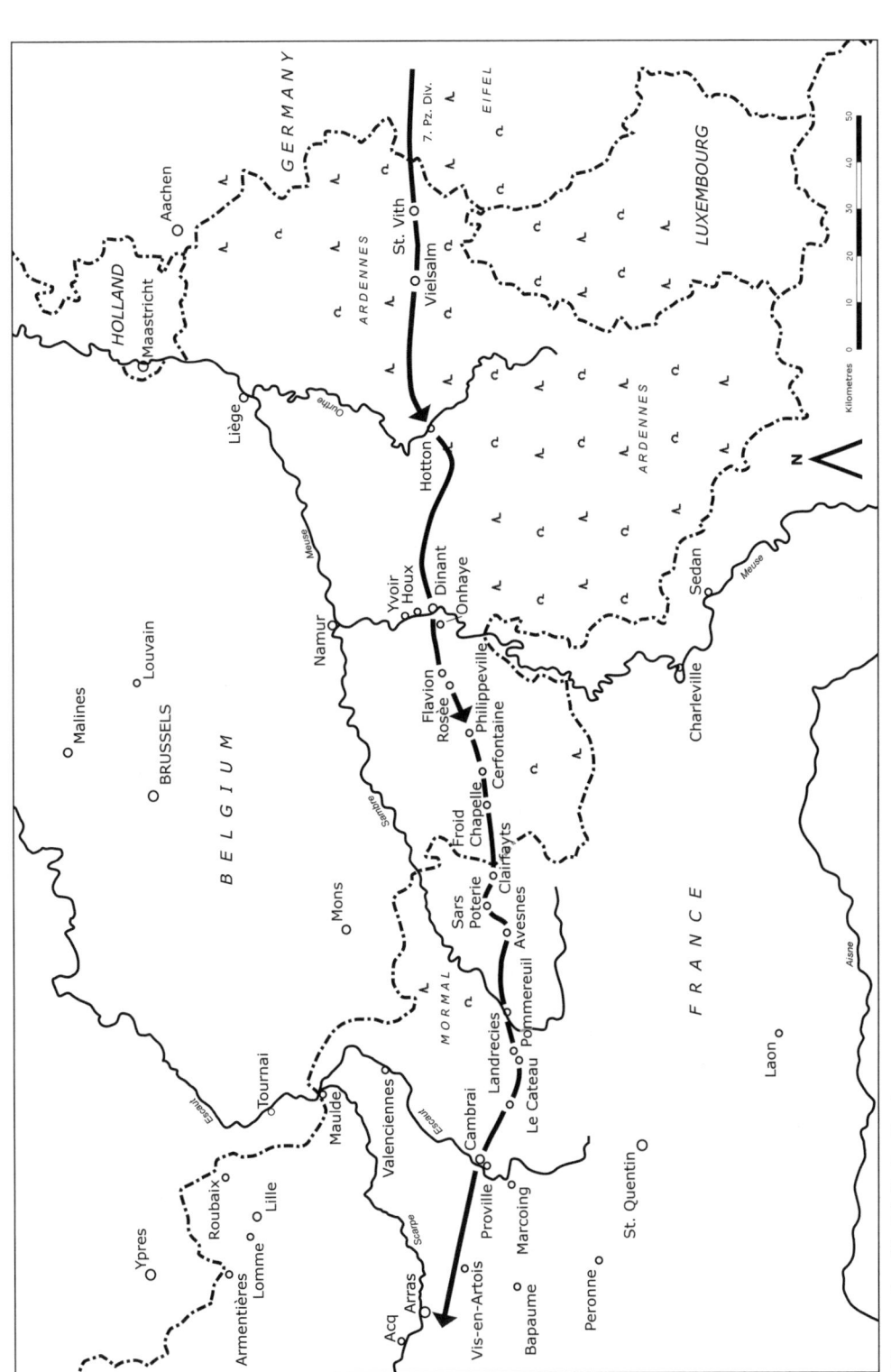

Maps produced by Mr Stefan Graeber

and engaging the resting enemy, Rommel gave the order to fire on the move with all barrels and drive on.

When the rifle regiments followed in the wake of the panzer regiment by dawn, they saw that the Avesnes road was littered with hundreds of smouldering trucks and tanks, and dead, wounded, and dazed Frenchmen. Rommel had correctly assessed the moral impact of his 'Ride of the Valkyries'. By midnight, the lead elements of the panzer regiment pushed through Avesnes, crowded with French troops and refugees, to the heights to the west of the town. Hearing the clattering of tank tracks in the dark, Rommel believed that these were his own panzers, but in fact these were the surviving tanks of the badly depleted French 1st Heavy Armoured Division, which now engaged the tail of Rommel's vanguard in street fighting. Rommel quickly manoeuvred into the rear of the unexpected enemy force and destroyed it. He could now have stopped, since he had reached the objective specified by the corps. Realising that he could push even further, however, he now decided to seize the Sambre bridge at Landrecies. Again, the panzer regiment ploughed through motorised French columns, completely taking the enemy by surprise. Rommel did not take the time to collect prisoners, but simply ordered the shaken enemy to lay down arms and march east. The bridge was taken at dawn. He then advanced even further until lack of fuel finally forced his vanguard to stop outside Le Cateau and go into all-round defence. It was only now that Rommel realised that he had not only far outrun his neighbouring divisions, but also the bulk of his own division. After Rommel had broken through the Maginot Line extension, a corps order had arrived to stop the advance until the next morning. Back in divisional headquarters, Rommel's operations officer, Major Heidkaemper, had therefore ordered the bulk of the division to stop and rest in the Sivry area. Rommel had even accomplished the rare feat of outrunning most of his own vanguard, as the battalions of the reinforced panzer regiment were scattered over many miles of road.

Isolated and far ahead with the panzer regiment, Rommel was now forced to retrace his route to collect his division. He travelled back through enemy-held territory in his armoured command car, accompanied only by a single panzer, which soon broke down. Undeterred, Rommel continued without even this minimal protection, relying entirely on his luck, his command presence, and quick thinking. French troops were on the move again on roads that the vanguard had traversed during the night. When he finally met lead elements of his division, he had a column of forty trucks full of armed Frenchmen trailing meekly behind him. Leading up the main body of his division to the panzer 'hedgehog' at Le Cateau was not simple, as enemy troops had meanwhile reoccupied the intervening space. In Rommel's absence, the panzer regiment marooned at Le Cateau, short of fuel and ammunition, had successfully defended itself against tank attacks. By the evening of 17 May, the area up to Le Cateau had been secured and prisoners and booty were collected.[17]

Rommel's feat was rewarded with the Knight's Cross and this established his reputation as a panzer leader. Beyond the breathtaking derring-do of his raid, the operational significance of this night advance lay in the fact that he maintained pressure on the enemy when other panzer divisions had to slow down due to the halt order. He had broken through the Maginot Line extension before it could be put fully into a state of defence. He had taken a bridge across the Sambre, thus making this river line untenable as a stop line. En route, he had badly mauled the troops of French II Corps which were supposed to man the Sambre line. His raid had also disrupted French attempts to shift troops south to counterattack Panzer Group Kleist. If the Avesnes raid had been Rommel's only notable feat of arms during the campaign, it would still have sufficed to establish him as a great commander.

On 17 May, General Halder, chief of staff of the army, regrouped the forces in the West. All panzer and motorised divisions came under command of Kluge's 4th Army to push to the Somme estuary. Army Group B was to become the anvil, and Army Group A the hammer. Hoth's command was reinforced and elevated to a Panzer Group.

Whilst Panzer Group Kleist was to swing round in a left hook to the Channel and then east via Dunkirk into the rear of Allied 1st Army Group, Panzer Group Hoth was to advance on Kleist's right flank via Arras. It was not until 19 May, however, that Halder could finally gain Hitler's permission to continue the unfettered advance to the coast.[18] In spite of the continued restrictions imposed on Panzer Group Kleist, Rommel was ordered to continue his advance to Cambrai on 18 May. In spite of a late start and several engagements on the way, the division reached Cambrai, but found it too heavily defended to capture. Nevertheless, the bridge across the Escaut Canal at Morenchies was taken. Once again, the division was out on a limb, since 5th Panzer Division was bogged down in fighting its way through the heavily defended Bois de Mormal. Again, Rommel accepted a high risk with his division deployed in a long salient with vulnerable flanks.[19]

On 19 May, the division found itself fighting against French units that tried to move through the division's salient. The area between Le Cateau and Cambrai was cleared and the left flank was secured by 8th Panzer Division's advance to Marcoing. A second crossing over the canal was taken at Proville. These two crossing points were to provide springboards for the advance to Arras.[20]

On 20 May, Panzer Group Kleist reached the Channel coast, thus completing the encirclement of Allied 1st Army Group. Panzer Group Hoth secured Kleist's right flank and squeezed the pocket from the south. In the small hours of 20 May, Rommel began the advance on Arras and overran marching columns of British 70th Brigade in the dark. An attempt to penetrate into Arras with panzers, however, was frustrated by the British garrison. Rommel now realised that the panzer regiment had once again advanced too quickly for the rest of the division to keep up. As on previous occasions, Rommel travelled back with his armoured car and a panzer to re-establish contact. This time, he almost over-taxed his luck when he met some tanks of a French Light Mechanised Division on the Arras-Cambrai road in Vis en Artois. The escorting panzer was destroyed and Rommel found himself in hiding for several hours. Possibly somewhat shaken by this experience, Rommel requested reinforcements from the Totenkopf Division to secure his long and exposed right flank along the Scarpe.[21]

The next day, 21 May, the division was ordered to circle around Arras in the south and south-west and reach the Scarpe at Acq. Fifth Panzer Division was ordered to advance on Rommel's right, north of Arras, Totenkopf Division was to advance on Rommel's left, whilst a motorised infantry formation would attack Arras itself. Accordingly, Rommel moved off with the panzer regiment, trailed at some distance by the rifle regiments and the artillery.

At this most inopportune time, when the division was on the move, strung out, and separated from its panzer regiment, General Martel launched what came to be known as the 'Arras Counterattack'. Luckily for 7th Panzer Division, the attack was very poorly prepared and coordinated, the attacking forces were weak, tanks and infantry were separated early on, elements of the attacking force accidentally clashed with supporting French forces, and other elements simply got lost and meandered across the battlefield. In spite of these shortcomings, the attack caused a dangerous tactical situation. Rifle Regiment 6 was shot up by tanks whilst still embussed. Quickly deployed anti-tank guns of the anti-tank battalion were unable to stop the heavily armoured Matilda tanks and were overrun. The tanks continued to push south deeper into the flank of the division. Rommel, once again impatient with the failure of the rifle regiments to keep up with the panzer regiment, had retraced his steps to hurry up his tardy troops when he witnessed the British attack unfolding. Immediately, he seized the reins. Standing on a hill at Wailly, he established several firing lines of artillery, anti-tank guns, light and heavy flak in depth in order to stop the tanks frontally, ordered the panzer regiment to turn back and strike the British into their deep right flank via Dainville, and requested Luftwaffe support. True to form, he ran from gun to gun to allocate targets, undeterred by the death of his orderly officer by his side, and bolstered the morale of his shaken men. Rommel's intervention was successful. The tanks were stopped, and Stuka attacked when the enemy was already withdrawing. The Totenkopf Division and 5th Panzer Division also had part in the defensive success. The flank attack by the panzer regiment was stopped by British anti-tank guns guarding the right flank of the attack force, and by French tanks in the same area. After heavy and costly fighting, the panzer regiment finally broke through, though too late to make its presence felt. Rather than permitting his division to lick its wounds, Rommel immediately went over to the counterattack.[22]

The Arras Counterattack was the only serious setback that Rommel suffered during this campaign. He had been caught by surprise and off balance. Spoiled by success and often indifferent enemy performance, he had failed to adequately protect his right flank whilst conducting a flank march close to a strongly garrisoned town. The heavy losses of eighty-nine killed, 116 wounded, and 173 missing were the result.[23] He can, however, take credit for his masterful handling of the crisis. It must also be borne in mind that he had reason to believe that 5th Panzer Division and a motorised infantry division would fix the British garrison in Arras.

After the battle, Rommel marred his tactically sound defensive success by sending exaggerated reports about attacks by 'hundreds of tanks' rather than the eighty-nine tanks that actually took part in the attack proper. Rundstedt and Hitler were already nervous about the possibility of powerful Allied counterattacks into the flanks of the exhausted and overstretched panzer divisions. Rommel's exaggerations added fuel to this fire, and resulted in decisions which foreshadowed the infamous Halt Order of 24 May: on 21 May, Guderian's corps' advance on the Channel ports was stopped for twenty-four hours, and XXXXI Corps was redirected east towards Arras, where the crisis had already passed, rather than continuing the advance towards the ports.[24]

On 22 May, Panzer Group Hoth continued the attack across the Scarpe that had been disrupted by Martel's counterattack on the previous day. Seventh Panzer Division quickly recovered from the shock and successfully fought its way across the Scarpe either side of Acq.[25]

On 23 May, most of Hoth's command tried to encircle the British garrison in Arras from east and west, whilst 7th Panzer Division and Totenkopf Division on its left were directed north towards the La Bassée Canal. The division reached the line Aix-Hersin-Barlin-Ruits, but then had to go over to the defence against armoured counterattacks by the French Cavalry Corps.[26] On 24 and 25 May, 7th Panzer Division reached the canal as ordered. British and Germans now faced each other across the canal, duelled with artillery, and conducted fighting patrols.[27]

On 26 May, the Halt Order was finally lifted and Hoth was ordered to advance across the canal and towards Tournai to encircle Allied formations south of Lille.[28] Seventh Panzer Division tried to cross the canal in two places between Préolan and La Bassée, with Totenkopf and 4th Panzer Division on the left, and 12th Infantry Division on the right. Whilst spirited British resistance prevented a crossing at the eastern crossing point, Rifle Regiment 7 successfully established a foothold at Guinchy. Even whilst the canal was still swept by machine-gun fire from flanking positions, Rommel immediately ordered his engineers to construct a bridge. True to form, Rommel spent the day leading from the front, directing guns and allocating targets, whilst men were killed and wounded next to him.[29]

In the early hours of 27 May, the division crossed the canal after having brushed off a weak infantry-tank counterattack. On the far bank, Rommel took his time to arrange his division in a large phalanx formation, with the three panzer battalions leading and the four infantry battalions following. The phalanx then moved off in the direction of Lille, crushing the resistance by British infantry, anti-tank guns, and some tanks, in its path. Ahead of 4th Panzer Division on the left and 5th Panzer Division on the right, the division reached Fournes at nightfall, and then the panzer regiment pressed on to Lomme, a western suburb of Lille. This time, Rommel stayed further back to ensure that the panzer regiment would not become isolated. The quick advance crossed British 2nd Division's line of withdrawal towards the Lys Canal and scattered its units. At Lomme, facing east, Rommel's division blocked the line of retreat of Allied forces attempting to fall back to the coast.[30]

On 28 May, breakout attempts by French 25th Infantry Division, the Moroccan Division, and 2nd and 5th North African Divisions were defeated by 7th Panzer Division. When Rommel made contact with 6th Army of Army Group B north of Lille, the encirclement was complete and elements of seven French divisions of IV and V Corps were trapped. Rommel can take considerable credit for this success.[31]

The battle for Lille was the end of 7th Panzer Division's part in Fall Gelb. After 29 May, the division was pulled out of the line for rest and refitting. This was very necessary as the panzer regiment had only eighty-four panzers still operable. Though the division was not brought back to full strength, some replacement panzers were received.[32]

Whilst German panzer divisions raced to the coast between 15 and 20 May, the Allies had redeployed forces in order to create a new front line running from the Channel, along the Somme and Aisne rivers, down to the Maginot Line. Since the Germans gave priority to eliminating the Dunkirk Pocket, French forces outside the pocket gained time to consolidate this line. In the first days of June, the panzer divisions redeployed for "Fall Rot", the second phase of the campaign. The plan envisaged that 4th Army, now part of Army Group B, was to cross the Somme, push west to Rouen and Le Havre and establish bridgeheads across the Seine. At the same time, 6th and 9th Armies, including Panzer Group Kleist, would cross the Aisne and then advance south, to the east of Paris. The decisive attack would be carried out by Panzer Group

Guderian of Army Group A further east, which would rush south-east towards the Swiss border and entrap the French divisions behind the Maginot Line.[33]

Seventh Panzer Division, with 5th Panzer Division and 20th Motorised Division part of Hoth's XV Corps, which was subordinated to 4th Army, was once again allocated to a supporting effort. On 3 and 4 June, the division moved into its jumping-off positions north of Amiens. At 0430h, on 5 June, 7th Panzer Division, with infantry leading, attacked across the Somme in two places and established a bridgehead. The crossing did not present a comparable challenge to that of the Meuse on 13 May, as French defences along the Somme were weakly held, the terrain was more open, and the French 5th Colonial Infantry Division had only just taken over this sector and had failed to demolish two railway bridges in Rommel's sector. Nevertheless, the village of Hangest was so stoutly defended that it had to be bypassed and could only be captured after a Stuka attack and hard fighting.

Since the French were too weak to hold a continuous frontline, Weygand, the French generalissimo, had adopted a checkerboard system of strongpoints based on villages and woods.[34]

Rommel, however, had no intention of delaying himself by fighting for villages. Instead, he deployed the division in a box formation, with the panzer regiment in the lead, the reconnaissance battalion protecting the flanks, and mounted or unmounted riflemen in the centre, the rest of the division following, whilst the artillery advanced by leaps and bounds, ready to deliver fire to the front or flanks as needed. In this formation, the division simply advanced cross-country, brushing off counterattacks into the flanks and suppressing enemy fire by firing on the move. Aided by the capture of the bridges, Rommel was soon ahead of 5th Panzer Division.[35]

On 6 June, Rommel's division continued the advance cross-country in box formation. A flank attack by a French tank regiment could be defeated by artillery alone. This time, Hoth did not wish 7th Panzer Division to surge ahead. Instead, 5th and 7th Panzer Division were ordered to advance side by side towards Forges-les-Eaux.[36]

By 7 June, XV Corps had advanced so far that French IX Corps, which held the line of the Bresle all the way to the coast, was cut off from the rest of 10th Army. British and French scratch forces were rapidly deployed to prevent 5th and 7th Panzer Divisions from reaching the Seine. En route, French 17th Light Infantry Division was overtaken on the march by Rommel's division and suffered heavy losses. By evening, the corps objective, the Paris-Dieppe highway between Forges-les-Eaux and Argueil, had been reached.[37]

On 8 June, French 10th Army had been irretrievably split in half. French IX Corps on the left began the withdrawal parallel to the coast towards Rouen, whilst the right wing of the Army folded back towards Paris. Hoth's panzer corps now had to seize Rouen and a crossing point across the Seine. Conscious of the need to capture a bridge, Rommel sped ahead with a light vanguard, clashed with British infantry at Sigy, and successfully took a bridge across the Andelle at Normanville. Following a corps order, Rommel then led the advance with the panzer regiment and the motorcycle battalion down the Seine valley towards Elbeuf. An attempted *coup de main* by the motorcyclists on the bridge at Elbeuf failed during the night. The reconnaissance battalion, meanwhile, arrived too late at Tourville to capture the bridge intact. A frustrated Rommel pulled back from the Seine and assembled his division in the Boos-Tourville-Sotteville area. In the meantime, 5th Panzer Division had likewise failed to take the bridges in Rouen.[38]

Though XVth Corps had failed to secure a Seine crossing, the advance to the Seine had severed French IXth Corps's line of retreat. This corps was now forced to withdraw towards Le Havre for embarkation.

On 9 May, the divisions of XVth Corps redeployed facing north, with 7th Panzer Division on the left, 2nd Motorised Division in the centre, and 5th Panzer Division on the right. The task of 7th Panzer Division was to intercept an Allied withdrawal to Le Havre, whilst the other two divisions had to prevent a breakthrough of IXth Corps to the south.

On 10 June, at 0430h, Rommel set off with a strong vanguard to the coast, advancing via Ourville to Veulettes. At the crossroads in Quainville, Rommel's vanguard arrived in time to stop the columns of French 31st Infantry Division of IX Corps which tried to reach Le Havre. The columns were scattered by rapid fire. In the early afternoon, lead elements of 7th Panzer Division reached the sea at Veulettes and les Petites Dalles. The rifle regiments, supported by artillery, meanwhile deployed further south along the Durdent, facing east, where they successfully repulsed breakthrough attempts towards Le Havre. Most of French IX Corps was

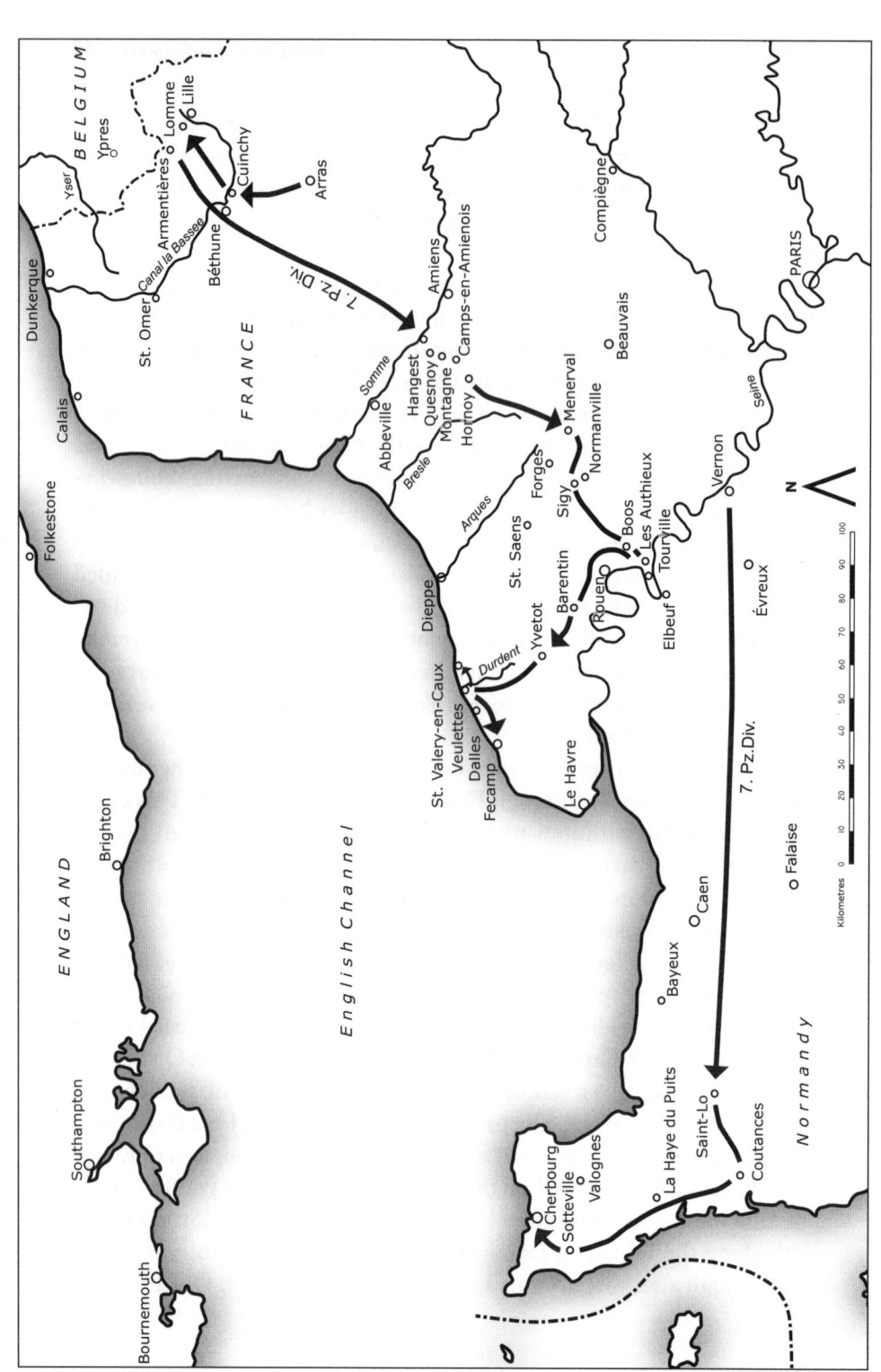

Maps produced by Mr Stefan Graeber

now trapped. The 51st Highland Division, which fought as part of this corps, had sent an improvised formation, called Arkforce, ahead towards Le Havre.

Further west, at Fécamp, the reconnaissance battalion took the high ground east of the town, but was unable to prevent Arkforce's successful withdrawal to Le Havre. Few prisoners were captured, but British ships were taken under fire, several were sunk, and a destroyer was damaged.[39] With the escape route to Le Havre blocked and the port of Dieppe made unusable by demolitions, IX Corps had to hold the tiny ports of St Valéry-en-Caux and Veules for the purpose of embarkation. Whilst 5th Panzer Division and 2nd Motorised Division closed in on St Valéry from the south, 7th Panzer Division approached from the west, along the coast.

On 11 June, in the afternoon, Rommel launched his attack with panzers and riflemen, supported by artillery. In spite of fierce resistance by battalions of the Highland Division, elements of 7th Panzer Division reached the western cliffs overlooking the port. With direct German observation of the harbour, embarkation had become impossible in broad daylight. When the Highlanders refused Rommel's demand to surrender and fortified the port instead, Rommel tried to penetrate into the town with panzers and infantry under cover of a heavy artillery bombardment, but failed in the face of stiff resistance. During the night, a combination of rain, fog, and harassment fire by Rommel's artillery and heavy weapons prevented embarkations in St Valéry, though about 3,000 Allied troops were evacuated from Veules.

On 12 June, British and French ships duelled with German heavy flak positioned on the western cliffs. It had now become clear that an evacuation was impossible. When Rommel renewed his attack into the port, the commander of IX Corps and his divisional commanders, including General Fortune commanding 51st Highland Division, had to surrender with 46,000 men and a vast quantity of vehicles and materiel. In conversation with the captured general officers, Rommel learned that his division had been dubbed '*la division fantôme*' due to its rapid and unpredictable movements. The encirclement of IX Corps was a signal achievement, but it must be born in mind that this was a success of XV Corps, not just of 7th Panzer Division, though Rommel's capture of the western cliffs was the decisive moment in the battle.[40]

The capture of St Valéry seemed to mark the high point and end of Rommel's part in the campaign. However, the services of 7th Panzer Division would be required one more time before the end of hostilities. On 17 June, XVth Corps ordered 5th Panzer Division to race to Rennes and Brest, whilst 7th Panzer Division was given Cherbourg as the objective. This order had been prompted by two developments: first, the concern that Allied forces might regroup in Brittany and turn the peninsula into a redoubt; second, Marshal Pétain's announcement that he was seeking a ceasefire made it desirable to improve the German bargaining position by making additional conquests.[41]

Seventh Panzer Division crossed the Seine at Vernon and advanced via St Lô to the foot of the Cotentin Peninsula. The division moved in two columns. Rommel led the left column up the western side of the peninsula, whilst the right divisional column, reinforced by Colonel von Senger's motorised brigade, moved up the eastern side of the peninsula. The advance from the Seine to the Cotentin peninsula met little opposition, even though the areas crossed were full of French troops. Obviously, the troops were under the impression that the war was already over and any further resistance was pointless.

Over twenty-four hours, 7th Panzer Division covered a record distance of 240 kilometres. The advance suddenly came to an end at La Haye du Puits, when the tip of Rommel's column rushed into a roadblock manned by French marines. He was forced to stop overnight and prepare a deliberate attack for the morning.

On 18 June, the defenders of the roadblock withdrew, and the left column of the division could resume the advance to Cherbourg, approaching the fortified port from the west and south-west. Losses were suffered when the fortress artillery opened fire, forcing Rommel to wait for the rest of his division to come up before resuming the attack. During the night, artillery arrived and the right-hand column completed the investment of the town from the south-east. On 19 June, the attack on Cherbourg recommenced with Stuka and artillery support and ended in the French surrender.[42]

At Cherbourg, Rommel could not repeat the success of St Valéry. Though large quantities of war materiel and thousands of French prisoners were captured, British troops of the 52nd Lowland and ad hoc Beauman Divisions had escaped, and many of the vehicles they had left behind had been rendered unusable. Nevertheless, the capture of this major port after a lightning-fast advance was a major military achievement. It must therefore have been galling to Rommel that Colonel von Senger had forestalled him in accepting the formal surrender of the fortress.[43]

After the surrender of Cherbourg, 7th Panzer Division was directed south and rushed via Rennes, Chateaubriant, Ancenis, Niort and St Jean to Saintes on the Atlantic coast, where the campaign finally ended on 24 June.

In statistical terms, 7th Panzer Division had performed magnificently: for a loss of 2,592 men and fifty-two armoured vehicles, the division had captured tens of thousands of prisoners, thousands of trucks and other motor vehicles, hundreds of tanks and guns, as well as vast stockpiles of ammunition, fuel, and military hardware.[44]

As a divisional commander, Rommel could only achieve as much as the instrument in his hands permitted. Even a commander of Rommel's ability could not have conducted the Avesnes Raid with an immobile or weak formation. A panzer division was the most powerful and versatile type of formation of the German Army. Whilst his panzers were not as well armoured or armed as the heavier French and British types, they were mechanically reliable, ergonomic in design, and well equipped with radio. In contrast to many French and British armoured formations, the German panzer divisions were also well-balanced formations, which lent themselves to the tactical and organisational integration of panzers, motorised infantry, artillery, and engineers. The allocation of short-range reconnaissance aircraft also proved very useful, as these increased Rommel's situational awareness, and therefore his ability to take calculated risks. Apart from these organic divisional assets, Rommel's command profited from Luftwaffe air support and was often reinforced by units subordinated from other divisions.

In the three months that Rommel had been in command of the division before the start of the campaign, he had to train his new command as well as learn the handling of a panzer division himself. In terms of tactical competence at the unit level, there is no evidence to suggest that the battalions of his division were not well trained. Enemy accounts suggest quick reactions and well-rehearsed drills. The various arms of his division also competently fought together in combined arms combat, the graduate level of conventional warfare. Examples for successful combined arms combat can be found during the Meuse crossing, the breakthrough of the extended Maginot Line, and the crossing of the La Bassée Canal. Rommel himself was not completely satisfied. He complained that panzer crews were too slow in opening fire on fleeting targets, that his men too often sought cover rather than suppressing the enemy with rapid fire, and that marching discipline was initially poor.[45]

Whilst successful enough in training his division, Rommel had less success moulding his regimental and battalion commanders and staff officers into his own image. The relationship between himself and his operations officer, Major Heidkaemper, a vital relationship in the German command system, was tense. Heidkaemper found it difficult to adjust to Rommel's thrusting and mobile style of leadership and did not see sufficiently eye-to-eye with his commander to divine Rommel's intentions when the latter was out of contact. There may have been a degree of animosity between Rommel, the self-educated field soldier, and Heidkaemper, the trained General Staff officer. Rommel also seemed disappointed by the inability of the commanders of his rifle regiments to keep up with the panzer regiment. Repeatedly, Rommel saw elements of his division performing less well when he was not personally present. At Elbeuf, the commander of the motorcycle battalion failed to take more energetic measures to capture the bridge intact. At Givenchy, a battalion of Rifle Regiment 7 had established a bridgehead but failed to take Givenchy and clear the banks of the canal as ordered.[46] Rommel was therefore forced to travel backwards and forwards to take direct control rather than trust in his subordinates. In the later stages of the campaign, however, the division began to act as a coherent formation.

There is no doubt that Rommel was an effective leader who impressed and inspired the men under his command with his energy and personal courage. By leading from the front and personally taking charge at the point of main effort, he had a direct and decisive impact on his division's success.[47] The personal risks that he took, however, put the effective command of his division in question. His death, particularly in the early stages of the campaign, would have left Major Heidkaemper struggling to take effective command of the often-dispersed division.

Rommel's skill as a combat leader is not in doubt, but how did he cope with the more mundane aspects of command? He probably paid less attention to logistics than he should have done. During the Avesnes Raid, he left his panzer regiment isolated and marooned, short of fuel and ammunition. During his advance on Lille, however, he was more circumspect and personally supervised the protected movement of fuel and ammunition to the most forward units. Sometimes, attention to detail was lacking: the Meuse crossing had to be conducted in full view of the enemy, because the divisional artillery did not have smoke shells available. On other occasions, however, he was more assiduous, for instance when personally supervising the deployment of heavy weapons.

How did Rommel's leadership style compare to official military doctrine as laid down in 'Truppenfuehrung', the keystone doctrine? Truppenfuehrung stressed the importance of leading from the front and the personal presence of the divisional commander at the point of main effort, even at the risk of courting death. It also stressed, however, that the divisional commander had to choose his place in such a manner that he could effectively lead his whole division, not just part of it. It also emphasised that the operations officer had to be in a position to take over command when the commander was incommunicado or incapacitated. Rommel was thus only broadly in line with established doctrine.[48]

There is little reason to doubt Rommel's tactical competence. He successfully conducted deliberately planned as well as hastily improvised engagements. His division crossed defended rivers, achieved breakthroughs, fought in wooded, hilly, and open country alike; it attacked, defended, and pursued. Of particular interest is Rommel's order of march. Rather than sending a lightly armoured vanguard ahead to scout, and following with the bulk of the combat power of his division, Rommel threw his most potent force, the panzer regiment, forward in order to maintain momentum and crush enemy opposition on the move. This tactic ensured that he could surprise and overwhelm the enemy with strong combat power on first encounter. The downside was the threat of ambush, as happened at Onhaye, and the risk of flank attack on the unarmoured elements of the division, as happened at Arras. Rommel was not a creature of routine, but rather organised the order of march depending on terrain and the overall situation. When time was of the essence, for instance when bridges had to be captured, or lines of retreat had to be intercepted, he sent the reconnaissance or motorcycle battalion ahead. When more than one road was available, he would advance in parallel columns, one of which was designated the main effort and had the panzer regiment allocated. When the enemy no longer had a continuous frontline and the terrain was open, the division advanced in a vast box formation.

German doctrine put a premium on the competent conduct of the all-arms battle. Rommel organised his division into several mixed formations, usually by reinforcing the panzer regiment with anti-tank guns, artillery, motorcycle troops, engineers, and reconnaissance elements, or by reinforcing his infantry regiments with some panzer and supporting arms. This organisation ensured that a mix of arms and capabilities was always at hand.

Rommel displayed his tactical competence on many occasions: for the Meuse crossing at Dinant, he combined the indirect fire of artillery with the direct fire of panzers to cover the assault by infantry. The breakthrough of the Maginot Line extension was a well-executed attack in which indirect fire suppressed the defender in depth, artillery fired smoke, engineers and infantry closed in under covering fire of panzer fire and smoke and created a breach, and the panzers then exploited in depth. At Arras he improvised an anti-tank front from anti-tank, flak, and artillery guns, ordered a flank attack by the panzer regiment, and arranged for air support. During the crossing of the La Bassée Canal, he used direct and indirect fire to suppress the defender and get his infantry across, and quickly defeated a counterattack by combining panzer and artillery fire. Remaining resistance between the canal and Lille was squashed by advancing with the panzer regiment in steamroller fashion, followed by unmounted infantry. Artillery advanced in waves to cover the division on the move, but was quickly concentrated on a single target when needed. In keeping with the spirit of 'Truppenfuehrung', he did not operate by template but solved each tactical problem individually.

In general, Rommel was a good judge of risk. He pursued without heed to flank security when he sensed that the enemy was faltering or uncoordinated.[49] At Flavion, he pushed past a French armoured division which potentially presented a fatal threat to his right flank, relying on French sluggishness and the expected arrival of 5th Panzer Division to protect his command. During the pursuit to the Seine, he advanced in box formation at high speed and relied on his artillery to brush off flank attacks. The advance to Cherbourg was conducted as a race through territory full of enemy troops, under the correct assumption that the French will to fight had, by and large, evaporated. At Cherbourg, he may have underestimated the risk posed by fortress artillery, and his infantry suffered accordingly, but he had reason to believe the risk worthwhile. At Arras, he seriously misjudged the risk presented by the British garrison, but can be exonerated as he had been led to believe that the garrison would be fixed by neighbouring divisions. On occasion, he was too rash; for instance when he pushed with armour from the line of march into Le Cateau, Arras, and Lille, only to be repulsed in the face of unexpected resistance.

Often, Rommel is given credit for innovation, such as using 88mm flak in an anti-tank role, the cross-country advance in box formation, mixed battlegroups, speculative firing on the move, and the Stosslinie. But how innovative was Rommel? Using 88mm anti-aircraft guns in a ground role was not unorthodox, as doctrine envisaged this possibility, the design of the Flak 36 reflected its dual purpose, and 5th Panzer Division did likewise.[50] Rommel's use of mixed battlegroups, based on a panzer or motorised infantry regiment, was by no means unusual either. Again, 5th Panzer Division operated in a similar manner. The cross-country advance with panzer leading on a broad frontage was reflected in doctrine and was also practiced by 5th Panzer Division.[51] Rommel's preference for firing on the move on identified or suspected enemy positions violated orthodoxy, which frowned on waste of ammunition. Guderian explicitly warned against untargetted shooting on the move and blithely relying on the psychological effect of tanks dashing through enemy positions, guns blazing.[52] Rommel's practice, however, was justified by his success. His willingness to conduct night advances with armour through enemy-held territory, even an armoured night attack on a fortified line, was unorthodox as well. Neither course of action would have been considered by more conventional generals. To continue the pursuit of a beaten enemy through the night, however, was part of doctrine.[53]

An invention that Rommel can exclusively take credit for is the 'Stosslinie'. The Stosslinie was a line arbitrarily drawn on the tactical maps. All orders could be given with reference to the Stosslinie. Since the enemy did not know the particulars of the Stosslinie, he could not make sense of geographical data communicated. Hence, radio transmissions could be sent in the clear, which simplified matters and accelerated the flow of orders and reports without compromising security.[54]

In summary, it seems fair to say that Rommel was innovative but not a revolutionary. Rommel was an imaginative commander. He often sought solutions to tactical problems that would not be out of place in Sun Tzu's *Art of War*. He used bluff and negotiations to undermine the resolve of his enemy and avoid unnecessary fighting. At other times, he confused the enemy: on two occasions, he let his panzers drive through an enemy-held forest with the crew sitting on top and waving white strips of cloth.[55] This stratagem was uncomfortably close to misusing the white flag.

For all his craftiness, Rommel was chivalrous by nature and not prone to order or condone acts of needless violence. At Cherbourg, he took precautions against looting and lapses of discipline.[56] He treated prisoners of war with consideration. On one occasion, he was forced to order the shooting of a French lieutenant-colonel for refusing to obey his captors.[57] Rommel's tactic of speculatively shooting on the move at potential enemy positions was tactically and psychologically sensible, but dangerous for the civilian population. On one occasion, the policy of shooting first led to the unintended destruction of an ambulance column.[58] Members of his division have been accused of murdering captured Black colonial troops at Arraines after the Somme crossing.[59] Arraines, however, was not in the sector of 7th Panzer Division. At Hangest, where elements of 7th Panzer Division encountered stubborn resistance by Black colonial troops, over a hundred prisoners were taken, some of whom were apparently shot.[60] It is unlikely, though, that Rommel ordered this atrocity or was even aware of it. On 8 June, during the advance to the Seine, Colonel Broomhall of British 1st Armoured Division was captured at Martainville, most likely by members of 7th Panzer Division, and used as a human shield on the lead panzer. Again, there is no evidence that Rommel knew or approved.[61]

A divisional commander must ensure that his actions contribute to the success of the parent formation. Did Rommel demonstrate an ability to think at the operational level of war? Rommel's scope for operational level decisions was limited. On the one hand, Hoth, his corps commander, set objectives, which were too specific to give Rommel opportunity to practice independent operational judgement, and too ambitious to easily exceed. On the other hand, Rommel's awareness of the larger picture at army, army group, or theatre level, was probably limited, which made it difficult to see the manoeuvre of his division in the larger context. For the most part, Rommel simply tried to reach the objectives specified by corps orders. During the Avesnes Raid, however, Rommel used his independent judgement to continue all the way to Le Cateau, well beyond the specified objective.

Rommel did not unduly focus on minor tactical success for its own sake and at the expense of momentum. He avoided combat if it threatened to needlessly slow down his advance. He merely checked French armour at Flavion rather than trying to destroy the whole formation, and he bypassed strongly defended towns and villages in order to penetrate as far and as fast as possible across open country. It is difficult to say, though, whether this emphasis on exploiting to the hilt was based on a sophisticated analysis of likely operational effects, whether he merely followed his stormtrooper instinct, or whether he simply tried to outrun any competitors in the race for honour and glory. On balance, it seems that Rommel's rapid rate of advance reflected his appreciation of the importance of momentum both at the tactical and at the operational levels.

Which personal qualities did Rommel display as a divisional commander? His personal courage was undeniable, often bordering on the foolhardy. His determination and energy inspired and compelled his men forward, even when exhausted or frightened. His personal fitness was a *sine qua non* for his style of command.[62] In moments of crisis, such as during the Meuse crossing and at Arras, he remained calm and decisive. At Arras, at the height of the crisis, he even found time to chastise members of the Totenkopf Division for failing to show proper respect to his rank.[63]

Rommel could be a benevolent commander. The services of his officers did not go unrecognised. The war diary lists the names of those who performed beyond the call of duty. Three of his regimental commanders received the Knight's Cross. On the other hand, he could be vindictive when he felt slighted. He was not above favouritism: during the attack on St Valéry he gave Lieutenant Hanke, state secretary in the propaganda ministry, a command that overtaxed his abilities and resulted in a bungled attack.

For all his desire to advance at the highest possible rate, Rommel was no butcher, willing to sacrifice his men needlessly.[64] At La Haye du Puits, he stopped overnight to prepare a well-supported attack for the next morning, rather than trying to force his way through a well-defended roadblock. At Cherbourg, he waited for reinforcements rather than expose his infantry to strong artillery fire.[65] Nevertheless, it must be noted that his division suffered heavier losses than 5th Panzer Division, even though the latter had to fight harder in some places, such as Flavion and the Fôret de Mormal.[66]

Rommel's benevolence did not extend to his peers. He did not give credit to other formations which had contributed to his successes, such as 5th Panzer Division at the Meuse and at St Valéry, to Brigade Senger at Cherbourg, or to the Luftwaffe, whose air support often made his task easier. He was ruthlessly competitive: on 14 May, he misappropriated a panzer unit from 5th Panzer Division and refused to give it back. He then failed to support this division in its fight against French 1st Armoured Division and added insult to injury by complaining that the sister division was hanging back.[67]

Relations with his superiors seemed good. Kluge, commanding 4th Army, wrote a very complimentary foreword to the divisional war diary, though he also remarked that Rommel had underplayed the achievements of other divisions. Rommel and Hoth also seemed to get on well with each other. Hoth even resented Hartlieb, commanding 5th Panzer Division, for being less thrusting than Rommel. Even so, Hoth was irritated by Rommel's efforts to blow his own trumpet, which is reflected in his rather ambivalent foreword to the war diary. Also, Hoth wrote a confidential report in which he warned that Rommel was too prone to act on impulse.[68] Rommel, for his part, was a loyal subordinate as long as corps orders gave him sufficient latitude. When he found orders restrictive or irksome, he found ways to circumvent them.

Sadly, Rommel was a glory hunter. He made sure that he had a senior representative of the propaganda ministry as well as the editor of the *Stuermer* in his division. He kept Hitler and *Wehrmachtsadjutant* Colonel Schmundt up to date on his latest exploits.[69] When he learned that the divisions on his left and right had stopped for the night during the advance on Lille, he was jubilant and pressed on in order to steal a march on his competitors.[70] He produced a prettified account of his division's part in the campaign, which exaggerated his own successes whilst slighting those of others. He rejoiced in the recognition and honours that he received from Hitler. His pursuit of personal recognition could be highly damaging to his own side: his exaggerated and self-serving account of the attack at Arras contributed to the infamous Dunkirk Halt Order. To use a sports analogy, Rommel was like the football player that charges at the goal without ever passing the ball to a teammate. To be fair, though, he did score the goal.

Overall, Rommel was a very successful divisional commander who made his name as a panzer leader during the campaign. His success was well deserved due to his personal courage, determination, and tactical skill, though it was at times marred by his selfish pursuit of glory and recognition. He regularly achieved or exceeded objectives set by his superiors and significantly contributed to the German victory in this campaign. Some of his feats of arms, such as the Avesnes Raid, remain textbook examples to this day. As Hoth rightly observed, however, Rommel's division did not fight alone and could at times only achieve its victories as part of a greater team, just as the division aided the success of the rest of the team.

### Notes

1. David Irving, *The Trail of the Fox: The Life of Field-Marshal Erwin Rommel* (London: Macmillan, 1985), p. 45.
2. A third artillery battalion joined the division on 5 June.
3. Karl-Heinz Frieser, *Blitzkrieg-Legende: Der Westfeldzug 1940* 3rd edn. (Munich: Oldenburg, 2005), p. 279; Thomas L. Jentz, *Panzer Truppen: The Complete Guide to the Creation and Combat Employment of Germany's Tank Force, 1933-1942* Volume 1 (Atglen: Schiffer, 1996), p. 121; Hasso von Manteuffel, *Die 7. Panzer-Division, 1935-1945: Die 'Gespenster Division'* (Friedberg: Podzun-Pallas, 1978), p. 24; Horst Scheibert, *Die Gespenster-Division: Eine Deutsche Panzer-Division (7.) im Zweiten Weltkrieg* (Friedberg: Podzun-Pallas, no date), p. 9.
4. Frieser, *Blitzkrieg-Legende*, p. 278; Irving, *Trail of Fox*, pp. 29, 36-38; Maurice Remy, *Mythos Rommel* 2nd edn. (Berlin: List, 2007), pp. 46-51; Ralf Georg Reuth, *Rommel: The End of a Legend*, translated by Debra S. Marmor and Herbert A. Danner (London: Haus Books, 2005), pp. 42-46.
5. Fraser, David, *Knight's Cross: A Life of Field Marshal Erwin Rommel* (London: Harper Collins, 1994), pp. 157-61; Jentz, *Panzer Truppen*, p. 106; Hans von Luck, *Panzer Commander: The Memoirs of Colonel Hans von Luck* (New York: Praeger,

1989), p. 27; Scheibert, *Gespenster-Division*, pp. 21-22.
6. Frieser, *Blitzkrieg-Legende*, pp. 100-06, 118-19, 278.
7. Frieser, *Blitzkrieg-Legende*, pp. 106-10, 162; G. Roton, *Années Cruciales* (Paris: Charles-Lavauzelle, 1947), p. 124.
8. Georges Hautecler, *Rommel and Guderian against the Belgian Chasseurs Ardennais: The Combats at Chabrehez and Bodange, 10 May 1940*, translated by G.F. Nafziger (West Chester: Nafziger Collection, 2003), pp. 31-53.
9. A. Doumenc, *Histoire de la Neuvième Armée: 10-18 Mai 1940* (Paris: Arthaud, 1945), pp. 44-45, 47, 51, 55; Frieser, *Blitzkrieg-Legende*, pp. 280-85; Imperial War Museum, AL596, *Kriegstagebuch, Ia, 7. Panzerdivision, 1940*, pp. 8-18.
10. Doumenc, *Histoire*, pp. 65-69, 83-88; Frieser, *Blitzkrieg-Legende*, pp. 285-88; *Kriegstagebuch*, pp. 19-22; B.H. Liddell Hart, *The Rommel Papers*, translated by Paul Findlay (London: Collins, 1953), pp. 7-11.
11. Frieser, *Blitzkrieg-Legende*, pp. 288-89; Plato, Anton-Detlev von, *Geschichte der 5. Panzer Division, 1938-45* (Regensburg: Walhalla, 1978), p. 51.
12. Doumenc, *Histoire*, pp. 111-24, 129-31; Frieser, *Blitzkrieg-Legende*, pp. 292-95; *Kriegstagebuch*, pp. 23-26; Liddell Hart, *Rommel Papers*, pp. 11-13; Roton, *Années Cruciales*, pp. 160-64.
13. Doumenc, *Histoire*, pp. 146-47, 155-56, 173-77; Frieser, *Blitzkrieg-Legende*, pp., 258, 276, 297, 299; A. Goutard, *The Battle of France, 1940*, translated by A.R.P. Burgess (London: Frederick Muller, 1958), pp. 165-74; *Kriegstagebuch*, pp. 27-30; Pierre Lyet, *La Bataille de France: Mai-June 1940* (Paris: Payot, 1947), pp. 49-60; Plato, *Geschichte*, p. 60; Liddell Hart, *Rommel Papers*, pp. 14-16; Roton, *Années Cruciales*, pp. 174-84.
14. Frieser, *Blitzkrieg-Legende*, pp. 318-22.
15. Frieser, *Blitzkrieg-Legende*, pp. 331-41.
16. Guy Heynen, *Le 84e RIF et la 1e DINA défendent L'Est de L'Avesnois* (Cerfontaine: no publisher, 1990), pp. 37-46; *Kriegstagebuch*, pp. 31-35; Liddell Hart, *Rommel Papers*, pp. 17-19.
17. Doumenc, *Histoire*, pp. 183-86, 195-201, 225, 238-40; Frieser, *Blitzkrieg-Legende*, pp. 331-40; *Kriegstagebuch*, pp. 35-37; Liddell Hart, *Rommel Papers*, pp. 20-26.
18. Frieser, *Blitzkrieg-Legende*, pp. 322, 343.
19. Doumenc, *Histoire*, pp. 263-70, 273; *Kriegstagebuch*, 40-44; Plato, *Geschichte*, p. 66; Liddell Hart, *Rommel Papers*, pp. 26-28.
20. *Kriegstagebuch*, pp. 45-46.
21. Gregory Blaxland, *Destination Dunkirk: The Story of Gort's Army* (London: William Kimber, 1973), pp. 129-30; L.F. Ellis, *The War in France and Flanders, 1939-1940* (London: HMSO, 1953), pp. 79-80, 88; *Kriegstagebuch*, pp. 47-50; David Rissik, *The DLI at War: The History of the Durham Light Infantry, 1939-1945* (London: Birchall, 1952), pp. 35-40; Wolfgang Vopersal, *Soldaten, Kaempfer, Kameraden: Marsch und Kaempfe der SS-Totenkopf Division*, Volume 1 (Bielefeld: Selbstverlag der Truppenkameradschaft, 1983), pp. 111-13.
22. Blaxland, *Destination Dunkirk*, pp. 132-137, 170-186; Ellis, *War in France and*

*Flanders*, pp. 87-97; Frieser, *Blitzkrieg-Legende*, pp. 344-57; *Kriegstagebuch*, pp. 51-55; Plato, *Geschichte*, pp. 69-71; Liddell Hart, *Rommel Papers*, pp. 30-33; Vopersal, *Soldaten*, pp. 115-35.

23. Ninety of the 173 missing men, however, reported back to duty. See Scheibert, *Gespenster-Division*, p. 36.
24. Frieser, *Blitzkrieg-Legende*, pp. 358-360; Army Group A War Diary, 22 May, quoted in Hans-Adolf Jacobsen (ed.), *Dokumente zum Westfeldzug 1940* (Goettingen: Musterschmidt, 1960), pp. 65-66; 'Halt Order', 24 May, quoted in ibid., p. 120.
25. Blaxland, *Destination Dunkirk*, pp. 175-77, 184; *Kriegstagebuch*, pp. 56-57; Plato, *Geschichte*, p. 73.
26. Blaxland, *Destination Dunkirk*, p. 184; *Kriegstagebuch*, pp. 58-59; Vopersal, *Soldaten*, pp. 139-46.
27. *Kriegstagebuch*, pp. 60-61; Plato, *Geschichte*, p. 77.
28. OKH Order, 26 May, quoted in Jacobsen, *Dokumente*, pp. 137-38.
29. *Kriegstagebuch*, pp. 62-64; Luck, *Panzer Commander*, p. 32; Liddell Hart, *Rommel Papers*, pp. 35-36.
30. Blaxland, *Destination Dunkirk*, pp. 268, 287-88; Ellis, *War in France and Flanders*, pp. 190, 194; Halder's Diary, 26 May, quoted in Jacobsen, *Dokumente*, p. 83; *Kriegstagebuch*, pp. 65-70; Plato, *Geschichte*, pp. 78-80; Liddell Hart, *Rommel Papers*, pp. 37-39.
31. Blaxland, *Destination Dunkirk*, pp. 289-90; *Kriegstagebuch*, pp. 70-72; Liddell Hart, *Rommel Papers*, pp. 40-41; Roton, *Années Cruciales*, pp. 237-38.
32. Jentz, *Panzer Truppen*, p. 135; Scheibert, *Gespenster-Division*, p. 39.
33. OKH Aufmarschanweisung, 31 May, quoted in Jacobsen, *Dokumente*, pp. 152-57; Umbreit, Hans, 'Der Kampf um die Vormachtstellung in Westeuropa', in Militaergeschichtliches Forschungsamt (ed.), *Das Deutsche Reich und der Zweite Weltkrieg*, Volume 2 (Stuttgart: Deutsche Verlagsanstalt, 1979), pp. 299-305.
34. Weygand, Order, 25 May, quoted in Roton, *Années Cruciales*, p. 245.
35. Michael Glover, *The Fight for the Channel Ports, Calais to Brest 1940: A Study in Confusion* (London: Leo Cooper, 1985), pp. 148, 154-55; *Kriegstagebuch*, pp. 75-81; Dominique Lormier, *La Bataille de France, Jour après Jour, Mai-Juin 1940* (Paris: Le Cherche Midi, 2010), pp. 424-26; Lyet, *Bataille de France*, p. 124; Plato, *Geschichte*, pp, 84-86; Liddell Hart, *Rommel Papers*, pp. 46-50; Roton, *Années Cruciales*, p. 254.
36. Glover, *Fight for Channel Ports*, pp. 155-57; *Kriegstagebuch*, pp. 82-83; Lormier, *Bataille de France*, p. 435; Lyet, *Bataille de France*, p. 124; Plato, *Geschichte*, p. 89; Roton, *Années Cruciales*, p. 254; Liddell Hart, *Rommel Papers*, pp. 50-52.
37. Ellis, *War in France and Flanders*, p. 280; Goutard, *Battle of France*, pp. 251-52; Basil Karslake, *1940: The Last Act, The Story of the British Forces in France after Dunkirk* (London: Leo Cooper, 1979), pp. 156-58; Lyet, *Bataille de France*, pp. 126-27; Liddell Hart, *Rommel Papers*, pp. 52-53; Roton, *Années Cruciales*, pp. 259, 261-63.

38. Blaxland, *Destination Dunkirk*, pp. 364-65; Bock Diary, 8 June, quoted in Jacobsen, *Dokumente*, p. 185; Ellis, *War in France and Flanders*, pp. 280-82; Glover, *Fight for Channel Ports*, pp. 161-64, 172, 190-191; Karslake, 1940, p. 167; *Kriegstagebuch*, pp. 87-88; Plato, *Geschichte*, pp. 91-93; Liddell Hart, *Rommel Papers*, pp. 54-57; Roton, *Années Cruciales*, pp. 263-66.
39. Blaxland, *Destination Dunkirk*, pp. 369-70; C.R.B. Knight, *Historical Records of The Buffs, 1919-1948* (London: The Medici Society, 1951), pp. 62-70; *Kriegstagebuch*, pp. 91-93; Luck, *Panzer Commander*, pp. 35-38; Liddell Hart, *Rommel Papers*, pp. 58-61.
40. Doherty, Richard, *None Bolder: The History of the 51st Highland Division in the Second World War* (Stroud: Spellmount, 2006), pp. 46-51; Glover, *Fight for Channel Ports*, pp. 176-78; *Kriegstagebuch*, pp. 94-97; Plato, *Geschichte*, pp. 96-97; Liddell Hart, *Rommel Papers*, pp. 62-66.
41. Bock Diary, 17 June, quoted in Jacobsen, *Dokumente*, p. 225.
42. Glover, *Fight for Channel Ports*, pp. 209-23; Karslake, *1940*, pp. 195-204; *Kriegstagebuch*, pp. 98-100; Plato, *Geschichte*, pp. 98-101; Liddell Hart, *Rommel Papers*, pp. 68-79; Frido von Senger, *Neither Fear nor Hope: The Wartime Career of General Frido von Senger und Etterlin, Defender of Cassino*, translated by George Malcolm (London: Macdonald, 1963), p. 28.
43. Glover, *Fight for Channel Ports*, p. 224; Karslake, *1940*, pp. 204-14, 220-224; *Kriegstagebuch*, pp. 103, 107; Liddell Hart, *Rommel Papers*, pp. 79-83; Senger, *Neither Fear nor Hope*, p. 29.
44. The 2,592 losses include 681 killed, 1,645 wounded, 266 missing. See *Kriegstagebuch*, p. 108; and Christian Zenter, *Der Frankreich Feldzug 10 Mai 1940: Daten, Bilder, Dokumente* (Frankfurt: Ullstein, 1980), p. 163.
45. Hautecler, *Rommel and Guderian*, p. 52; Liddell Hart, *Rommel Papers*, p. 18.
46. Liddell Hart, *Rommel Papers*, p. 36.
47. Fraser, *Knight's Cross*, pp. 172-73, 208.
48. *Truppenfuehrung*, Heeres-Dienstvorschrift 300/1 (Berlin: Mittler, Berlin, 1936), paragraphs 109-15, 119.
49. Fraser, *Knight's Cross*, p. 37.
50. Plato, *Geschichte*, p. 78; *Truppenfuehrung*, paragraphs 758, 812.
51. Plato, *Geschichte*, p. 73.
52. Guderian, Heinz, 'Kraftfahrkampftruppen', in Hermann Franke, *Handbuch der neuzeitlichen Wehrwissenschaften*, Volume II, pp. 382-401, at p. 390
53. Taysen, 750; *Truppenfuehrung*, paragraphs 40, 410, 542.
54. Liddell Hart, *Rommel Papers*, p. 15.
55. Irving, *Trail of Fox*, pp. 42-46.
56. Fraser, *Knight's Cross*, p. 206.
57. Liddell Hart, *Rommel Papers*, p. 22.
58. Irving, *Trail of Fox*, p. 42.
59. Julien Fargettas, 'Les Massacres de Mai-Juin 1940', in Christine Levisse-Touzé (ed.), *La Campagne de 1940: Actes du Colloque, 16 au 18 Novembre 2000* (Paris: Tallandier, 2001), pp. 448-64 at pp. 454-55.

60. Raffael Scheck, *Hitler's African Victims: The German Army Massacres of Black French Soldiers in 1940* (New York: Cambridge University Press, 2006), p. 26.
61. Karslake, *1940*, p. 160; *Kriegstagebuch*, pp. 87-90.
62. Ronald Lewin, *Rommel as Military Commander* (London: Batsford, 1968), pp. 19, 239, 241.
63. Vopersal, *Soldaten*, p. 124.
64. Fraser, *Knight's Cross*, p. 44; Lewin, *Rommel*, p. 242; Luck, *Panzer Commander*, p. 35.
65. Fraser, *Knight's Cross*, p. 205.
66. Fifth Panzer Division suffered 1,838 losses compared to 2,592 for 7th Panzer Division. See Plato, *Geschichte*, p. 106.
67. Frieser, *Blitzkrieg-Legende*, pp. 284, 289; Irving, *Trail of Fox*, pp. 51-52.
68. Irving, *Trail of Fox*, p. 51.
69. Fraser, *Knight's Cross*, p. 191.
70. Fraser, Knight's Cross, p. 178; Irving, *Trail of Fox*, p. 48.

CHAPTER THREE

# Rommel in the Desert: 1941

*Niall Barr*

While the exploits of Rommel's 'Ghost Division' in France had certainly gained him a reputation for boldness and daring, it was really in North Africa that Rommel became famous, indeed perhaps the most celebrated of all of Germany's generals of the Second World War. Throughout his military career, Rommel had craved the recognition and rewards that went with successful battlefield command and, during two years of intense mechanized warfare in the barren deserts of Libya and Egypt, Rommel proved that he was indeed an outstanding commander. Joseph Goebbels, Hitler's Propaganda Minister, highlighted Rommel's talent and achievements in North Africa, and his status was even accepted by his British opponents. Rommel became a household name in Germany *and* Britain and it was this fact which ensured that he achieved a rare accolade for any military commander: he became a legend in his own life time as the 'Desert Fox'.

It is interesting to speculate whether Erwin Rommel would have reached these heights of fame if he had served on the Eastern Front, where the reputations of many German generals were swallowed up by the vastness of the theatre and the barbarity of the conflict. As a junior general officer, without the benefit of staff training and education and facing the hostility of many other German officers, Rommel may well have struggled to stand out from the crowd on the wide steppes of Russia.

Ironically, Rommel came to fame in a theatre which held almost no strategic interest for Hitler whatsoever. It was Benito Mussolini, the Italian Duce and Hitler's close ally, who made a grandiloquent and opportunistic declaration of war on Britain and France on 10 June 1940.

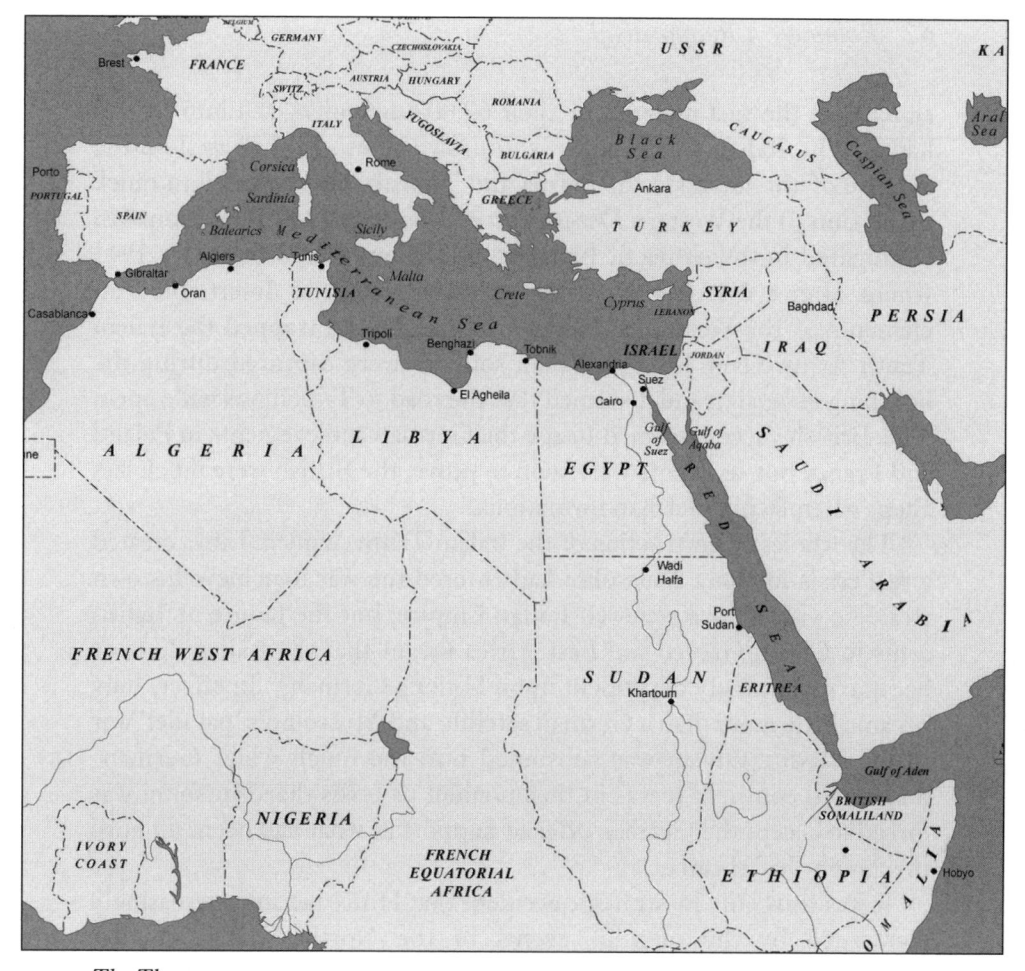

*The Theatre*

Mussolini expected a rapid and victorious end to his 'parallel war', but he soon found that his armed forces were in no position to deliver the glorious result he had envisaged. The Italian Tenth Army, under Marshal Rudolfo Graziani, eventually invaded Egypt on 9 September 1940, but only managed to stagger forwards sixty miles before halting at Sidi Barrani. In the period of relative quiet which followed, the vastly outnumbered British Western Desert Force raided and patrolled the front while their commander, Lieutenant General Richard O'Connor, laid his plans for a 'five day raid'. When the Western Desert Force attacked the Italian camps around Sidi Barrani on 9 December 1940, they rapidly inflicted a stunning defeat on them. Within two days, the Italian camps, along with the vast majority of their 60,000 defenders, fell into British hands. The Italian forces began withdrawing into Libya based on the defence of the fortresses of Bardia and Tobruk, but these fell in quick succession to the Western Desert Force in January 1940. The campaign culminated in the climactic battle of Beda Fomm on 5 February 1941 where, after a dramatic chase across unreconnoitred desert, the lead elements of the Western Desert Force caught and trapped the Italian Tenth Army. Over 140,000 Italian soldiers were captured during the lightning campaign and it seemed that the road to Tripoli was wide open. This British success seemed to ape the German achievements in Poland and France but, as events were soon to prove, the British were much less adept when facing German formations.

The wholesale destruction of the Italian Tenth Army in Libya created a real crisis for Italy. Mussolini had entered the war to achieve his own strategic vision for a renewed Italian Empire, but the failure of Italian arms in Libya, Greece and East Africa meant that the Italian dictator became increasingly dependent upon Hitler's Germany.[1] In effect, Italy became little more than a German satellite and Mussolini's 'parallel' war in the Mediterranean was subsumed into the much wider German-dominated conflict.[2] It was in this moment of crisis that Mussolini was forced to accept the German offer of support in what had been, up until this point, 'his' theatre.

It was thus only by strategic accident that Hitler became increasingly concerned by the turn of events in the North African theatre. Notwithstanding the efforts of Admiral Raeder to convince him of the opportunities that beckoned in the Mediterranean, Adolf Hitler, the German Fuehrer and the dominating will of Germany's strategic ambitions, considered the theatre of entirely secondary importance to the Third Reich. Nonetheless, he also knew that he could not be seen to merely stand and watch as his oldest ally suffered a catastrophic military defeat.

It was in this context that Hitler despatched strictly limited military resources to shore up the Italian position in the Mediterranean. Fliegerkorps X of the Luftwaffe was ordered to bases in Sicily, while it was decided to send a small 'special military blocking' force, consisting of a scratch force – the 5th Light Division – to Tripoli in February 1941.[3] General Halder, the chief of staff of the German Army, selected Major

General Hans Freiherr von Funck to command this small force and he arrived in Tripoli in early February to assess the situation. Von Funck's swift prognosis was gloomy: he doubted whether even significant German intervention could prevent disaster in Libya.[4]

In the event, Funck's pessimistic assessment cost him the command of the German force. What Hitler wanted was a commander who could 'carry away his troops', which he considered 'an absolute essential for an army leader of a unit which has to fight under particularly difficult environmental conditions such as in North Africa'.[5] Hitler overrode Halder's objections and settled on his favoured bright star, Generalleutnant Erwin Rommel, to take charge of the German force in Libya. Rommel's assignment at Hitler's request over the heads of many equally experienced and highly qualified officers simply reinforced the prejudice of many German General Staff officers that Rommel was a 'parvenu' who owed his position to Hitler's patronage. Yet although Rommel did indeed owe this new post to Hitler's influence, he had already proven himself as a very talented tactical commander who understood innately the opportunities inherent in armoured warfare. Rommel had shown the drive and energy necessary to command a force in such unfamiliar conditions and, over the next two years of combat in the desert, would prove himself a master of armoured warfare and a daring and bold commander who, although far from infallible himself, never hesitated to punish mistakes made by his opponents.

On 6 February 1941, the day after the battle of Beda Fomm, Rommel was briefed by Field Marshal Walter von Brauchitsch, the Supreme Commander of the German Army, on his new mission. He was to go Africa immediately to assess the situation and await the arrival of the first German troops, who would reach Tripoli in mid-February. The whole of the 5th Light Division would arrive by mid-April and the 15th Panzer Division would be complete by the end of May. Rommel was firmly told to confine his activities to reconnaissance until the bulk of his troops had arrived.[6] That evening, Rommel wrote to his wife that his 'new job is very big and important'. Rommel had every reason to be excited by his new command. The ability of large military forces to move, live and fight in the desert was unprecedented and Rommel's forces, along with their British rivals, were only able to sustain high-intensity operations in the middle of an arid desert for months on end due to the mechanisation of warfare. The seemingly endless canvas of the desert offered real opportunity for a bold, hard-driving commander who understood the new tools of war – the tanks, trucks and aircraft which offered unlimited movement across hundreds of miles.

However, excited as he was by the prospect of an entirely independent command, Rommel misunderstood its importance to the German Reich. While he consistently saw the advantages and opportunities offered by the desert war, that perspective was not shared in Berlin. Whatever victories Rommel might win, as far as Adolf Hitler was concerned the war in the desert, and indeed the entire theatre of the Mediterranean, was never more than secondary and of little importance compared to the coming struggle with the Soviet Union. Rommel soon came to realise that his repeated requests for reinforcements, supplies and transport fell on deaf ears in Berlin. Rommel's case was not assisted by the fact that it took ten times the level of transport to keep Rommel's three divisions in the field compared to three divisions in Russia. Even providing Rommel with an extra regiment, let alone another division, would have placed a disproportionate strain on the Wehrmacht's resources. In the event, Rommel's Afrika Korps never consisted of more than two armoured and one mechanized division until September 1942. Yet at the same time, for the British, the defence of the Mediterranean and Middle East was central to their ability to continue the war and thus the importance of the theatre was considered 'second only to the United Kingdom itself'.[7] Indeed, the asymmetric importance of the Mediterranean theatre to its main protagonists would eventually decide the outcome of the conflict.

After discussions in Rome with his Italian allies, Rommel arrived in Tripoli on 12 February 1942. He was accompanied by Colonel Schmundt, one of Hitler's key Wehrmacht adjutants. However, after a quick assessment of the situation, and a realisation that the Italian commanders were 'sluggish', Rommel decided to depart from his instructions and 'to take the command at the front into my own hands'.[8] Right from the start of his command in Africa, Rommel had decided to exert his own authority and make his own decisions rather than be bound by orders or agreements made by others who were not on the spot. This characterised his command and leadership throughout the following years in the desert. From his initial reconnaissance trips to the front, Rommel had realised that to await passively any British advance on Tripoli was to invite disaster; the British could only be stalled through boldness. Thus, right from the start, Rommel had understood many of the dynamics of warfare in the desert, but also the psychology of his opponent. These were insights which he exploited to dramatic effect over the next two years.[9]

Rommel was only too well aware of the Axis vulnerability in Libya and he utilised clever deception and sleight of hand to conceal the weakness of his force. When the leading tanks of 5th Light Division arrived in Tripoli they were driven around many times in the parade that marked their arrival, to suggest to British agents that the Germans had arrived in strength. Rommel's use of dummy tanks – mounted on Kubelwagens – paid an unconscious compliment to the origins of the panzerwaffe, which had first trained with cardboard tanks in the early thirties.

However, the greatest deception was inflicted by the British themselves. General Sir Archibald Wavell, the British commander-in-chief in the Middle East, had quite consciously denuded the Western Desert Force in order to provide troops for the expeditionary force to Greece. The British 2nd Armoured Division, which held the front at El Agheila, contained just one armoured brigade, which was itself 'an armoured brigade in name only'.[10] Moreover, its ranks were filled with inexperienced soldiers who were new to the desert. Perhaps most importantly, Wavell had based his calculations on excellent intelligence of German troop movements and intentions. From late February, Brigadier Shearer, Wavell's chief intelligence officer, was receiving first-class intelligence based on the decrypted radio messages of Fliegerkorps X and the Fliegerfuehrer Afrika. This was one of the first uses by the British of their code-breaking of the German Enigma machine, which the Germans believed ensured that all their radio traffic was undecipherable. Yet the possession of direct intelligence of German orders and intentions in this case proved highly misleading.[11] The intercepts gave the British 'proof' that the Afrika Korps could not be ready to mount an attack before May, which gave them confidence that there would be time to train, equip and bolster the formations in the desert before any serious threat from the German forces could emerge.

Having forestalled any potential British drive on Tripoli, Rommel returned to Germany where, on 19 March 1941, he was awarded the oak leaves to his Iron Cross for his service in France, but also received instructions from von Brauchitsch that there was 'no intention of striking a decisive blow in Africa in the near future'. Furthermore, the commander-in-chief made it clear that Rommel could expect no further reinforcements.[12] Yet within days of his return to the desert, Rommel began planning an attack to drive the British out of Cyrenaica. Rommel had already decided to ignore his instructions from General Gariboldi, the new Italian commander-in-chief in Libya, and now he was willing to disobey his German superiors at *Oberkommando der Heeres* (OKH),[13] by launching an attack at Mersa Brega on 31 March 1941. However, the German troops, in their first action in Africa, soon became bogged down and it was only after a day of hard fighting that the 8th Machine Gun Battalion of the 5th Light Division managed to outflank the British defences. Instead of mounting an immediate counter-attack, the British forces, confused and disorientated by the unexpected attack, began to pull out. This quickly degenerated into a precipitate retreat which offered Rommel the perfect opportunity to exploit his success.

Rommel sent his forces along four axes of advance into the Cyrenaican 'Bulge' and forced them into rapid movement. Using his Fiesler Storch to fly above the battlefield and personally scout the terrain and opposition, Rommel hounded his commanders into greater activity. The Axis pursuit into Cyrenaica became a chaotic uncoordinated rush forward, but it had the desired effect. If the British had been in greater strength and had acted with greater determination, Rommel might have found himself in serious trouble, but his emphasis on speed never gave the British the chance to recover. It was during this pell-mell advance that Rommel captured two British items which soon became part of his legend. At Mechili he found the armoured British command truck, which was quickly christened 'Mammut', and the sand goggles which he placed on his General's cap.[14] In fact, Rommel soon encouraged his men to make good deficiencies in their equipment by using British items. German units had never previously operated in desert conditions and although much of their equipment was robust and practical, some items, designed for service in Europe, failed in the desert conditions. Filters had to be fitted to tank engines to ensure that they did not choke from the constant clouds of dust, while German trucks were found to be much inferior to British ones for traversing the desert. Ultimately, these relatively minor equipment problems were overcome rapidly through improvisation.

Rommel later wrote:

> One of the first lessons I had drawn from my experience of motorised warfare was that speed of manoeuvre in operations and quick reaction in command are decisive. Troops must be able to carry out operations at top speed and in complete co-ordination. To be satisfied with norms is fatal. One must constantly demand and strive for maximum performance, for the side which makes the greater effort is the faster – and faster wins the battle.[15]

Rommel had no time for subordinates who failed to match up to his expectations and he quickly taught his units what he expected of them. When the 5th Light Division reported that it required a four-day halt to replenish its supplies of petrol, Rommel simply ordered that every available divisional vehicle was to be used to replenish petrol, rations and ammunition and that the division was to be ready to move within 24 hours. After one day's halt, then, the division was ready to continue its advance.[16] This was an early demonstration of Rommel's cavalier attitude to the 'rules' of supply and also to the advice of the quartermasters who kept the German soldiers in Africa supplied and on the move. While Rommel's methods often demonstrated that improvisation could triumph over 'the norms', his often barely concealed contempt for the opinions of his supply officers would lead him into enormous difficulty during the desert campaigns.

This was because the freedom and tactical possibilities offered by the desert also enhanced the importance of supply. Both sides had to transport virtually all their supplies, equipment, ammunition, food and fuel into the theatre to sustain their armies. This placed an enormous burden on the armies' administrative services, which made any sustained advance difficult. Both armies had to rely on motor transport, since without the internal combustion engine the high tempo and speed of the desert campaigns simply could not have been sustained. The distances involved in the deserts of Libya and Egypt were also unprecedented. An advance of 268 miles had seen Rommel's panzers reach the Channel coast in France, but Tripoli, the main Axis port and supply base, was 1,415 miles away from the Egyptian city of Alexandria, the home of the Royal Navy's Mediterranean Fleet. The further an army advanced from its main base, the greater was the distance – and the consumption of fuel - that its motor transport had to travel to sustain the spearhead units. This law of diminishing returns placed an increasing brake on the progress of an advancing army in the desert. The sheer difficulty of maintaining a fast-moving mechanised army in the desert was consistently underestimated by Rommel.

Nonetheless, in its first campaign the Afrika Korps overcame these difficulties and bundled the Western Desert Force out of Cyrenaica in a matter of days. Perhaps the worst loss suffered by the British during this debacle was the capture of Lieutenant General Richard O'Connor and Brigadier Combe, two of the most experienced and skilled of Britain's desert commanders. The British loss of Cyrenaica was due primarily to Rommel's audacity in mounting an attack with inadequate forces. Rommel had torn up the orthodox military rulebook and achieved an astonishing success precisely because of his boldness.

Not only did Rommel believe that his methods of command had once again been vindicated, but this initial experience in the desert also confirmed that: 'the principles laid down for tank warfare have been entirely justified and should be applied unchanged. The desert is ideal tank country with unlimited space for manoeuvre.'[17]

The Germans may not have possessed deep knowledge of desert conditions, but they did possess a clear and well-defined doctrine for armoured warfare which had been developed and refined during the Polish and French campaigns. When the 5th Light Division arrived in Libya it was able to execute those methods without change. The all-arms combination of the panzer divisions had been tested and proved during the early years of the war. Each division was a fine balance of all-arms, consisting of a reconnaissance unit, a panzer regiment composed of two tank battalions, a rifle regiment of three battalions and an artillery regiment. The backbone of the panzer regiments was provided by the Panzer III and IV, which were relatively well armed, armoured and reliable tanks which generally outmatched their British counterparts. There was also a generous allocation of anti-tank and anti-aircraft guns along with engineers and support services within each division. All of these different units were bound together not only by a strong collective sense of belonging to an elite, but also by excellent radio communications.[18] Thus, even in his first assault in Africa, Rommel possessed a force of considerable power and flexibility.

Rommel now believed that the British forces had entirely collapsed and that it was a matter of pursuing them all the way to the Suez Canal, but he soon found his advance stalled at Tobruk. While most of the 2nd Armoured Division fell back in disorder to the Egyptian frontier, the 9th Australian Division pulled into the formidable defences of Tobruk and soon demonstrated that they could defend its positions with real tenacity. Rommel repeatedly mounted hasty attacks because he did not expect to have to fight hard to take the town. On each occasion, these ill-prepared assaults broke down against the determined Australian defence. The first attack on 11 April 1941 was quickly stopped, but a more serious effort was soon organised. On the night of 13 May, German engineers managed to cut a small bridgehead into the Tobruk perimeter and the 5th Panzer Regiment and 8th Machine Gun Battalion quickly passed through. However, the attack quickly turned into a disaster during the next day of fierce fighting. The panzers soon outran their infantry support and were brought under heavy artillery fire. Pushing deeper into the defences, the panzers then fell victim to well-placed British tanks, which knocked out sixteen of the thirty-eight German panzers. Meanwhile, the Australian infantry, which allowed the panzers to pass through their positions, cut down the advancing German infantry.[19]

Rather than accepting that the reduction of Tobruk required a more methodical approach, Rommel blamed General Streich, the commander of the 5th Light Division, for the disaster. Streich had already attracted Rommel's ire and the failure of this assault led to sharp words between the two generals. Lieutenant Schmidt, Rommel's ADC, witnessed the argument in which Rommel shouted at Streich: 'Your Panzers did not give of their best and left the infantry in the lurch!'. Schmidt recalled that Rommel 'gave vent to his anger openly and used blunt words, such as presumably only one general may use to another'.[20] Streich was soon relieved of command and sent back to Germany as the first general officer casualty of Rommel's method of command. As Schmidt explained, Rommel had already become an inspirational figure to the men in the Afrika Korps, and radiated 'enthusiasm and energy wherever he appeared'. However, Rommel also had high standards: 'He could not tolerate subordinates who were not as enthusiastic and active as himself, and he was merciless in his treatment of anybody who displayed lack of initiative. Out! Back to Germany they went at once.'[21] In this instance,

Rommel really had no one to blame but himself: he had underestimated the nature of the Tobruk defences. Thus Rommel could be a difficult, even unreasonable commander, but his blunt methods also meant that he shaped the Afrika Korps into a formidable instrument.

Rommel had thus placed himself – and his army - in a very difficult position. Rommel ardently desired to continue his advance into Egypt, but this was impossible while Tobruk was held against him. Not only could the garrison mount sallies against his supply columns, but also, without the port capacity which Tobruk represented, any advance into Egypt would soon grind to a halt. Instead, Rommel was forced into an awkward defensive posture in which he needed to besiege Tobruk with sufficient forces to prevent a break-out by the garrison, while simultaneously watching the frontier to ensure that a major British relief force did not break through to Tobruk. Instead of driving forward to victory, Rommel was forced to settle down for a lengthy siege, which tested the endurance of his army.

Rommel found this deadlock intensely frustrating, but the source of his frustration was wider than he realised. Rommel's surprise attack in March 1941 had coincided with perhaps the period of Britain's greatest vulnerability in the Middle East. Virtually simultaneously, the British Middle East Command had to cope with Rommel's attack in the desert and the Greek campaign, which was soon followed by evacuation and the subsequent German airborne attack on the island of Crete. These events were followed closely by Raschid Ali's rising in Iraq and the arrival of German Luftwaffe units in Syria. Meanwhile, the war in Ethiopia and East Africa was still being waged. Thus, the period from March to June 1941 saw perhaps the greatest series of challenges to Britain's position in the Middle East, but none of the threats were individually sufficient to overwhelm the British. Perhaps the best chance of breaking the British hold over Egypt Rommel ever had occurred fleetingly during the spring of 1941, but throughout this period he was stalled by the defences of Tobruk.

Meanwhile, General Franz Halder, the chief of staff of the German Army, was furious about Rommel's flagrant disobedience and sent his deputy chief of the General Staff, General Friederich Paulus, to assess the situation in North Africa. Halder wanted Paulus to make recommendations which would hopefully restrain 'this officer, who has gone mad'.[22] Halder was understandably concerned that Rommel had exceeded his remit – he understood, even if Rommel did not, that there simply was not sufficient logistic support to maintain a larger German force in North Africa and that Rommel's positions around Tobruk invited a British counter-attack. Although Paulus initially gave a favourable report on the situation at the beginning of May 1941, he became deeply concerned by the exposed positions at Sollum and the heavy demands made on the troops by the harsh conditions. Rommel attacked Tobruk again on 30 April but, after three days of fierce fighting, although the Axis forces widened their breach in the perimeter, they were once again held by the Australian defence.[23] Paulus subsequently reported to OKH that the Afrika Korps was far too weak to attack again, which resulted in Rommel receiving direct orders forbidding any further assaults without higher authority. Paulus's final report on the situation was pessimistic and placed the blame for the parlous state of the Axis troops squarely on Rommel's shoulders. He also recommended that the Axis forces should withdraw from Tobruk to hold a line at Ain el Gazala just to the west of Tobruk.[24] Rommel, characteristically, ignored both Paulus's report and Halder's increasing anger at the situation. However, Paulus's visit served notice to Rommel that he was under increasing scrutiny from the 'desk soldiers' he despised: any further failure would result in his immediate removal.

Yet if Rommel was under increasing scrutiny, Wavell also faced intense pressure from Winston Churchill, the British Prime Minister, to retake Cyrenaica. Wavell's first attempt, Operation 'Brevity', was, as its name suggested, hasty and ill-prepared. The British assault was launched on 15 May 1941, and saw a three-pronged thrust with the objective of taking Sollum and Cappuzzo on the frontier. Although the Western Desert force had managed to scrape together only twenty-nine cruiser tanks and twenty-four Matilda Mark II infantry tanks, the British assault managed to threaten Rommel's grip on Tobruk. The 7th Armoured Brigade, with just two squadrons of cruiser tanks, mounted a sweep through the desert, while the 22nd Guards Brigade Group, supported by infantry tanks, advanced to clear the top of the Halfaya Pass and seize Capuzzo.[25] The Axis positions above the Halfaya Pass were quickly overrun, while the 7th Armoured Brigade pushed through the desert towards Sidi Omar, but radio intercepts warned Rommel and the Afrika Korps of the British intentions. British radio procedure was notoriously lax and Rommel's radio intercept service, known as Unit 621 under the command of Captain Alfred Seebohm, gave him plenty of warning of the British attack. Throughout the battle, Rommel was concerned that the Tobruk garrison might stage a break-out and this fixed many of the Axis forces into defence, but he realised that he needed to assemble a large armoured force for a counter-attack, even though he knew that there was insufficient fuel to sustain the force in an extended engagement. The first panzers on the scene promptly ran out of fuel, but their eventual counter-attack at Capuzzo drove the 7th Armoured Brigade back to the frontier. As a sequel, on 26 May some 160 German panzers with only limited fuel threw the British garrison out of their positions above the Halfaya Pass: 'Brevity' had failed to change the calculus around Tobruk.

The fresh German garrisons quickly developed their defences on the frontier into formidable positions of all-round defence. Rommel put his previous experience of utilising the German 88mm anti-aircraft gun in the anti-tank role to good effect. These powerful guns were dug in to the German defences at the Halfaya Pass so that only their barrels showed above ground.

Reinforced by tanks delivered by the 'Tiger' convoy, Operation 'Battleaxe' on 15 June 1941 was a serious attempt to drive the Axis forces away from Tobruk. However, Rommel was already alive to the danger and the German frontier defences were ready. This time, when the lumbering Matilda infantry tanks – which had proven invulnerable to every Italian anti-tank and artillery gun – rumbled forwards to assault the German defences at Halfaya Pass, they were knocked out at long range by the well dug-in German 88mm guns. A simultaneous advance through the desert by 7th Armoured Brigade was held up by a determined German defence. German reinforcements from Tobruk then arrived and counter-attacked the British armour, which resulted, after two days of heavy fighting, in a British withdrawal. Not surprisingly, the result of 'Battleaxe' was 'sadly disappointing' to the British, but for Rommel the battle was a considerable personal vindication.[26] Although the Axis forces remained pinned to their ground around Tobruk, Rommel had avoided defeat. Indeed, Rommel's position as a successful commander and a darling of Goebbels's Propaganda Ministry was confirmed by the June fighting. Lieutenant Berndt, who served on Rommel's headquarters staff, had previously worked for Goebbels at the Propaganda Ministry. Berndt took a personal interest in developing Rommel's profile and he 'knew how to turn Rommel's success into excellent propaganda, and he did a good deal to further Rommel's popularity in the field. His exploits were publicized in Germany as well.'[27] Rommel certainly basked in the fame which Berndt's efforts brought him, and this defensive success silenced his critics at OKH. Yet while 'Battleaxe' brought Rommel fame in Germany, it also represented his last moment of undivided attention in the limelight. Three days after the end of 'Battleaxe', Hitler began Operation 'Barbarossa', his long-planned invasion of the Soviet Union. Launched with 166 divisions and over 3.9 million men, Barbarossa was a truly gargantuan military endeavour which dwarfed the Axis effort in the Mediterranean.

However, if Hitler's attention was now fixed on the events in the east, the battles in the Western Desert remained of the utmost importance for the British. Churchill had expected 'Battleaxe' to clear the Axis forces out of Cyrenaica altogether and its failure led to the replacement of Wavell with General Sir Claude Auchinleck. If Rommel had become a household name in Germany, his capability, and that of his men, was also growing in the minds of his opponents. The lightning attack in the spring of 1941, combined with his adroit handling of his armoured forces in 'Brevity' and 'Battleaxe', meant that Rommel was beginning to be seen as an exceptional commander by his British counterparts. However, for the British soldiers fighting in the desert, the aura surrounding Rommel was also combined with the shocking realisation that the Germans now possessed anti-tank guns with the extreme range and lethality of the German 88mm gun. Not only were German tactics superior, but British tank crews also came to see their cruiser tanks as disappointingly unreliable, under-armoured and under-gunned compared to their German opponents. All of these themes seemed to coalesce in an aura of invincibility that came to surround Rommel's name and that of his soldiers: the Afrika Korps.

Rommel was promoted to General der Panzertruppe in June 1941, and was further rewarded with the creation of the Panzergruppe Afrika in the next month. This meant that Rommel was now in full command of a much larger formation, and, perhaps more importantly, OKH was no longer in operational control of the German forces in Africa. Rommel now had the Afrika Korps, commanded by General Ludwig Crüwell, and the Italian XX Motorised Corps under his command, but the Italian XXI Corps remained under the command of the Italian General Bastico, cruelly nicknamed 'Bombastico' by Rommel. Rommel, who had been close to being removed, was now in full command, yet he had no intention of sitting back as a higher-level formation commander and letting others lead from the front.

Rommel was also disdainful of the General Staff officers who now filled his expanded headquarters. Major-General Alfred Gause was 'of reflective and thorough habits' and proved an excellent chief-of-staff for the new formation. Lieutenant-Colonel Siegfried Westphal, the Ia (chief of operations), proved 'wide-awake' and 'competent', while Major von Mellenthin served as Rommel's intelligence officer for the rest of the campaign.[28] In fact, Rommel's habitual suspicion of staff officers was misplaced; over time, the staff officers of the Panzergruppe were welded into a highly efficient team which served Rommel well even in the face of his explosive temper and frequent abuse.

Yet, just as the Axis began to reorganise their forces in Africa, so too did the British. Indeed, Auchinleck laid careful plans for a deliberate offensive to relieve Tobruk. He refused to be harried into a premature attack by Churchill and steadily built up his forces throughout the autumn of 1941. The expanded Western Desert Force was renamed the Eighth Army and placed under the command of Lieutenant General Alan Cunningham, and benefitted from a major transfusion of strength during the autumn of 1941. By mid-November, both sides had almost completed their preparations for a major offensive: the British to relieve Tobruk, and Rommel for a final assault on the fortress which had frustrated his plans. Fixated on his own schemes, Rommel refused to recognise the growing signs of an imminent British offensive. In fact, the British had assembled a formidable array of men, tanks and aircraft, while also doing their best to choke off Rommel's supply lines.

Rommel certainly did not pay due heed to the increasingly parlous state of his army's supply function, or recognise it as a warning sign of an imminent British offensive. Rommel simply cursed the Italians for their inability to supply his army's needs, while the British used their temporary air and naval superiority to cut off the Axis supply convoys to North Africa. It was no accident that the basing of Force 'K', composed of two Royal Navy light cruisers and two destroyers, at Malta in October saw Rommel's supply situation deteriorate to the point of collapse just before Auchinleck launched Operation 'Crusader' on 18 November 1941. In fact, the Italian Navy was being forced to fight an intense battle to ship supplies to North Africa and suffering crippling losses in the process. On 8-9 November, the actions of Malta-based aircraft and submarines, in combination with the surface ships of Force 'K', sunk every ship in an important Italian convoy to Tripoli. These events forced the Italian Navy to halt all convoys to Tripoli and to consider the port practically under blockade. Rommel's supplies dwindled to a trickle at this critical moment.

The British offensive actually began with a commando raid on what was thought to be Rommel's headquarters – a house at Beda Littoria – which had been occupied by him for a few weeks in July and August 1941. Of course, the British commandos found that Rommel was gone, but the raid demonstrated the importance the British now attached to Rommel's person, even if it also showed a misunderstanding of his methods of command. Eighth Army, now composed of two corps, drove across the frontier on 18 November 1941. This time, due to strict radio silence during the approach march, the British achieved considerable surprise. While Crüwell, the commander of the Afrika Korps, recognised these moves as the start of an offensive, Rommel remained fixated on his planned Tobruk assault and refused to see the British advance as anything other than a reconnaissance in force.[29]

The British drove forwards to Gabr Saleh, where they expected to meet the Afrika Korps head-on in a great armoured clash. Yet although the British had seized the initiative, they became uncertain because Rommel had not reacted in the way they expected. The British captured Sidi Rezegh airfield, which would later prove the fulcrum of the battle, but rather than remaining concentrated and setting the pace of events, the British armour began to disperse as they moved off in different directions in search of the Afrika Korps. As late as the evening of 19 November, Rommel remained preoccupied with Tobruk and seemed oblivious to the danger. However, after a conference with Crüwell that night, he ordered the Afrika Korps to destroy the British armoured columns that now threatened to interfere with his offensive. On 20 November, the first clash of armour took place at Gabr Saleh, in what was to become the biggest battle so far in North Africa. The Crusader battle became a vast, swirling and bloody battle of attrition, in which both sides were worn down to the point of exhaustion by three weeks of intense fighting. The battle was also one of the most confused and confusing battles of the entire war, ranging over a vast area of open desert in which neither Rommel, nor his rival Cunningham, had a clear picture of the dispositions of his own troops – let alone those of his opponents. Frequently, fierce fighting boiled up during the battle whenever the two sides collided with one another.

Over the next three days there was a series of clashes between armoured forces around Sidi Omar and south of Sidi Rezegh, in which the German and Italian forces generally came off better than their British opponents. However, in these confused and swirling engagements the Afrika Korps also became dispersed. By 20 November both sides had begun to converge on Sidi Rezegh, where the fighting reached a crescendo. On 21 November, the Tobruk garrison mounted a serious break-out attempt but this was held – just – by German and Italian forces which had been preparing to mount their own attack. Meanwhile the 2nd New Zealand Division and 4th Indian Division of XIII Corps had broken through on the Sollum front, and Cunningham ordered the New Zealanders to press forward along the coastal escarpment towards Tobruk.[30] The fighting at Sidi Rezegh reached a crescendo on 23 November, known to the Germans as Totensonntag (the German day of remembrance for the dead of the First World War), in which the 5th South African Brigade was destroyed, but the Afrika Korps had, by this time, also suffered heavy losses. 'Crusader' had transformed from a swirling battle of manoeuvre into an all-out attritional slugging match.

Throughout that day of heavy fighting, Rommel and Crüwell had been out of touch and they were only able to meet at 6am on 24 November. Rommel now made one of his most controversial command decisions. Instead of dealing with the looming threat of the 2nd New Zealand Division, he decided to order the 21st Panzer Division to drive to the frontier in pursuit of the retiring elements of the 7th Armoured Division, with the intention of relieving the isolated frontier garrisons and panicking the British into a full-scale withdrawal. Rommel, along with his chief-of-staff General Gause, put himself at the head of his troops in what he thought would be the decisive blow, and with Crüwell caught up in the swirling fight at Sidi Rezegh, command of the Panzergruppe headquarters devolved upon Lieutenant-Colonel Westphal. Rommel – and his chief-of-staff – were completely out of touch with headquarters for several critical days. Rommel's habit of leading from the front had many advantages, but during the 'Crusader' battle his behaviour proved that he had not fully made the transition to higher command.

In what became famous as his 'dash to the wire', Rommel set off at the head of the 21st Panzer Division at 10am on 24 November. This advance narrowly missed the remaining British armour but caused a 'flap' amongst large numbers of British support troops and lorries, which stampeded in front of the advancing panzers. After an advance of sixty miles in six hours and numerous skirmishes with British forces, Rommel had reached the frontier. Yet over the next few days, with the panzer divisions strung out over sixty miles with no secure supply route, Rommel's attacks to relieve the frontier garrisons achieved little. The rapid move and multiple orders emanating from both Rommel and Crüwell simply added to the confusion amongst the Afrika Korps.

Rommel's 'dash to the wire' certainly unnerved Cunningham, who was ready to order a full withdrawal, but although Cunningham was on the verge of a nervous breakdown, so intense had been the strain of the fighting, Auchinleck held his nerve. He was convinced that Rommel was reaching the end of his resources and instead relieved Cunningham, replacing him with Major-General Neil Ritchie, and insisted that the British continued the fight. Thus Rommel's bold, perhaps foolhardy gambit, had almost worked, but ultimately it did not lead to the crushing victory he desired. Instead, while the panzers had been disorganised and depleted, the British armour had been given a chance to repair some of the damage of the earlier fighting.

Meanwhile, the New Zealand Division had advanced to Sidi Rezegh after heavy fighting, and the Tobruk garrison had managed to effect a successful break-out. Westphal was by now the only German officer with a relatively clear picture of the threat developing at Sidi Rezegh and, with no means of contacting Rommel, Gause or Crüwell, he ordered 21st Panzer to return to the Tobruk front on his own authority. Rommel was furious, but eventually realised that Westphal had taken the right decision. Indeed, the Afrika Korps may only have been saved from destruction by Westphal's brave intervention in the chaos of battle.

As the Afrika Korps streamed back towards the vital ground of Sidi Rezegh, the fighting flared up once again on this already bloody battlefield and was to rage for another five days. The New Zealand Division suffered serious casualties at the hands of the panzers, but although the British hold over Sidi Rezegh was weakening, and the Axis counter-attack forced the Tobruk garrison to re-enter their perimeter, the fact was that the British were still receiving reinforcements and Rommel was not. Eventually, on 7 December, Rommel, in discussion with Crüwell, had to face the fact that his Afrika Korps was nearly at the end of its strength. While the British were still very much in the fight, the lack of petrol and ammunition meant that the Afrika Korps was rapidly becoming untenable. After a bloody trial of strength, in which he had very nearly broken the Eighth Army, Rommel realised that he could only save the Afrika Korps by mounting a fighting withdrawal back to the Gazala line.

It has to be said that the 'Crusader' battle was not Rommel's finest hour. He had been slow to recognise the nature of the British threat and did not handle his forces with consistent skill. His constant need to lead from the front was not equal to the challenge of commanding enlarged armoured forces over a vast battlefield – he simply could not be everywhere at the same time. Rommel had been unable to control the chaotic fighting, but his 'dash to the wire' may have cost him a narrow victory. Interestingly, Rommel never wrote up this tense, fractious and unsuccessful episode in his memoirs.[31] In fact, Rommel was strangely fortunate that the German Army in Russia suffered a serious setback in December 1941. OKH was too busy with the crisis caused by the Soviet counter-offensive around Moscow to give much attention to Rommel's misfortunes in the desert. That month also saw a 'purge' of senior army officers, including von Rundstedt, Guderian and even von Brauchitsch. From 18 December 1941, Hitler assumed direct command of the army, which limited the influence of Rommel's critics yet further.[32] Ultimately, Crusader resulted in a British victory. Tobruk was relieved, Cyrenaica retaken and Rommel had been humbled, but all of this had taken three weeks of intense and exhausting combat, which left the Eighth Army just as damaged as its opponent.

On 10 December, the siege of Tobruk was finally lifted and Rommel found it impossible to remain for long at Gazala. His stated intention to withdraw to El Agheila was greeted with dismay by Mussolini and many of the Italian commanders, but in the end there was little they could do to prevent it. The Axis forces executed a skilful withdrawal and fought numerous sharp rearguard actions in Cyrenaica. The message 'Wait some months and we'll be here again! Wish you a happy Christmas.' was chalked on a hotel sign by a wag in the Afrika Korps before he left Benghazi in December 1941.[33] This seemed to sum up the fact that the war in North Africa had already witnessed rapid changes in fortune and was far from finished. Rommel had gained a reputation, but he had failed to change the strategic balance in North Africa. After nine months of exertion and hard fighting, the men of his Afrika Korps found themselves back at El Agheila on 6 January 1942, where they had begun their campaign in Africa.

## Notes

1. Gerhard Schreiber, Bernd Stegemann and Detlef Vogel, *Germany and the Second World War: Volume III, The Mediterranean, South-east Europe, and North Africa 1939-1941* (Oxford: Clarendon Press, 1995), p. 181.
2. Macgregor Knox, *Mussolini Unleashed, 1939-1941* (Cambridge: Cambridge University Press, 1986), p. 272.
3. Schreiber et al, *Germany: Volume III*, pp. 654-55.
4. Ibid, p. 655.
5. Quoted in Ralf Georg Reuth, *Rommel: The End of a Legend* (London: Haus Books, 2008), p. 47.
6. B.H. Liddell Hart, *The Rommel Papers* (London: Collins, 1953), p. 98.
7. Michael Howard, *The Mediterranean Strategy in the Second World War: The Lees-Knowles Lectures at Trinity College, Cambridge 1966* (London: Weidenfeld & Nicholson, 1968), p. 9.
8. Liddell Hart, *Rommel Papers*, p. 101.
9. Ibid, p.100.
10. I.S.O. Playfair, *The Mediterranean and Middle East, Volume II: The Germans Come to the Help of their Ally* (1941) (London: HMSO, 1956), p. 32.
11. F.H. Hinsley, *British Intelligence in the Second World War: Its Influence on Strategy and Operations, Volume I* (London: HMSO, 1979), pp. 191-223; Ralph Bennett, *Ultra and Mediterranean Strategy 1941-1945* (London: Hamish Hamilton Ltd, 1989), pp. 15-30.
12. Liddell Hart, *Rommel Papers*, pp. 105-06.
13. German Army High Command.
14. Heinz Werner Schmidt, *With Rommel in the Desert* (London: Constable, 1997), p. 34.

15. Liddell Hart, *Rommel Papers*, p. 225.
16. Ibid, p. 110.
17. Australian War Memorial (AWM), Australian Intelligence Diary, Morshead Papers, 3DRL 2632 6/28, School for Armoured Troops, Wunsdorf, 16 Oct.41 – Experiences from the African Theatre of War.
18. W. Heinemann, 'The Development of German Armoured Forces 1918-40', in J.P. Harris and F.H. Toase (eds), *Armoured Warfare* (London: Batsford, 1990), p. 58.
19. Playfair, *Mediterranean and Middle East*, p. 35.
20. Schmidt, *Rommel in the Desert*, pp. 43-44.
21. Ibid., p. 42.
22. Halder, quoted in Martin Kitchen, *Rommel's Desert War* (Cambridge: Cambridge University Press, 2009), pp. 95-96
23. Playfair, *Mediterranean and Middle East*, p. 156.
24. Kitchen, *Rommel's Desert War*
25. Playfair, *Mediterranean and Middle East*, p. 160.
26. Ibid, p. 170.
27. Schmidt, *Rommel in the Desert*, p. 65.
28. Ibid, p. 84.
29. I.S.O. Playfair, *The Mediterranean and Middle East, Volume III: British Fortunes Reach their Lowest Ebb (September 1941 to September 1942)* (London, HMSO, 1960), pp. 38-39.
30. Ibid, p. 48.
31. The account of 'Crusader' in Rommel's published memoirs was written by Lieutenant General Fritz Bayerlein. See Liddell Hart, *Rommel Papers*, pp. 154-72.
32. David M. Glantz and Jonathan House, *When Titans Clashed: How the Red Army Stopped Hitler* (Lawrence, KS: University Press of Kansas, 1995), p. 90.
33. George Forty, *Afrika Korps at War: The Road to Alexandria* (Shepperton: Ian Allan, 1998), p. 159.

CHAPTER FOUR

# Rommel in the Desert: 1942

## *Niall Barr*

Over the course of 1942, Rommel's career described an arc rather like that of a Greek tragedy. Like Icarus, Rommel made the choice to go higher and further than ever before but with ultimately tragic consequences. Within the space of a few months of intense combat, Rommel achieved one of the greatest battlefield victories of the Second World War, only to taste the bitterness of a comprehensive defeat and the end to his hopes of conquering Egypt in yet another climactic battle.

The year began with perhaps the swiftest reversal of fortune of the desert war. Almost as soon as Rommel had been forced to retreat due to lack of supplies, events began to turn in his favour. Virtually every ship of Force 'K', the British flotilla which had sunk so many Italian ships, was lost in an uncharted minefield off Tripoli on 18 December. In the same month the Luftwaffe deployed Fliegerkorps II to Sicily, under the command of Albert Kesselring, to 'neutralise' the island of Malta. Suddenly, the British stranglehold on Rommel's sea lines of communication was released. Axis supply convoys started to reach Tripoli, bringing Rommel a much-needed transfusion of strength at the very same time that the British forces were becoming progressively weakened by their need to supply their troops over a distance of 900 miles. At the same time, the Japanese assault on Pearl Harbour and Malaya meant that British reserves which were badly needed in Cyrenaica had to be diverted to the Far East.

It did not take Rommel long to scent the opportunity for a counterstroke against the weakened forward units of the Eighth Army. When,

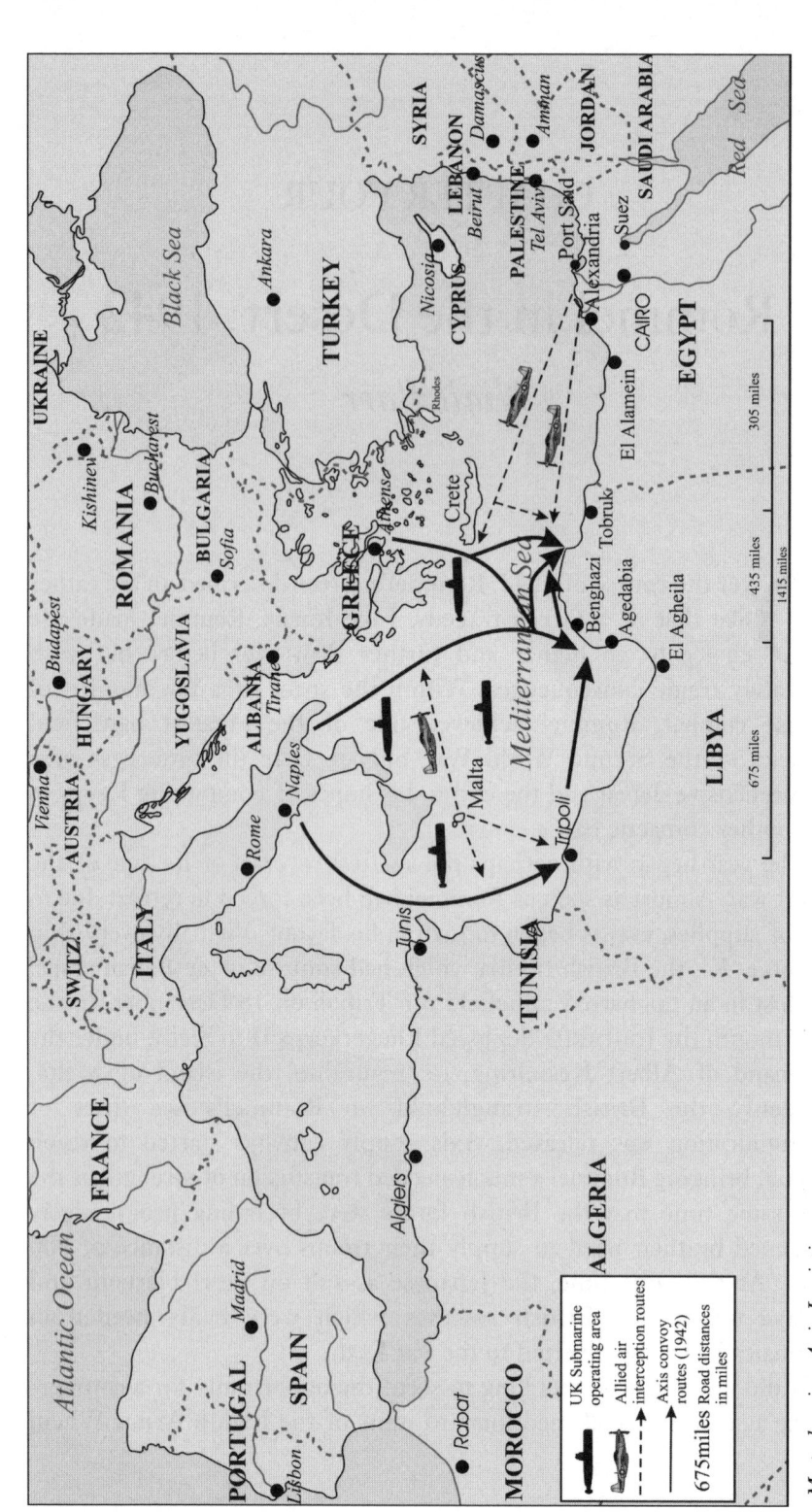

*Map showing Axis Logistics*

on 21 January 1942, Rommel's newly renamed and reinvigorated *Panzerarmee Afrika* attacked at El Agheila, the British units pulled out 'as though they'd been stung'.[1] Rommel's men quickly drove the Eighth Army back to Ain el Gazala, which lay just west of Tobruk. Rommel had once again ignored the protestations of his Italian superior, General Cavallero, who had wished the attack to be no more than a sortie. However, although the British had pulled out of Cyrenaica precipitately, they had prepared a position at Gazala, and the line stabilised there for a number of months, as both sides built up their strength for the next trial. The loss of the Cyrenaican airfields made the Royal Navy's task in running convoys through to Malta yet more difficult. Churchill began to harass Auchinleck with demands for an immediate offensive to recapture Cyrenaica and thus relieve the pressure on Malta, which under Fliegerkorps II bombardment had become the most bombed place on earth. Meanwhile, the Axis commanders began to plan their own offensive to take Tobruk.

The plans for Operation 'Venezia' had been thrashed out between Marshal Count Ugo Cavallero, the chief of the Italian General Staff, Field Marshal Albert Kesselring, the German commander-in-chief in the south, and Rommel. The official plan was that, once the Panzerarmee had defeated the Eighth Army and seized Tobruk, its advance would be halted on the Egyptian border. This operational pause would enable the Panzerarmee to be resupplied for a sustained advance into Egypt. Meanwhile, air and naval assets would be redeployed for Operation 'Herkules', the long-planned conquest of Malta. Once the island fortress was in Axis hands, the supply routes to Africa would be considerably safer and the Panzerarmee could then be unleashed in an invasion of Egypt with the Suez Canal as its ultimate objective. The agreed Axis strategy was ambitious but, for once, coordinated the demands of this complex air, land and maritime theatre.

The Eighth Army stood on the Gazala line with 100,000 men, 849 tanks and 604 aircraft. Rommel's *Panzerarmee Afrika* had 90,000 men and only 561 tanks (228 of which were inferior Italian designs) and 542 aircraft. Although the Eighth Army stood on the defensive, it remained poised to seize the initiative. The Eighth Army's offensive plans, codenamed 'Acrobat', were to defeat the *Panzerarmee* and destroy the Axis presence in North Africa. However, enormous 'mine marshes' had been laid to channel any advance by the Axis forces and some of its armoured units had just been re-equipped with the powerful new American Grant tank, which outclassed all of the German and Italian models. Meanwhile, the new British 6-pdr anti-tank gun – a match for the German 50mm Pak 38 – was just reaching the Royal Artillery's anti-tank batteries. Rommel's men would no longer have quite the qualitative advantage in weaponry which they had enjoyed during the previous year.

Yet although both commanders – Rommel and Major General Neil Ritchie – had planned their own offensives, it was Rommel who struck first. On 12 May, Rommel wrote to his wife that, with his coming attack, he hoped that 'we'll be able to bring the war to an end this year'.[2] The *Panzerarmee* began its opening moves on the afternoon of 26 May 1942, and by dusk British patrols had observed the long columns of tanks, trucks and guns heading towards Bir Hacheim. Yet even though the Eighth Army now possessed knowledge of the German attack and its probable direction, little was done to capitalise on the intelligence.

The next day, the concentrated power of the Afrika Korps descended on the strung-out elements of the 7th Armoured Division and scattered them. Fourth Armoured Brigade, after inflicting considerable loss on the advancing 15th Panzer Division, retired north to El Adem, having lost much of its strength. That afternoon, more British armour engaged in a fierce action with the panzer divisions, but the British armoured brigades were coming into action individually and without their supporting infantry and anti-tank guns. This meant that the British armoured brigades simply did not have the stamina or strength to sustain the fight against the combined forces of the Afrika Korps. However, by the end of 27 May the *Panzerarmee* was also beginning to run into serious difficulties. The panzer divisions had lost a third of their strength in the heavy fighting, and their forces were now scattered over a wide area – on the British side of the minefields. This meant that the Axis supply columns were completely out of touch and unable to reach the fighting units.

By the end of 28 May, General Ritchie was becoming confident that the tide of battle was flowing in his favour. The units of the Afrika Korps remained separated and were still having to fight off the attentions of the British armoured brigades. By the following day, Rommel's forces were in a critical situation. Rommel later admitted that he 'was seriously worried that evening'.[3] The fact was that if the British had been able to press their advantage, and use their superior numbers, Rommel's forces would have been crushed. The Eighth Army had trapped the Afrika Korps against its minefields and it seemed that the main striking force of the *Panzerarmee* would wither and die over the next few days. But even in this moment of crisis, Rommel did not despair. Hemmed in by the minefields to the south, and the British armoured brigades to the north and east, Rommel concentrated his forces in an area that became known the 'cauldron'. The Axis forces deployed a heavy anti-tank gun screen to hold off the British armoured forces and began to cut a gap in the minefields to the east to restore communication with the rest of the *Panzerarmee Afrika*.

It was only on 30 May that Rommel realised that his route to the west was barred by the 150th Brigade, which was well dug in and supported by thirty tanks from the 1st Army Tank Brigade. Now desperate to cut a gap in the minefields, Rommel shifted forces from the north and east and threw them against the beleaguered 150th Brigade. It was not until the afternoon of 1 June that the defenders were finally overcome. Meanwhile, the British armoured brigades had put in numerous piecemeal attacks, but met with the concentrated fire of the Axis anti-tank gun screen and made no progress. None of these attacks had prevented Rommel from switching troops to launch against the 150th Brigade.

The slow reactions of Eighth Army Headquarters meant that the eventual recognition of the plight of 150th Brigade came too late for any effective action to be taken. Ritchie seemed to be making decisions in slow motion; it was not until the night of 1/2nd June that he finally decided to put in an attack on the Axis forces holding the 'cauldron', and the hastily organised attack which followed achieved nothing but loss. This failure, and the belated realisation that 150th Brigade had been destroyed, led Ritchie to make fresh plans for an attack on the Cauldron in '48 to 72 hours'. Ritchie had lost the initiative and his best chance for defeating Rommel.

Rommel wasn't willing to wait patiently for Ritchie to develop his attack. Having secured his supply lines, he sent the 90th Light and the Trieste Divisions south to deal with Bir Hacheim. He knew that once this outpost had fallen, little could prevent his onward rush to Tobruk and the encirclement of the British forces holding the weakened Gazala line. Stuka dive bombers hammered the Free French defenders of Bir Hacheim in swirling sandstorms while the soldiers of the 90th Light and Trieste Divisions probed the defences. General Koenig's Free French put up fierce resistance, but while battle raged at Bir Hacheim, there was little pressure exerted against the Axis defenders of the 'cauldron'. Although small British columns continued to raid and harass the Axis supply lines, this could not dislodge the really dangerous Axis forces in the 'cauldron', or save Bir Hacheim. Both sides were reorganising and preparing for the next blow, but Ritchie's passivity doomed Bir Hacheim to slow strangulation and capture. One by one, piece by piece, Rommel's army was destroying the units of the Eighth Army.

When, finally, the Eighth Army acted to crush the German forces in the 'cauldron', it was far too late. Operation 'Aberdeen', which began in the early hours of 5 June, was an unmitigated disaster. The attack made by 7th Armoured and 5th Indian Divisions became a blow into the air and the German reaction was fierce and caused heavy losses amongst both the armour and infantry. The Indian infantry battalions that had advanced deep into the German positions were all overrun and captured. The artillery batteries which had been brought forward and concentrated for the barrage were caught without armoured support and destroyed by the advancing German panzers. By the end of this fiasco, the Eighth Army had not only lost the initiative, but had also lost its ability to control Rommel.

After days of aerial bombardment and fierce fighting, Bir Hacheim was finally evacuated by the Free French on 10 June, who managed to escape with most of their force intact. With his southern flank secure, Rommel could now return to his planned northward thrust. Fatal disaster struck the Eighth Army on 12 and 13 June, when both sides' armour met in action once more around the 'Knightsbridge' area. Once again, the British armoured units suffered from fatal lapses in command. Confusion descended upon the commanders of the British divisions at the very moment that the Germans attacked. In the swirling fight that developed, the Germans gained the upper hand and capitalised upon it; the panzers encircled the British armour and attacked from three sides. Confused and fierce fighting in the middle of a severe dust storm continued during 13 June, which saw the

'Knightsbridge' position captured and the British Armoured Brigades reduced to mere shadows of their former selves. By the end of 13 June, the Eighth Army could only muster fifty cruiser and twenty infantry tanks, and, because the armoured brigades had been forced to withdraw, they could not recover the hundreds of wrecked and damaged tanks which littered the battlefield. This disaster sealed the fate of the Eighth Army.

Without the power to halt, let alone defeat, the *Panzerarmee*, the Eighth Army fell back to the Egyptian frontier. This exposed the fortress of Tobruk to a full-scale attack. While the Eighth Army was withdrawn to the Egyptian frontier in the hope that it could rest, reorganise and, most importantly, rebuild its armoured formations, the 2nd South African Division and supporting troops were left in Tobruk to accept a 'temporary' siege. For Rommel, this was a moment of supreme opportunity. Having been repeatedly frustrated by Tobruk's resistance in the previous year, he was determined 'to finish with it for good'.[4] While the British fondly hoped that Tobruk could resist a one or two-month siege, Rommel planned a lightning-fast attack to seize the prize immediately. On 20 June, wave after wave of German and Italian bombers attacked Tobruk with impunity. At dawn, Rommel's tired men moved into the attack against the fortress and found that the defences were not what they had been: many of the mines had been lifted and placed in the ineffectual Gazala line. By midday, the vital crossroads of King's Cross was in Axis hands and it was only a matter of time before the fortress fell. Major General H.B. Klopper, commander of the 2nd South African Division, vacillated between fighting on, breaking out and surrender. The decision was made for him when German panzers broke through to the port. Almost 35,000 men were taken prisoner and vast quantities of supplies and stores were either captured or destroyed.[5]

The port, which had held out for over nine months against Rommel the year before, fell after just two days of fighting. For Rommel, this was the supreme moment of his career. He had inflicted a crushing defeat upon the larger and more powerful Eighth Army and had seized Tobruk within a matter of days. As he later remembered, 'For every one of my "Africans", that 21st of June, was the high point of the African war.'[6] And with the capture of Tobruk, Rommel was free to contemplate his long-held ambition of invading Egypt.

## 88  Rommel: A Reappraisal

Rommel now had no intention of waiting for the reduction of Malta before invading Egypt. Kesselring met with Rommel on the afternoon of 21 June to discuss future plans and reminded Rommel of the agreed strategy, while also warning Rommel that his supplies during the offensive had only been assured because Malta had been neutralised in preparation for the assault. Kesselring had already ordered his air units back to Sicily for 'Herkules'. The next day, Rommel met with General Count Barbasetti, the chief of the Italian Liaison Staff, who informed him that General Bastico, the Italian commander in chief in North Africa, had ordered Rommel to halt. Rommel, who had just heard of his promotion to Field Marshal that day, told Barbasetti that he would not accept this 'advice'.

Faced with intractable opposition from both his German and Italian superiors, Rommel simply short-circuited the Axis command chain. He made a direct appeal to Mussolini on 22 June, which was then passed on to Hitler. The German Fuehrer had never been an enthusiastic supporter of 'Herkules', perhaps due to the legacy of the costly operation on Crete, and was happy to postpone the operation indefinitely. Hitler also believed that the British had lost the opportunity to grab Tripoli from the Italians in January 1941, so he had little hesitation in sanctioning Rommel's continued advance. He signalled to Mussolini that 'It is only once in a lifetime that the Goddess of Victory smiles.' Mussolini was only too happy to be convinced and, against the protests of Cavallero, gave his blessing to Rommel's continued advance. Rommel received Mussolini's approval in the first hour of 24 June but the units of the *Panzerarmee* had been on the march since 22 June. The entire Axis strategy for the Mediterranean theatre had been derailed.

Yet Rommel's decision to pursue the Eighth Army was based not only on his own intuition and thirst for military glory, but also on crucial American reports of British frailty. Rommel had come to rely on intelligence received from what he called his 'Good Source', which provided him with detailed information concerning the plans and operations of the Eighth Army. Unfortunately for the British, the 'Good Source' was none other than Colonel Bonner F. Fellers, the military attaché in the United States Embassy in Cairo. Unbeknown to Fellers or the authorities in Washington, the Italian Military Intelligence Service

Rommel, on the left, during the First World War, with an unknown fellow officer.

Rommel, on the right, with Major Sprosser. Italy, 1917.

Rommel with Major General Fortune at the surrender of the 51st Highland Division, Cherbourg 1940.

Rommel in a formal photograph, early 1940s.

Rommel in North Africa, 1941.

Rommel in North Africa with Italian officers and men, 1941.

A view of the Sidi Rezegh battlefield, November 1941.

Rommel during a tour of inspection, Western Desert, 1941.

A characteristic photograph of Rommel in his staff car, Western Desert, 1942.

British Commander-in-Chief Middle East General Claude Auchinleck, Cairo, 1941.

Probably the most famous portrait photograph of Rommel as commander of the Afrika Korps.

Rommel conferring with commanders, Western Desert, 1942.

General Bernard Montgomery, Eighth Army commander, 1942, wearing a slouch hat decorated with the emblems of various army units.

Rommel with Bayerlein and Kesselring, North Africa, 1942.

Hitler greeting Rommel at a formal Nazi Party gathering.

Rommel in Normandy during one of his tours of the Atlantic Wall, 1944.

Rommel's funeral, with von Rundstedt, on the left, delivering the eulogy.

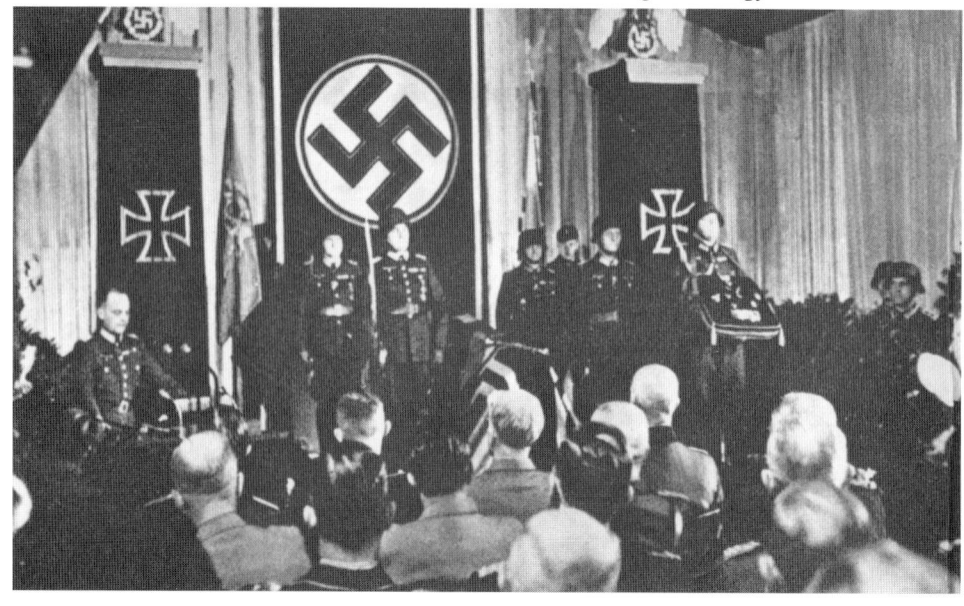

(SIM) had broken the American diplomatic cipher. Thus every detailed report that Fellers sent back to Washington was intercepted and read by the Italians. The information which was received from the 'Good Source' was considered of critical importance, and was quickly sent on to the intelligence staff of the *Panzerarmee Afrika*.

Although the British came to realise that the American diplomatic code had been compromised and moved swiftly to limit the damage, Rommel received his most critical information from the 'Good Source' in June 1942. On 16 June, Fellers detailed the full extent of British tank losses, explaining that although the British had begun the battle with 742 tanks, they now had only 133 tanks left.[7] This gave Rommel the invaluable intelligence that, weakened though his panzer divisions were, the British had virtually no tanks left to stop them. In another report, Fellers gave a full listing of the remaining British forces. Detailed intelligence of this nature very rarely finds its way into the hands of a commander and Rommel was determined to make full use of it. Fellers even ended his report with the observation that 'If Rommel intends to take the Delta, now is the time.'[8]

There was a heavy irony that it was an American officer who gave Rommel the advice that if his *Panzerarmee* was to destroy the Eighth Army at its weakest, it had to strike now. Rommel was thus able to make an informed calculation concerning the risks of continuing his pursuit of the British. Rommel's drive into Egypt was not the blind rush of a gambler, but was based on the full knowledge of the British weakness. However, although it was indeed 'a plan with a chance of success', by driving on into Egypt, Rommel was also taking the biggest risk of his career.[9] Nonetheless, Rommel believed that his victorious troops could drive the British out of Egypt altogether, and on 21 June he issued a general Order of the Day which made his intentions clear:

> Soldiers of the *Panzerarmee Afrika*! Now for the complete destruction of the enemy. We will not rest until we have shattered the last remnants of the British Eighth Army. During the days to come, I shall call on you for one more great effort to bring us to this final goal.[10]

The calm rebuilding of the Eighth Army behind the frontier very soon turned into a confused rout and Rommel's men experienced little or no delay in their pursuit. Rommel knew that speed was essential; if the British were given any respite they might be able to recover, so he drove his men on and on deeper into Egypt. The remnants of the Eighth Army fell back towards the little coastal town of Mersa Matruh, where Ritchie was determined to fight the final battle to save Egypt or suffer irretrievable defeat.

However, at this moment of crisis, General Auchinleck decided to relieve Ritchie and take command of the Eighth Army himself. He realised that the Eighth Army would probably be destroyed if it fought at Matruh. Auchinleck instead planned to pull back the army to the El Alamein position, which: 'offered by far the strongest position in the Western Desert as both its flanks rested on impassable obstacles'.[11] With the impassable salt marshes of the Quattara depression on one flank, and the sea on the other, there remained a narrow neck of desert 40 miles wide at Alamein. This limited the opportunities for Rommel's characteristic outflanking sweep through the desert. Given the reduced state of the Eighth Army, El Alamein was the only place which offered the Eighth Army an even chance of holding Rommel before he reached Alexandria.

Ultimately, there was still a messy fight at Mersa Matruh, in which the Afrika Korps burst through the centre of the Eighth Army's positions. The battle of Mersa Matruh turned into another fiasco for the British. Caught by Rommel's spearheads between defence and withdrawal, the Eighth Army did not really had a chance to fight properly. With one of the wings of the Eighth Army threatened with encirclement, the British pulled out hurriedly towards Alamein, with the lead elements of Rommel's forces hot on their trail. The result was the loss of two badly needed infantry divisions. Rommel seemed as unstoppable as ever.

Even after the disasters of Gazala and Tobruk, the British had remained confident that the iron laws of time, space, distance and logistics would eventually bring Rommel to a halt. In every previous desert offensive, the attacker had become progressively weaker as they drove forwards, yet Rommel had ploughed past the frontier, rushed the defences of Mersa Matruh and was now close to El Alamein. According to British expectations Rommel's offensive capacities should have dimmed and the prospects of the Eighth Army brightened. Yet, instead, Rommel's aggressive push seemed as fierce as ever, while the strength of the Eighth Army faded away.

The explanation lay in the fact that virtually all of the fighting stores, clothing, food, petrol and ammunition which the Eighth Army had needed had been based forward around Tobruk and Belhamed. The speed of the German advance led to hasty withdrawals from some dumps and panic demolitions in others. In dumps from Tobruk and Belhamed, Sollum and Capuzzo to Mersa Matruh and El Daba, the Eighth Army lost thousands upon thousands of tons of food, ammunition, engineer stores, petrol and supplies. The quantities of ammunition which were either captured or destroyed were staggering and as Eighth Army had haemorrhaged its lifeblood, so the *Panzerarmee* had received a substantial transfusion of supplies. The normally iron laws of logistics, which should have forced Rommel's army to grind to an undignified halt, had been bent. The wholesale capture of British arms, equipment and supplies pushed the culminating point of Rommel's advance further than either side had believed possible. It was estimated that in July 1942 the Germans had as many as 6,000 usable lorries which had formerly belonged to the Eighth Army. Similarly, German and Italian artillery units, which had lost numerous guns during Gazala, supplemented their firepower with captured British 25-pdr field guns and ammunition. The spearhead units of the *Panzerarmee*, eating 'Imperial Tinned Peaches' and driving Canadian Ford trucks with Iraqi petrol in their tanks, pushed on towards Alamein.

Yet in pushing his *Panzerarmee* as far and as fast as it could go, Rommel had completely outrun Kesselring's ability to provide air cover. The Axis air forces had put forth an enormous effort during the battle of Gazala and for the attack on Tobruk, but could not sustain this level of activity indefinitely. Furthermore, the air forces had been planning to prepare for the projected invasion of Malta, not the immediate invasion of Egypt. Even as Rommel's men crossed the Egyptian frontier on 23 June, the air support which they depended upon evaporated. By pushing deep into Egypt, Rommel forced Kesselring to send squadrons to his aid at the same time as he had to provide squadrons to neutralise Malta. There simply was not enough fuel or transport to bring the squadrons forward quickly and, even though Rommel attempted desperate measures by removing transport from Italian units to give to the Luftwaffe, it took days for the squadrons to reach the forward landing grounds at Fuka and Daba. Meanwhile, there was now insufficient Axis airpower devoted to the suppression of Malta, which meant that the island could revitalise its battered defences and offensive power. Although the squadrons of the *Regia Aeronautica* and Luftwaffe struggled forwards into Egypt, the skies above the two armies were completely clear of Axis aircraft from 23 June until 26 June. Rommel's impetuous advance meant that his army lacked the air support which could have completed his victory.[12] If the Luftwaffe was conspicuous by its absence during the retreat to Alamein, the same could not be said of the Desert Air Force. Instead, the squadrons of the Desert Air Force dominated the skies above the Eighth Army.

On 29 June, as his men raced towards the little railway halt, Rommel wrote to his wife that: 'Now the battle of Mersa Matruh has also been won and our leading units are only 125 miles from Alexandria. There'll be a few more battles to fight before we reach our goal, but I think the worst is well behind us.'[13] Rommel knew it was only a matter of time before British and American reinforcements reached Egypt. His fighting formations and transport columns were being subjected to increasingly heavy bombardment from the air, but none of these problems would matter if he could drive through the last defensive positions held by the Eighth Army around Alamein. Rommel was confident that, after one last supreme effort of will, Egypt would be his.

Rommel knew that speed was of the utmost importance if he was to bounce the British out of their last defensive line. Unfortunately, in taking no time to reconnoitre the Eighth Army's positions at El Alamein, he made the same mistake that he had made at Tobruk the year before. Given what seemed to be a similar British deployment to that at Mersa Matruh, Rommel decided to replicate his plan of attack. While mounting a feint attack towards the southern flank of the Eighth Army, Rommel planned to penetrate the centre and encircle the Eighth Army just as he had done at Matruh. Rommel knew that there was little chance of breaking the Eighth Army in a frontal assault, but he hoped that, with luck and daring, his troops might encircle the Eighth Army and panic it into 'headlong flight'[14] in a repeat of Mersa Matruh.

However, when the *Panzerarmee* began its attack on 1 July 1942, the Afrika Korps ran straight into the positions of the 18th Indian Brigade at Deir el Shein, which had been completely missed by Axis intelligence in their hurried assessments of the British defences. Rather than motoring forwards into the rear of the Eighth Army, the Afrika Korps had to spend a day of hard fighting reducing the resistance of the defenders of Deir el Shein, and the last positions were not overrun until the evening. Although 18th Indian Brigade had finally succumbed to the Afrika Korps, its determined resistance had halted Rommel's drive for a few vital hours. Without this breathing space, it is unlikely that the British troops defending the Alamein line would have been able to shake themselves into the semblance of order which was vital if the Eighth Army was to hold off Rommel's tired but victorious troops. The sacrifice of the brigade had bought critical time. Although few, if any, observers recognised it at the time, the resistance of 18th Indian Brigade had stemmed the tide.

Just as the main thrust of the Afrika Korps had been halted, so too had the drive of the 90th Light Division around the Alamein 'box' to the coast. By the late afternoon, the division had made little progress and Rommel went forward to encourage his men, but soon found that he had to stem a rout of his own most trusted soldiers.[15] This was a clear demonstration that Rommel had pushed his men beyond the limit of their endurance.

Far from being over, as Rommel had hoped, the battle for Egypt had only just begun. In fact, although the units of the *Panzerarmee Afrika* continued their attacks over the next two days, they were met with increasingly steadfast resistance. Rommel had thrust his men into the Alamein line in the hope that the British defence would collapse, but they now faced an unexpectedly stubborn and determined resistance. The possibility arose that, far from thrusting into the rear of a defeated army, the *Panzerarmee* had placed its head and neck into a noose. By 2 July there were only thirty-seven tanks left to arm the two panzer divisions,[16] and while the Luftwaffe was still nowhere to be seen, the Desert Air Force continued its systematic bombing of the *Panzerarmee*. On the third day of battle at Alamein, the Afrika Korps continued its thrust along the Ruweisat ridge but it became clear, after a day of heavy fighting, that the Eighth Army would not give up its positions. The 90th Light's entry in its war diary gloomily commented that:

> the enemy gave no sign of withdrawing. On the contrary, he gave the impression that he was trying with all his force to stop the *Panzerarmee* from storming the Alamein position. It seemed that

the German forces, exhausted by the heavy fighting and the hardships of the past days and weeks ... would not be able by their own strength, to force this last British fortification.[17]

The truth was that Rommel's attack at Alamein could only have succeeded against a comprehensively demoralised force. After a day of heavy fighting, the last gasp of Rommel's offensive had been held. Rommel was forced to accept that the flame of his offensive, which had burnt so brightly at Gazala, Tobruk and Mersa Matruh, had finally gone out. Now the *Panzerarmee Afrika* was 1,400 miles from its main logistic base with no further strength to defeat the Eighth Army. The Axis forces could no longer go forwards, but nor could they withdraw for lack of fuel and they could hardly fight for lack of ammunition. Although no one could know it at the time, the fighting at Alamein over the first three days of July 1942 marked the high water mark for Rommel and his army. After a run of extraordinary success, Rommel would never achieve another full-scale victory and he would never reach the Nile delta, which had seemed so close just a few days before.

The two armies had fought each other to a standstill and Rommel was now faced with an unenviable set of operational and strategic choices. There were strong military arguments to suggest that Rommel's best course of action was to mount a phased withdrawal back to the Libyan frontier. This would shorten his lines of supply and wrong-foot the already exhausted Eighth Army. Unfortunately, while captured petrol and supplies had allowed the *Panzerarmee* to reach El Alamein, there was now not enough petrol to make an orderly and phased retreat. Once his offensive had been held, Rommel found himself trapped at El Alamein; he could not go forwards or back. Rommel had staked his personal reputation and standing with Hitler in making the advance into Egypt. Rommel's insistence that he should continue his advance into Egypt had derailed the existing Axis strategy, and he could hardly admit failure now. Instead, Rommel had little choice but to grimly hang on at El Alamein, in the hope that his logistic difficulties could be surmounted and that he could find another way out of the labyrinth of his own making.

Over the next few days, both armies caught their breath, but although Rommel attempted a further attack on 9 July, it became a blow in the air. It was Auchinleck who launched the 9th Australian Division in an attack near the coast on 10 July, which not only destroyed the Italian Sabratha Division but also overran and captured *Nachrichten Fernsehsendung Aufklarungs Kompanie* 621[18] commanded by Captain Alfred Seebohm. Since April 1941 NFAK 621 had provided Rommel with vital tactical intelligence by 'listening in' to British radio traffic, translating and interpreting the messages and sending important signals direct to Rommel, and now it was lost. Rommel was furious when he learnt the news – and with good reason, since Seebohm and NFAK 621 had provided him with an unparalleled wealth of tactical intelligence.[19] Rommel has often been credited with an inspired tactical sense – a 'fingertip feel' for the shifting patterns of battle – but much of this vaunted ability rested on the efforts of Alfred Seebohm and NFAK 621. The 'Good Source' provided by Bonner Fellers was stopped on 29 June, and NFAK 621 was destroyed on 10 July. The airwaves, which had provided Rommel with superb operational and tactical intelligence, fell silent. Rommel's 'fingertip feel' left him and never returned.

Rommel made one last attack against the defences of the Alamein box on 13 July, writing to his wife that: 'Today is to be another decisive day in this hard struggle. Things are already on the move all over the desert.'[20] In fact, Rommel's counter-stroke failed comprehensively against the South African defence. Having been balked, he tried again against the Australian positions near the coast but, once more, his troops were held by a determined defence.

Rommel had done everything he could to lever the Eighth Army out of its positions and for the rest of the month the *Panzerarmee* had to hold on to its own positions as Auchinleck launched a series of attacks to break Rommel's army. Rommel had no option but to hold his ground at Alamein and the British attacks became set-piece assaults on a fixed defence. On each occasion, on 15, 22 and 28 July, New Zealand, Australian and British infantry tore great gaps in the *Panzerarmee*'s line. These attacks caused great damage – particularly to the Italian infantry units – only to be savaged in their turn by a rapid counter-attack by the panzers of the Afrika Korps. Rommel's men held the line but only at the cost of heavy casualties.

The strain of this defensive fighting told heavily on all of the Axis troops and on Rommel himself. His letters to his wife had generally been optimistic and full of fresh ideas for military exploits, but on 17 July

Rommel wrote:
> Things are going downright badly for me at the moment, at any rate, in the military sense. The enemy is using his superiority, especially in infantry, to destroy the Italian formations one by one, and the German formations are much too weak to stand alone. It's enough to make one weep.[21]

The Eighth Army had chewed its way through four Italian infantry divisions, which seriously weakened the position of the *Panzerarmee*. This constant attrition forced Rommel to adopt new defensive methods, whereby German infantry was interspersed amongst Italian formations in a process he called 'corseting'. Rommel used this procedure to stiffen his defences and ensure that there would be no easily identified weak points in the *Panzerarmee*'s line.

General Nehring's comments on the nature of the July fighting acknowledged the strain that the entire *Panzerarmee* was facing:

> Officers and men had passed difficult hours rich with crises, which they mastered conscious of the fact that everything was at stake. If D.A.K. collapsed the *Panzerarmee* was lost. Once again the overtired and exhausted troops fighting in contrary climatical conditions had made superhuman efforts to restore the situation.[22]

That the Afrika Korps had once again survived a supreme crisis demonstrated the tough resilience of the German troops. However, both armies suffered severely during the July fighting. The Eighth Army suffered over 13,000 casualties, while at least 7,000 German and Italian troops had been captured during the month of heavy fighting.[23] Neither army had achieved its goal. By the end of the month, both armies were simply incapable of further offensive effort and the front at El Alamein settled into an uneasy lull.

During August 1942, Rommel was beset by myriad problems, but the worst was what can only be described as a quartermaster's nightmare. Having advanced to El Alamein and survived the repeated attacks mounted by the Eighth Army, the *Panzerarmee* was stranded in the desert. Rommel had never expected to spend so long at the gates of Egypt, but now the Axis quartermasters had to try to find a solution to the problems of an army which had long passed its culminating point.

Throughout the July fighting, the *Panzerarmee* had passed from crisis to crisis and had survived only on a hand-to-mouth basis. Much of the petrol, ammunition, food, mines, tools and even uniforms used by the army had come from captured British stocks. Supplies were certainly available, but the problem now lay in transporting those supplies across the Mediterranean to North African ports and then moving them all the way to the front at El Alamein.

Ultimately, the *Panzerarmee* depended on the Italian navy and merchant marine running the gauntlet of increased British air and submarine attacks mounted from Malta and Egypt. The power of the Desert Air Force to mount powerful raids against the Axis lines of supply also severely reduced the quantities of supplies which the *Panzerarmee* was receiving. During July, 20,000 tons of Axis shipping was sunk, mainly as a result of air attack from Malta and Egypt, but the losses climbed to 65,000 tons in August.[24] Greater Luftwaffe protection was demanded but this simply took limited air resources from one task to another. The neutralisation of Malta, protection of convoys in the Mediterranean, patrols over the extended desert line of communications and close support of the *Panzerarmee Afrika* simply could not all be delivered simultaneously by the overstretched Luftwaffe and *Regia Aeronautica* units in the Mediterranean theatre. Even in the face of these attacks, the Italian Navy still found it possible to escort the majority of supplies safely across the Mediterranean. However, once a convoy had reached Tripoli, Benghazi or Tobruk there remained the problem of getting the resources to the front. The supplies had to be unloaded from the ships, dumped on the quays and then loaded onto trucks for a drive of nearly 1,400 miles to the front.[25]

Naturally, the movement of supplies from these far distant ports consumed vast quantities of petrol and placed great wear and tear on the motor transport involved. In fact, there was a chronic shortage of motor transport within the *Panzerarmee*. At any one time, 25 per cent of the *Panzerarmee*'s motor transport was under repair and, since 85 per cent were captured British vehicles, the lack of spare parts created an enormous problem.[26]

Air transport was the one method which promised to short-circuit the strictures of logistics, but the Luftwaffe could never provide sufficient air transport to fulfil anything more than a small percentage of the daily needs of the *Panzerarmee*. Air transport could never provide a complete answer to the complex and voracious appetite of a mechanised army in the field. [27] In fact, although Rommel later complained bitterly that insufficient efforts had been made to sustain his army during this critical period, the Italian supply organisation met many of the demands – particularly in tanks and ammunition – of the *Panzerarmee* during August 1942. Reinforcements were flown in by the Luftwaffe and although insufficient motor transport was shipped, supplies in accordance with Rommel's priority lists for ammunition, tanks and guns were generally met. By 28 August, the strength of the army had been rebuilt and compared favourably with the forces that had begun Operation Venezia on 26 May. The army now held 84,000 German and 44,000 Italian personnel with 234 German and 281 Italian tanks. Given the difficulties inherent in its transportation, this rapid build-up of men and materiel represented a considerable achievement by the Axis supply organisation.[28]

However, the army remained desperately short of fuel, which was the one resource Rommel needed to launch his attack. In fact, it was no accident that Italian tankers were sunk with depressing regularity. The British air and naval effort from Malta and Egypt was necessarily limited, but it was focused on sinking the tankers bringing fuel to Rommel's army. The British decryption of German and Italian radio traffic gave complete details of ports of departure, and expected times of arrival of these high-value targets. This enabled attacks to be planned and targeted precisely. The security of Ultra intelligence was guarded by the standard procedure that every convoy had to be visually sighted by an aircraft before an attack could be mounted. While by no means all of the attacks were successful, Ultra enabled the British to target Rommel's tankers. [29] This meant that the limited resources that the British could afford to devote to the air and naval campaign against Axis shipping had a disproportionate and sometimes crippling effect upon the *Panzerarmee*'s logistic chain. [30]

During the build-up to the offensive, Rommel's doctors became increasingly worried about his health. The Field Marshal was now suffering from low blood pressure, which precipitated fainting fits, brought on by chronic stomach problems. On 21 August, Rommel informed OKH of his condition and requested that a replacement be sent out as soon as possible. Rommel asked for Panzer General Heinz Guderian as his replacement.[31] Guderian had masterminded the creation of the *Panzertruppen* in the 1930s and had led the XIX Panzer Corps to victory in 1940. However, during the Barbarossa campaign of 1941, Guderian had quarrelled violently with Hitler and he remained out of favour. Berlin's excuse was that no suitable replacement with tropical experience could be found and Rommel had to steel himself to continue until the offensive had been carried through.

Even with his health problems and supply difficulties, Rommel knew he needed to attack again before the British were reinforced. After repeated postponements waiting in vain for additional fuel shipments, Rommel finally decided to launch his army in one last attempt to take the Delta. He wrote to his wife: 'There are such big things at stake. If our blow succeeds, it might go some way towards deciding the whole course of the war. If it fails, at least I hope to give the enemy a pretty thorough beating.'[32] He decided to avoid the heavily defended northern sector and mount his main attack in the south, cutting gaps in the British minefields and then using his armour and mobile forces to encircle and destroy the Eighth Army in a repeat of Gazala. Ultimately, Rommel made the decision to attack in the full knowledge that he lacked the fuel to make the attempt. Not only was Rommel gambling on repeating another Gazala, but he was also relying on the mere promise of fuel to complete his advance to the Delta.

On 29 August 1942, the tanks, half-tracks and trucks of 21st Panzer Division rumbled southwards along desert tracks towards their assembly points. That night, the divisional staff received a short message from the Afrika Korps: 'X Day 30 Aug'.[33] However, this time the Eighth Army, now under the command of Lieutenant General Bernard Montgomery, was ready. Warned by Ultra intelligence of Rommel's intentions, Montgomery had dug his armour into position on the Alam Halfa ridge to block the most likely path of the Afrika Korps' advance. Even progress through the British minefields proved slow, due to repeated British air attacks and a skilful delaying action by the 7th Armoured Division. Rommel soon realised that: 'All possibility of taking the enemy by surprise – an essential condition for the success of the operation – had now disappeared.'[34] The unexpected delay had increased fuel consumption but, although Rommel considered breaking off the attack, this would mean halting, turning around and withdrawing through narrow minefield gaps in the face of active opposition. Perhaps not surprisingly, Rommel decided to continue the offensive, but with a modified plan. There was insufficient fuel to make a wide sweep to the east, as he had originally intended, so he decided to turn the panzer divisions to the north-east immediately. Their objective was now Point 132 on the Alam el Halfa ridge.[35] Unwittingly, Rommel had chosen to drive his Afrika Korps onto the waiting British armour. When the Germans attacked the ridge, they fell into a long-prepared trap. The fighting on 31 August was fierce, and casualties on both sides were heavy, but Rommel's panzers were held by determined resistance and heavy artillery fire. As darkness fell, the panzers drew off to the south and Colonel Lungerhausen, who had by now taken command of 21st Panzer Division, assessed that any 'frontal attack on the enemy positions forward of the division will be very costly'.[36] During the evening, Fritz Bayerlein, now commanding the Afrika Korps, suggested to Rommel that both panzer divisions should withdraw from contact, drive east and then swing round to take Height 132 from the flank.[37] This is almost certainly what the Afrika Korps would have attempted the next day, but the fuel tanks of the panzers were nearly empty. The fuel situation not only made any outflanking move impossible, but placed the whole of the Afrika Korps in a very precarious situation. As von Mellethin commented: 'an armoured division without gasoline is little better than a heap of scrap iron'.[38] The panzer divisions could not manoeuvre without fuel and without manoeuvre they could not dislodge the Eighth Army from the Alam el Halfa ridge.

As the panzer divisions took up all-round defensive positions in the Ragil depression they, and the Axis transport moving slowly through the minefield gaps, were hammered constantly by air attack. The Afrika Korps met with no success on 1 September either. Kesselring made good his promise to fly in fuel in the dire emergency that faced the *Panzerarmee*, but almost all of it was swallowed up simply transporting it to the front. Meanwhile, British attacks on the desperately needed tankers meant that, just as before the 'Crusader' offensive, combined air and naval attacks strangled the *Panzerarmee*'s supply lines. There was now no hope of receiving sufficient fuel to continue the attack and Rommel had to take the painful decision to begin a withdrawal. Rommel's hopes of victory had disappeared like a mirage.

The orders to withdraw came as a shock for most of the officers and men of the Afrika Korps. They had expected to resume their attack after a temporary pause and did not understand the wider reasons which forced the withdrawal. On the night of 2 September, the *Panzerarmee* had to inform OKW and the Commando Supremo of its failure.[39] The *Panzerarmee* had been repulsed by an unexpected combination of rigid defence by the Eighth Army and continual attacks by the Desert Air Force. One British commentator later argued that: 'In effect, the guns and armour of the Army made a ring and the air gave the punch inside the ring.'[40] Montgomery had been highly cautious during his first battle, but his approach had maximised the damage inflicted on the *Panzerarmee* for very little cost.

The 'six days race', as the Axis troops called the battle, was soon over. Rommel had not broken the Eighth Army or reached the Delta and it was the *Panzerarmee* which had received 'a pretty thorough beating'.[41] The Axis also had no wish to point out the fact that their last all-out attempt to reach the Delta had failed disastrously and Goebbels's Propaganda Ministry referred to the events merely as a 'reconnaissance in force'. Rommel had made a fundamental mistake; he had committed his main striking force to an advance deep behind the Eighth Army's lines with insufficient fuel to complete the movement. Yet Rommel never seems to have fully understood the true reasons why his offensive failed. He certainly recognised the significance of the power of the Desert Air Force, but to the end he always maintained that his supply problems were ultimately and primarily due to Italian failures of organisation and inefficiency. He seems never to have understood the full complexity of the interdependencies that ensnared the *Panzerarmee*'s logistics.

Once the *Panzerarmee* had withdrawn, it still remained pinned to the stretch of desert around El Alamein. Having conclusively beaten off the Axis offensive, the Eighth Army could now prepare to mount its own. Rommel was bitterly disappointed and increasingly ill. Eventually, his doctor insisted that he return to Germany for a rest cure. On 22 September, Rommel handed over command of the *Panzerarmee* to General der Kavallerie Georg Stumme, who had served with distinction in Russia. Although his offensive had failed, Rommel returned to a hero's welcome in Germany. On 30 September 1942, Hitler personally presented Rommel with his Field Marshal's baton. At fifty years of age, he was the youngest Field Marshal in the Wehrmacht, and without question Hitler's favourite military commander. Rommel had received the oak leaves to the Knight's Cross in March 1941 for his service with 7th Panzer Division and been promoted to General der Panzer Truppe that June. In the following January, Rommel's command became the *Panzerarmee Afrika* and he was promoted to full Generaloberst in the same month as the youngest officer ever to have attained this rank. That February, Hitler awarded him the swords to the oak leaves of the Knight's Cross and, on 23 June 1942, Rommel heard that he had been promoted to Field Marshal. 'Medals, promotions and other marks of Hitler's favour' had indeed 'piled up during Rommel's "African years" in a way no other Wermacht general could match'.[42] Yet when he received his baton, Rommel remarked to his wife: 'I would rather he had given me one more division.'[43] Rommel had indeed received the special favour of the Führer, but not the resources he had required to achieve lasting success. Indeed, it might even be said that the strenuous efforts of Rommel and his men – both German and Italian – had been a useful propaganda coup for Hitler and little else.

As Rommel recovered his health in Germany, the *Panzerarmee Afrika* had to prepare to meet the coming British offensive. In fact, Rommel had already set in train the measures necessary to blunt any attack by the Eighth Army. His engineers worked hard to lay 445,358 mines in what were known as Rommel's 'Devil's Gardens'.[44] In amongst the mines, the Axis infantry held a chequerboard of strong points laid across the front and up to five kilometres in depth. No other army had incorporated this quantity of mines into its defences up to this point in the war and all of this hard labour was designed to ensure that the Eighth Army would be confronted by a series of mine boxes which hemmed in any attacking force so that it could be counter-attacked by the *Panzerarmee*'s mobile reserves. These deep defences certainly presented the Eighth Army with a severe challenge.

After months of intense preparation, the Eighth Army finally struck its blow after dusk on 23 October 1942. The attack opened with the biggest artillery bombardment of the desert war, then four British and Commonwealth infantry divisions advanced deep into the Axis defences. However, the subsequent advance of the British armour was held up by a combination of hard fighting and the deep minefields. On

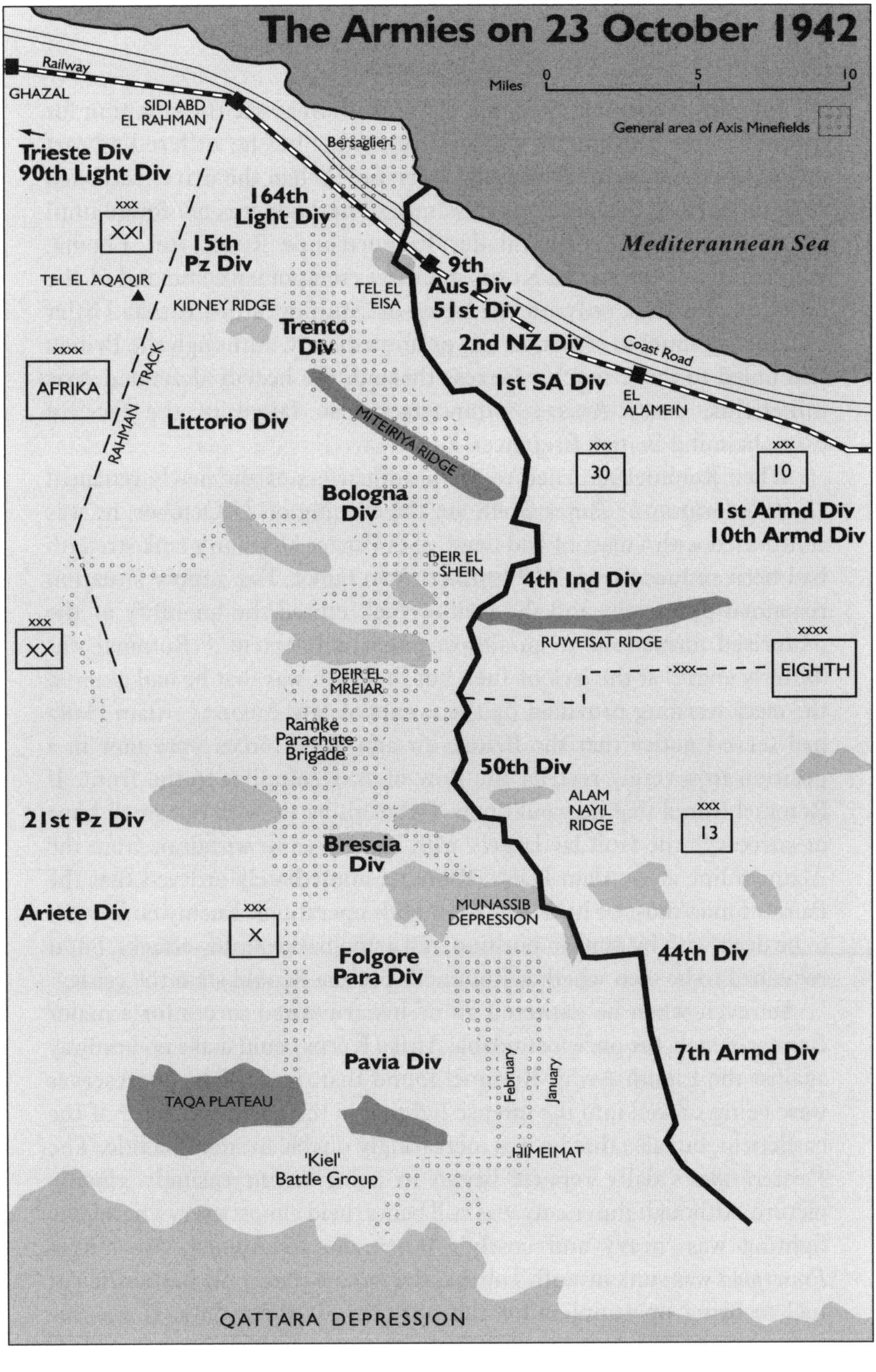

The Armies on 23 October 1942
Miles
0
5
10
General area of Axis Minefields
Railway
GHAZAL
SIDI ABD EL RAHMAN
Trieste Div
90th Light Div
Bersaglieri
164th Light Div
XXX
XXI
15th Pz Div
Mediterannean Sea
TEL EL AQAQIR
KIDNEY RIDGE
TEL EL EISA
9th Aus Div
51st Div
Trento Div
2nd NZ Div
Coast Road
XXXX
AFRIKA
RAHMAN TRACK
1st SA Div
EL ALAMEIN
Littorio Div
MITEIRIYA RIDGE
XXX
30
XXX
10
Bologna Div
1st Armd Div
10th Armd Div
DEIR EL SHEIN
4th Ind Div
XXX
XX
RUWEISAT RIDGE
XXXX
EIGHTH
XXX
DEIR EL MREIAR
Ramke Parachute Brigade
50th Div
ALAM NAYIL RIDGE
XXX
13
21st Pz Div
Brescia Div
MUNASSIB DEPRESSION
Ariete Div
XXX
X
44th Div
Folgore Para Div
7th Armd Div
Pavia Div
February
January
TAQA PLATEAU
HIMEIMAT
'Kiel' Battle Group
QATTARA DEPRESSION

the following morning, Stumme drove forward to see the situation for himself – just as Rommel would have done – but he suffered a heart attack when his car was brought under fire. When the driver returned to headquarters, Stumme was missing and his body was not found until the following day.[45] General der Panzertruppe Ritter von Thoma, commander of the Afrika Korps, took over temporary command of the army. It was thus only on the news of Stumme's death that Hitler ordered Rommel to return to Egypt immediately. Although the British had failed to make much progress through the heavily defended Axis minefields, every Axis counter-attack also failed in the face of overwhelming British firepower.

When Rommel returned to the headquarters of the newly renamed *Deutsch-Italienische Panzerarmee* on the evening of 25 October, he was confronted with a mass of bad news. 15th Panzer Division's tank strength had been reduced from 119 to thirty-two tanks. The supply situation remained precarious and the lack of fuel limited the 'mobility of the motorised formations to an almost unbearable extent'.[46] Rommel was 'bitterly angry' at the lack of fuel, but the truth was that he had ignored the clear warning provided by the events of late August.[47] Alam Halfa had served notice that the British air and naval forces were now in a position to severely restrict the flow of Axis supplies to the front. If Rommel feared that he would now 'fight this battle with but small hope of success'[48] the fault lay largely with his refusal to withdraw from the Alamein line after Alam Halfa. Rommel immediately ordered that the Panzer forces must be held back for mobile operations. Enemy tanks were to be dealt with by guns in position, not armoured counter-attacks, but it remained to be seen whether Rommel's presence could stem the crisis.[49]

Yet even when he gathered all of his armoured forces for a major counter-attack, the once formidable Afrika Korps could make no headway against the Eighth Army. Rommel found that, inexorably, his reserves were being sucked into the intense fighting in the northern sector of the battlefield, but also that he was increasingly unable to stem the tide. The *Panzerarmee*'s daily reports began to paint an increasingly gloomy picture. Although the enemy was still being 'held almost everywhere', the fighting was 'heavy and costly'. When, on 27 August, the tanker *Proserpina* was sunk just off Tobruk, the *Panzerarmee* only had sufficient fuel to bring up supplies for the next two or three days. It was re-emphasised to Berlin that: 'Unless every possible assistance is given in bringing over fuel the defensive battle cannot be brought to a successful conclusion.'[50]

With his main attack held, Montgomery launched the 9th Australian Division in an attack towards the coast which, over the next few days, saw some of the fiercest fighting of the desert war. Rommel launched counter-attack after counter-attack to try to stem the Australian advance to no avail. He later bemoaned the fact that at Alamein: 'Rivers of blood were poured out over miserable strips of land which, in normal times, not even the poorest Arab would have bothered his head about', but there was little doubt that the tide of battle was inexorably flowing in Montgomery's favour.[51] On 28 October Rommel exhorted his men thus: 'The present battle is a life and death struggle. I therefore require that … every officer and man will give of his utmost and thereby contribute to its success', but the blunt fact was that willpower alone was no longer enough against the British superiority in numbers and, above all, firepower.[52]

Rommel's attention was increasingly fixed upon the coastal sector, where the fight between 90th Light Division and the 9th Australian Division reached a furious intensity in the last days of October. Through their stubborn, repeated attacks and dogged resistance the Australians drew in the last reserves of the *Panzerarmee* into a wild mêlée. Meanwhile, although Montgomery's initial plan for a rapid breakthrough had failed, by launching the 9th Australian Division towards the coast he had managed to retain the all-important initiative since the successive Australian attacks against the vulnerable yet vital coast road forced an Axis response. Each time the Australian infantry seized ground and threatened future attacks, Rommel mounted counter-attack after counter-attack in a desperate attempt to stabilise the situation. This fighting wore down the 9th Australian Division to a virtual skeleton, but it sucked in all of the Axis reserves and concentrated them in the far north. The Australian soldiers could have been forgiven for thinking that they were fighting the battle alone, but their series of attacks gave the Eighth Army vital time to prepare its next blow. Instead of regaining the initiative, Rommel had been dragged into a costly fight which wore his army down while Montgomery prepared for another blow.[53]

Operation 'Supercharge' began on the night of 1 November with a massive bombardment and infantry assault on a compact 4,000 yard front.

This assault bit deeply into the remaining Axis defences and the British momentum was continued by the 9th Armoured Brigade's 'Balaclava' charge against the dug-in positions of the Afrika Korps anti-tank gun screen. These all-out hammer blows weakened but did not break the tenacious defence of the *Panzerarmee*. Even though Rommel had been expecting the British breakthrough attempt to take place along the coast road, it did not take long for the Afrika Korps to assemble for its counter-attack. For Rommel and his men, this really was the last ditch: for the rest of the morning and afternoon, there was the greatest clash of armour seen at El Alamein. The Axis gunners redoubled their fire into the congested British salient while the two German panzer divisions drove forward to stem the tide. Observers in the 90th Light Division commented that:

> During the morning the fighting reached its climax. Smoke and dust covered the battlefield, and visibility became so bad that the general picture was of one immense cloud of smoke and dust. Tanks engaged in single combat; in these few hours the battle of Alamein was decided.[54]

Although the German tank crews pressed home their attacks they made no headway: the German counter-attack 'broke down in the face of the massed British armour.'[55] The British had failed to break through, but the 15th and 21st Panzer Divisions were virtually destroyed during the day of intense fighting. On the evening of 2 November, after a desperate day of fighting, Rommel telephoned von Thoma to discuss the situation. Von Thoma reported that he had managed to close the gap with scanty forces, but he also estimated that no more than thirty-five tanks would be available for use the next day – and the British had at least four times that number at the front.[56] The infantry and artillery had fought bravely but were now reduced to one third of their strength.[57] Von Thoma believed that if the British attacks continued in the same strength a breakthrough would be unavoidable because there were no longer any reserves available. The moment that Rommel had feared for so long had finally arrived: he would have to withdraw to save what he could of his army. The *Panzerarmee*'s daily report tried to put the best possible light on the desperate situation:

> After ten days of uninterrupted fighting our own losses are exceptionally high, due to the overwhelming superiority of the

enemy's infantry, tanks and artillery and the unremitting use he has made of his Air Force. … In the coming night and on 3 November we expect new attempts to penetrate by strong armoured forces … our forces are no longer sufficient to prevent new breaks through. As from 3 November the Army is therefore preparing to fight its way back step by step in face of the enemy pressure.[58]

The Eighth Army had not broken through during Operation 'Supercharge' but the skilful positional defence put up by the British units during the morning and afternoon of 2 November had doomed the *Panzerarmee* to defeat. By forming a new salient, the Eighth Army had invited counter-attacks and these had worn down the strength of the panzer divisions to the point that they could no longer resist. Rommel was finally forced to admit that his army would have to withdraw from El Alamein before it was completely destroyed.

Rommel, having taken this painful decision, worked quickly to give the retreat the best chance of success but, at 13.30 on 3 November, *Panzerarmee* H.Q. received a direct order from Adolf Hitler. When the *Panzerarmee*'s daily report for 2 November had reached OKW, now installed in the Wolfschanze in East Prussia, the news of Rommel's imminent withdrawal had struck like a 'thunderclap'.[59] Hitler sent a grandiloquent message forbidding any withdrawal:

> The German people joins with me in following, with full confidence in your leadership and in the bravery of the German and Italian troops under your command, the heroic defence in Egypt. In your present situation nothing else can be thought of but to hold on, not to yield a step, and to throw every weapon and every warrior who can be spared into the fight. …Despite his numerical superiority the enemy must have exhausted his strength. It would not be the first time in history that the stronger will has triumphed over stronger enemy forces. You can show your troops no other road but that to victory or death.[60]

There was a certain ironic echo of Rommel's own order of 28 October in Hitler's words, but Rommel, so used to complete freedom of action in his theatre, was shocked to receive a direct order forbidding retreat.[61] Instead of sensibly ignoring this impossible order, Rommel obeyed it. The orders for further withdrawal were cancelled and all formations were ordered to 'defend their present positions to the last'.[62] Unsurprisingly, this sudden change in orders caused considerable confusion amongst the units of the *Panzerarmee*. Hitler's order completely disrupted what had been a relatively ordered withdrawal and doomed the non-motorised Italian infantry to capture. Rommel felt an 'overwhelming sense of bitterness' when he realised that: 'even the greatest effort could no longer change the course of the battle'.[63]

However, although Rommel attempted to execute Hitler's order, von Thoma protested that his Korps would be destroyed if it continued to hold its present positions. He demanded that his men should be allowed to move back to the line which had been arranged on 2 November. Rommel hesitated but eventually agreed to pull the Afrika Korps back.[64] Rommel also sent off Lt Berndt, his personal assistant, to the Wolfshanze to persuade Hitler to change his mind. Von Thoma's intervention ensured that the Afrika Korps would be able to escape, but although some of the German forces were able to slip away, the Italian forces of the *Panzerarmee* were doomed to destruction.

The next morning, von Thoma, who had reputedly said to one of his officers that: 'Hitler's order is a piece of unparalled madness. I can't go along with this any longer', bravely commanded the rearguard until he was captured.[65] By the evening of 4 November, the issue was no longer in doubt. After twelve days of intense fighting, the resistance of the *Panzerarmee* had finally been broken and what was left of the Axis army was in full retreat.

The remnants of the Afrika Korps were actually able to disengage from the pursuing elements of the Eighth Army by making a night march on the night of 5 November.[66] However, 21st Panzer Division was immobilised for lack of fuel the next day[67] and only really saved by the rain storm which fell in the early afternoon and turned the desert into a quagmire. The rain and subsequent floods on 6 and 7 November meant that the Eighth Army's pursuit ground to a halt. Ultimately, although a number of attempts were made to cut them off, the remnants of the *Panzerarmee* were able to escape. However, Rommel did not escape with anything recognisable as an army. Casualty figures for the *Panzerarmee* will only ever be estimates given the confusion that reigned amongst its units in the early stages of the pursuit. British estimates, based on intercepts, gave German casualties as 1,149 killed, 3,886 wounded and 8,050 captured. Italian losses amounted to 971 dead, 933 wounded and 15,552 captured. By 11 November the number of Axis prisoners had risen to 30,000 as more were netted during the pursuit.[68] The Eighth Army claimed to have destroyed or captured 259 Axis tanks and 254 guns during the fighting, although these were incomplete estimates.[69] The vital support structure of the army, along with the headquarters of the formations, did survive, but the fighting element was reduced to little more than a weak regimental group. In these circumstances, the wreck of the *Panzerarmee* only survived by making a headlong flight out of Egypt.

Hitler later remarked to Rommel that his retreat was 'exemplary and fantastic', but it still represented a heavy defeat.[70] Goebbels also attempted to put the best gloss on these events. Berlin radio even reported that: 'Rommel is advancing westwards; he still holds the initiative in that he frustrates all British efforts to deal him a decisive blow.' This desperate twisting of the facts opened Goebbels to ridicule and nothing could conceal the fact that Rommel's retreat from Alamein represented the destruction of the Axis ambitions in Africa. It was not until Rommel's forces reached El Agheila that they were able to make a brief stand in the positions they had first occupied in 1941, but this time there could be no counter-offensive. Caught between the advancing Eighth Army and the Anglo–American landings in French North Africa, Rommel's force could no longer stand in Libya. On 23 January 1943, Rommel's men relinquished Tripoli to the advancing forces of the Eighth Army.[71] Italy's North African colony had been lost and, with it, all of Rommel's African ambitions.

Rommel later mused on the course of the fighting in the desert that: 'With only three German divisions, whose fighting strength was often ludicrously small, we kept the British Army busy in Africa for eighteen long months and gave them many a trouncing, until our strength finally ran out at Alamein.'[72] While Rommel's comments do a serious disservice to the major Italian effort in the desert, they do perhaps hit upon an important truth. The fact that General Jodl could speak of 'Rommel's little shooting expedition in North Africa' at the Nuremberg trials revealed what a low priority was accorded to the theatre by the German

High Command.[73] Rommel constantly railed against the lack of attention paid to his theatre and refused to be bound by the limits of logistic reality. In so doing, Rommel won for himself and his army laurels of imperishable military glory, but also doomed himself to ultimate defeat.

### Notes

1. Basil Liddell Hart, *The Rommel Papers* (London: Collins, 1953), p. 181.
2. Ibid, p. 188.
3. Ibid, p. 208.
4. Ibid, p. 225.
5. The best estimated figures give the totals as 19,000 British, 13,400 South African and 2,500 Indian troops. See J.A.I. Agar-Hamilton and L.C.F. Turner, *Crisis in the Desert: May-July 1942* (Oxford: Oxford University Press, 1952), p. 221.
6. Liddell Hart, *Rommel Papers*, p. 231.
7. US National Archives, RG457/1035, Fellers to Washington, 16 June 1942, in 'The Contribution of the Information Service to the May-June 1942 Offensive in North Africa'.
8. Ibid.
9. Liddell Hart, *Rommel Papers*, p. 233.
10. Ibid, p. 232.
11. The National Archives (hereafter TNA), WO 32/10160, Auchinleck's Despatch.
1 Air Historical Branch (hereafter AHB), RAF Narrative (First Draft), *The Middle East Campaign, Operations in Libya and the Western Desert 21st January 1942 to 30th June 1942* (London: Air Ministry, n.d.), pp. 193-203.
12. Liddell Hart, *Rommel Papers*, p. 239.
13. Ibid.
14. Ibid.
15. New Zealand National Archives (hereafter NANZ), WAII/1/DA438.23/1, DAK War Diary, 2 July 1942.
16. NANZ, WAII/1/DA438.24/2, NANZ, 90th Light Division War Diary, 2 July 1942.
17. Translates as 'Strategic Signals Intercept Company'. Seebohm's unit was previously called the 3rd Intercept Company of Signals Battalion No.56 (3/N/56) but changed to the more important title on 17 April 1942. See TNA, WO201/2150, German Wireless Intercept Organisation.
18. Hans Otto Behrendt, *Rommel's Intelligence in the Desert Campaign* (London: William Kimber, 1985), p. 170.
19. Liddell Hart, *Rommel Papers*, p. 255.
20. Ibid, p. 257.
21. NANZ, WAII/1/DA438.23/2, Walther Nehring, *Der Feldzug in Afrika*, p. 33.

22. John Rylands Library, Dorman O'Gowan Mss, 1/27/9, Taylor to Barnett, 18 January 1965.
23. AHB, *Middle East Campaign, July 1942-May 1942*, p.140.
24. Martin van Creveld, *Supply in War: Logistics from Wallenstein to Patton* (Cambridge: Cambridge University Press, 1977), p. 197.
25. Ibid, p. 42.
26. TNA, CAB 146/14, EDS Appreciation No.9. pp. 43-45.
27. Ibid, pp. 58-62.
28. Bennett, *Ultra and Mediterranean Strategy*, pp. 148-151; Hinsley, *British Intelligence: Volume 2*, p. 417-425.
29. In mid-August, the Italians lost the *Lerici* on 16 August, *Rosolino Pilo* on 17 August, the cargo of the auxiliary sailing vessel *Agia Maria* on 19 August and the tanker *Pozzarica* on 21 August. See AHB, *Middle East Campaign, July 1942-May 1942*, p. 140.
30. Liddell Hart, *Rommel Papers*, p. 271.
31. Ibid, p. 275.
32. NANZ, WAII/11/23, 21st Panzer Division War Diary, 29 August 1942.
33. TNA, CAB 146/14, Enemy Documents Section Appreciation No.9. p. 106.
34. German maps referred to the high point on the Alam el Halfa ridge as Height 132, while British maps showed it as Point 102.
35. NANZ, WAII/11/23, 21st Panzer Division War Diary, 31 August 1942.
36. NANZ, WAII/11/23, Nehring, *Feldzug in Afrika*, p. 65.
37. F.W. von Mellenthin, *Panzer Battles, 1939-45: A Study of the Employment of Armour in the Second World War* (London: Cassell, 1955), p. 145.
38. Australian War Memorial (hereafter AWM), AWM54 492/4/77, *Panzerarmee Afrika* Daily Report, 2 September 1942.
39. AHB, *Middle East Campaign, July 1942-May 1942*, p. 193.
40. Liddell Hart, *Rommel Papers*, p. 275.
41. Ralf Georg Reuth, *Rommel: The End of a Legend* (London: Haus Books, 2008), p. 49.
42. Liddell Hart, *Rommel Papers*, p. 232.
43. AWM, AWM54 492/4/77, Pz Army Engineer HQ to Pz Army G Branch, 20 October 1942, Translation of Appendices to *Panzerarmee Afrika* War Diary September to October 1942.
44. Liddell Hart, *Rommel Papers*, p. 305.
45. TNA, CAB 146/17, Enemy Documents Section Appreciation No.9, pp. 24-25.
46. Liddell Hart, *Rommel Papers*, p. 304.
47. Ibid, p. 305.
48. TNA, CANB 146/17, Enemy Documents Section Appreciation No.9, p. 26.
49. Ibid, p. 52.
50. Liddell, Hart, *Rommel Papers*, p. 306.
51. NANZ, WAII/11/20, DAK War Diary, 28 October 1942.
52. Imperial War Museum, Montgomery Mss, BLM49/1, Montgomery to Brooke, 1 November 1942.

## 112   Rommel: A Reappraisal

53. NANZ, WAII/11/23, 90th Light Division War Diary, 2 November 1942.
54. AWM, AWM 54 423/4/103, 15th Panzer Division Report on the Battle of Alamein and the Retreat to Marsa el Brega, 23rd October – 20th November 1942.
55. TNA, CAB 146/17, Enemy Documents Section, Appreciation No.9, pp. 91-92.
56. Ibid.
57. AWM, AWM54 492/4/74, Translation of German Official War Narrative, 23 October – 5 January 1943.
58. Walter Warlimont, *Inside Hitler's Headquarters 1939-45* (London: Weidenfeld and Nicolson, 1964), p. 268.
59. AWM, AWM54 492/4/74, Translation of German Official War Narrative, 23 October – 5 January 1943.
60. Liddell Hart, *Rommel Papers*, p. 322.
61. AWM, AWM54 492/4/74, German Official War Narrative, 23 October – 5 January 1943.
62. Liddell Hart, *Rommel Papers*, p. 322.
63. NANZ, WAII/11/20, DAK War Diary, 3 November 1942.
64. William Richardson and Seymour Freidlin, *The Fatal Decisions* (London: Michael Joseph, 1956), p. 106.
65. AWM, AWM 54 423/4/103, 15th Panzer Division Report on the Battle of Alamein and the Retreat to Marsa el Brega, 23rd October – 20th November 1942; Ibid., AWM 423/4/103 (Pt 93), 21st Panzer Division Report on the Battle of Alamein and the Retreat to Mersa el Brega.
66. Ibid.
67. TNA, CAB106/2291, Middle East Strategy.
68. Ibid., WO 201/439, 8th Army Claims up to 2359 hrs 3 November.
69. Reuth, *Rommel*, p. 57.
70. Ibid, p.48.
71. Liddell Hart, *Rommel Papers*, p. 192.
72. Reuth, *Rommel*, p. 188.

# CHAPTER FIVE

# Rommel in Normandy

## *Peter Lieb*

**Intermezzo: 'Führer Headquarters' and Italy, May to October 1943**

When Rommel left Africa in March 1943 his career seemed to be broken. The most popular German commander was relieved of his post in the face of a huge defeat. Hitler was well aware that it would be unwise for all sorts of reasons to link the downfall of Army Group Africa to the name of Rommel, the child of Joseph Goebbels's propaganda machinery. The German minister had put a lot of effort into the construction of this Rommel myth. A 'military authority such as Rommel cannot be created at will and again disposed of at will',[2] he once stated. For a while he deluded the German public into thinking that Rommel would remain in Africa, because for Goebbels Rommel's name was 'invaluable for the future course of the war'.[3]

In reality Rommel was jobless for the time being. He stayed at his home in Wiener Neustadt and bemoaned his unsatisfactory situation. His close relationship with Hitler was blemished after several clashes over the war in North Africa; he confided to his son Manfred that he had 'fallen into disgrace and could expect no important job for the present'.[4] From a distance he had to watch the capitulation of Army Group Africa on 13 May 1943. Over 300,000 German and Italian soldiers fell into captivity. Only three months after Stalingrad the Germans had suffered another crushing defeat, this time at the hands of the Western Allies.

Hitler tried to re-establish the broken relationship with his former favourite general and called him to Berlin on 9 May 1943. Over the following weeks Rommel accompanied Hitler to the 'Führer

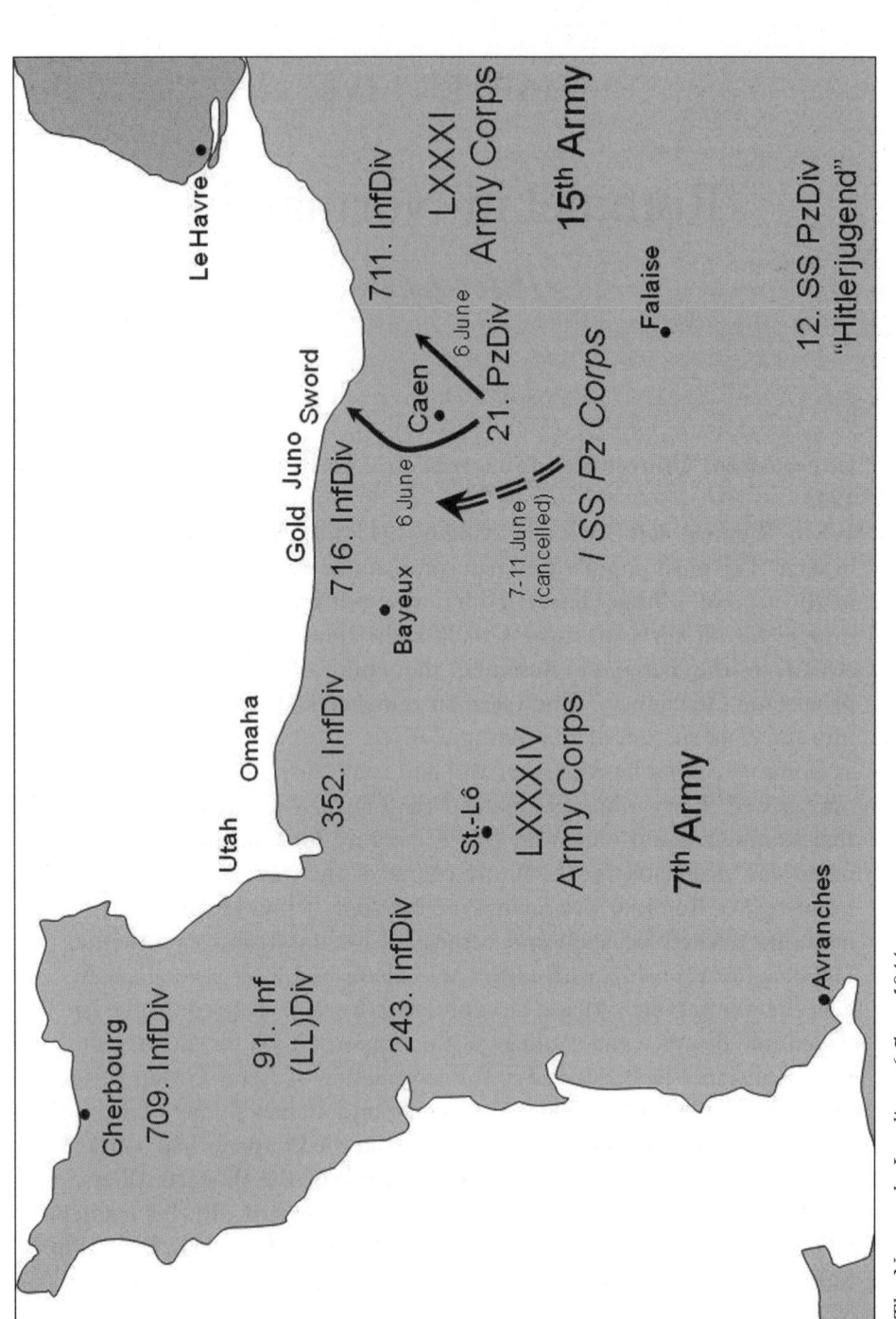

*The Normandy Landings, 6 June 1944*

Headquarters' and served him as a kind of military advisor – but without any real power and influence. The close personal proximity of the men still did not alter the situation fundamentally; they remained estranged and even clashed once more about the future of the war. Rommel aired his pessimistic view on Germany's economic output against the Western powers' industrial might. Allegedly, Hitler admitted he had never wanted to wage war against the West, but now had to live with the consequences.[5] Rommel said of the Führer 'sometimes you feel that he's no longer quite normal'.[6]

In early summer 1943 Hitler's main strategic concern was Italy. Due to the long series of heavy and costly defeats in North Africa the Axis partner had become war weary, a weakness the Allies soon exploited. On 10 July 1943 US, British and Canadian forces attacked the 'Fortress Europe' and landed on Sicily. Hitler was hesitant about how to react. Personally, he favoured a combined German-Italian supreme command in Italy under Rommel, all the more as, according to Jodl, the field-marshal was the only German commander 'numerous officers and soldiers in Italy would willingly subordinate to'.[7] But Rommel's appointment was too closely linked to internal power struggles amongst the Führer's entourage. Opposition came particularly from diplomats and the Luftwaffe. They favoured Göring's protégé, Luftwaffe Field-Marshal Albert Kesselring. In the end they prevailed: Kesselring became commander-in-chief of the German forces in Italy.

Hitler appointed Rommel instead as supreme commander of the German and Italian forces in the Balkans, where another Allied landing was expected. On 25 July Rommel flew to Thessaloniki in Greece. It was the shortest command of his career: on the same day at 23.15hrs he received a telephone call from the Führer Headquarters in Rastenburg and was urged to come back. He was now to assume command of Army Group B, initially under the codename 'I.A. OKW/Auffrischungsstab München' (OKW/Refreshing Staff Munich), with headquarters in Pullach south of Munich. What had happened?

On the same 25 July the Fascist Council overthrew Mussolini. King Victor Emanuel III relieved the Duce of all of his posts and placed him in 'protective custody'. Italy's exit from the Axis alliance was only a question of time. In anticipation of this the Germans silently prepared for the disarming of the Italian forces under the codename 'Achse'

(Axis), because they rightly distrusted their ally's lip service claiming Italian loyalty to the German Reich. In reality, since the Duce's overthrow the Italians had established secret contact with the Allies and negotiated an armistice. However, it would take until 8 September 1943 for the Italian government under Marshal Pietro Badoglio to officially declare the armistice after the Allied landing on mainland Italy. The Germans felt 'betrayed' once more, just as in 1915 when Italy had declared war on the Central Powers despite the Triple Alliance.

The Germans executed 'Achse' with swiftness and firm determination. Rommel was to play a crucial role in disarming the Italian forces in Northern Italy. His Army Group B was actually not worth its name in summer 1943, as it had only three divisions under its command: 44th Infantry Division, 26th Panzer Division and SS Panzer Grenadier Division "Leibstandarte SS Adolf Hitler". All three divisions had crossed the Brenner Pass from Austria into Italy in the previous months and the Italians had been led to believe these forces would help to ward off a potential Allied landing in Northern Italy. In reality, Rommel had prepared for operation 'Achse' and after the Italians declared the armistice his modest force quickly disarmed 5th, 8th and parts of 4th Italian Army without major bloodshed.[8]

After the threat from the Italian Army was removed, the Germans reconsidered the operational plans for the defence of the Italian peninsula. Rommel always believed the Allies would land as far north as possible, and hence suggested a series of delaying actions by Kesselring's Army Group in Southern Italy. These forces would gradually withdraw northwards and finally meet Rommel's Army Group B north of Rome, where he himself would take over the supreme command of all German and remaining loyal Italian forces; Kesselring's Army Group would be dissolved.

Hitler had initially approved this plan, but events unfolded differently over the coming weeks. On 11 September, Kesselring reported to Hitler that he intended to hold a line in Southern Italy just north of Salerno where the Allies had landed. He could support his arguments with his latest military success. With relatively few troops he had been able to slow down the Allied advance from the Salerno beachhead and particularly had been able to prevent an Allied breakthrough. Hitler was more than pleased with Kesselring's performance and as a consequence revoked the subordination of Kesselring's forces under Rommel.

On 30 September, Hitler met personally with the two antagonists, Kesselring and Rommel, in order to discuss the future conduct of the war in Italy. Rommel insisted on a defence line north of Rome. In contrast, Kesselring painted a much more positive picture of the German situation and advocated a defence line south of Rome. Hitler's choice was thus easy: given the option of a pessimistic Rommel or an optimistic Kesselring it was obvious that the Führer favoured the latter.

Rommel's downbeat attitude soon became evident to other representatives of the Third Reich. Goebbels blamed Rommel for seeing the war from a 'defeatist angle' and claimed that 'many even take the view that Rommel would be solely a retreat general'.[9] On 19 October 1943 Hitler ultimately decided that Kesselring would become Supreme Commander South for all German forces in Italy. Rommel's time in Italy ended with a humiliating internal defeat against his old rival Kesselring. For a few days his fate was undecided, before he finally received a new command appointment on 5 November: Inspector for the Defence Fortifications in the West. It was to become one of his most challenging missions and also the last military post of his life.

## Preparing for the Storm: Commander of Army Group B, November 1943 to May 1944

Rommel's appointment coincided with a fundamental change in German strategy. On 3 November 1943 Hitler issued his Directive Nr. 51, in which he shifted the focus away from the Eastern Front. Even though the danger from the Red Army was not gone, a much bigger one was looming: the 'Anglo-Saxon landing'. Hitler rightly realised that a successful Allied landing threatened Germany's industrial heart, the Ruhr, whilst in the East he could still trade space for time. As a consequence, the German dictator decided to reinforce the defence in the West.[10] The Allied landing should be warded off before Germany would turn eastwards again. The Directive Nr. 51 introduced 'the last big phase of Hitler's strategy' in the war.[11]

As one of the first obvious symbols for his new strategy, Hitler sent Rommel to France, where the Allied landing was most likely to happen. For the German public at home and the ordinary soldiers on the front the name Rommel was still surrounded by the myth of invincibility. His arrival in the West would bolster German morale and revive fading optimism to win the war. Goebbels considered Rommel as 'undoubtedly the suitable man' in the West and also expected a big moral impact on the Allies.[12] They knew they would soon meet again the erstwhile 'Desert Fox', the most stubborn German senior commander they had ever faced during the war. Amongst all senior German generals Rommel had collected by far the most experience in fighting the Western Allies. His appointment in the West was hence a clever move, both in military and political terms.

Rommel's bulky title was soon dropped and his former Army Group B officially reconstituted. The army group was subordinated to Army Group D (later Supreme Commander West), which was commanded by sixty-nine-year-old Field-Marshal Gerd von Rundstedt. The oldest and the youngest Wehrmacht field-marshals had to cooperate and agree on a defence plan against the Allies. This proved to be a rather difficult task, as the officers had different ideas about how to ward off an invasion, in particular with regard to the employment of the armoured divisions. Rundstedt's ally in this question was the commander of the Panzergruppe West, General Leo Geyr von Schweppenburg, who had been military attaché in London in the 1930s and spoke six foreign languages.[13]

The debate between Rommel, Rundstedt and Geyr later became known as the 'Panzer Controversy'.[14] Officially, German military doctrine had never considered the need for defences against an amphibious landing; the German Field Manual 300/1, *Truppenführung*, had nothing to say about it. Thus the commanders had to rely on previous experiences in the war in comparable situations. In the West the crux turned out to be employment of what was seen as the German trump card: the armoured reserves. A veteran of the war in North Africa, Rommel knew all too well the disastrous impact Allied airpower had had on his ability to freely manoeuvre his forces, particularly in the later stages of the campaign. In contrast to many of his colleagues, he did not belittle the Allied military achievements and once stated: 'Our friends from the East cannot imagine what they're in for here. [...] Here we are facing an enemy who applies all his native intelligence to the use of his many technical resources, who spares no expenditure of material and whose every operation goes its course as though it had been the subject of repeated rehearsal.'[15]

Rommel's defence concept centred round the 'Atlantic Wall'.[16] Expecting no substantial support from either the Luftwaffe or the Kriegsmarine, he wanted to destroy the Allied landing forces on the beaches, i.e. at the weakest moment of any amphibious operation. The armoured reserves should be split up and deployed as close as possible to the coast so that they could join the battle in the earliest stages. This concept meant a fundamental violation of German military doctrine with its core belief of concentrating forces and destroying the enemy with a single mighty blow.

Rundstedt, in contrast, still fixed his ideas on this very concept. For him the Atlantic Wall was not useless, but only an instrument to delay the Allied landings or at best to disrupt some of the enemy's forces. The main battle should be fought in the hinterland, out of the Allied naval gunfire range. For the implementation of his concept he received Geyr's Panzergruppe West, which was a staff for the operational conduct of armoured forces. Geyr, an Eastern Front veteran, developed Rundstedt's ideas even further and wanted to defeat the enemy in central France with all armoured divisions available. Several times Geyr and Rommel seriously clashed about this issue, to the extent that Rommel requested Geyr's direct subordination[17] – but to no avail.

Both plans seemed to have their strengths and weaknesses and hence each idea had its supporters. In January 1944 Rundstedt asked his army commanders for their opinion on this question; as expected he received mixed answers.[18] In the end, however, all depended on Hitler. The dictator personally favoured Rommel's plan, yet for a different reason. He objected to the idea of giving up a single kilometre of once-conquered terrain. But eventually Hitler stuck to his divide-and-rule principle and shied away from a definite decision. This resulted in a compromise: half of the armoured divisions were subordinated to the individual armies or army groups and would be deployed near the coast, while the other half were concentrated with Panzergruppe West further in the hinterland.

Rundstedt and Rommel did not only differ on their defence ideas in the West, they also personified two distinct generations of officers with two completely different styles of command. Rundstedt mostly remained in his headquarters and delegated much of his work to his very capable chief-of-staff, General Günther Blumentritt. In contrast, Rommel was a typical field commander and sought personal contact with his troops. During his numerous inspection tours along the Atlantic Wall he was always fully focused on his work; the rich French cultural heritage meant little to him. His operational officer, Colonel Hans-Georg Tempelhoff, once wrote in his diary: 'On our journeys with the field-marshal we always drive straight past the monuments and fine architecture. He's so wrapped up in his job that he's totally uninterested in anything else except the military needs of the moment.'[19]

A camera team frequently accompanied Rommel on these trips. He was still a media star and many of his colleagues considered him a pompous parvenu and doubted his military skills.[20] Furthermore, his behaviour towards his subordinates was often rough. After one of his tours the commander of 84th Army Corps, General Erich Marcks, summarised his impressions of Rommel: 'He is a choleric who often explodes and the commanders are terribly scared of him. The first one, who has to report to him in the morning, receives a chewing out[21] as a matter of principle.'[22]

Notwithstanding these personal flaws, Rommel's hard and restless work on the defence preparations bore fruit. In October 1943 the commander of 15th Army, Colonel-General Hans von Salmuth, had pointed out the alarmingly poor state of the Atlantic Wall,[23] but by mid-1944 this had changed fundamentally. For example, the number of mines laid weekly rose from about 25,000 in 1943 to 250,000 in 1944.[24] Systematically flooded areas, barbed wire, minefields, foreshore obstacles (such as the so-called 'Czech hedgehogs'), concrete bunkers, field fortifications, communication trenches, heavy batteries, machine-gun emplacements, flamethrowers, and grenade launchers would transform the beaches into massive areas for killing Allied troops. A few kilometres in the hinterland a second line of defence was erected and would stop any enemy forces that managed to break through the first defences on the coast. On D-Day, however, this defence line was far from complete. A peculiar anti-airborne obstacle was even named after the man who was the indefatigable driver of all these changes: the 'Rommel asparagus'. These were wooden stakes connected by wire and rammed into the ground with a mine on top. If a glider or a parachute force came into contact with the wires, the explosives would detonate. On his inspection tours Rommel also stressed the need for mental preparation of the German soldiers for the 'progressing modernisation of the war',[25] i.e. the overwhelming Allied firepower.

Rommel's defence plans and ideas stemmed, at least partly, from his experiences with the 'Devil's Gardens' in North Africa where he had denied the enemy large areas with relatively cheap and simple minefields. Of course, Rommel did not conceive all these devices himself, but he encouraged his subordinates to come up with new ideas and improvisations. His engineer general Wilhelm Meise once called Rommel 'the greatest engineer of the Second World War. There was nothing I could teach him.'[26] In April 1944 Rommel promised Hitler that he would have finished the defence preparations along the Atlantic Wall by 1 May.[27] The field-marshal should have known better. On D-Day the German defences in the West were far from being complete. Even worse, the ammunition supply in the bunkers of the Atlantic Wall was insufficient and the quality of many German troops questionable. Some of them were so called Osttruppen, former Soviet prisoners who now fought in German service for a lost cause. In summer 1944 the Wehrmacht was a mere shadow of itself compared to 1941.

Yet Rommel was confident he could defeat the Allies at the Atlantic Wall. The great optimism he spread was contagious and the vast majority of the German soldiers in the West, as well as the population in the Reich, still believed that the coming Allied landing would be Germany's last, but at the same time promising, chance to turn the tide of war.

## Fighting the Storm: Commander of Army Group B during the Normandy Battle, June/July 1944

In the morning of 6 June 1944 the long-awaited Allied invasion commenced, but Rommel missed the start of his last battle.[28] He had not believed in an imminent Allied landing due to the bad weather forecast and, hence, had decided to fly to Germany to celebrate his wife's birthday at home in Herrlingen. His defence plan deemed the first hours of the invasion critical, but ironically he was not present in these important moments to coordinate the German counter-measures. Moreover, most German commanders, including Rommel, had expected a landing at the Pas-de-Calais, but the Allies had deceived their enemies and chosen the Normandy beaches instead. This gave them the element of surprise.

Only a few hours after the amphibious landings, British, Canadian and US forces broke through the German defences with relative ease in four of their five landing sectors. Only at Omaha Beach did the Wehrmacht come remotely near to driving the enemy back into the sea. Rommel's idea of defeating the Allies on the beaches was shattered into pieces on the very first day. Vast amounts of Allied firepower from the air and from the sea paralysed the German defenders in the bunkers. Heavily outnumbered, they either surrendered or died in their emplacements.

Rommel's internal opponents could not hide their satisfaction as the events were unfolding. For instance, the chief-of-staff of Army Group G in distant southern France, Major General Heinz von Gyldenfeldt, wrote in his personal diary that the 'Atlantic Wall as such was overrun in a few hours as could have been expected'.[29] The German initial response was ill-coordinated and lacked overall direction. The only element available for an immediate local armoured counter-attack on 6 June was 21st Panzer Division. As this division could have played a vital role in the eastern landing sector, it is worth scrutinising its actions on this day.

Before D-Day 21st Panzer Division had been deployed in the area around Caen and split up into four battle groups. After the war Geyr called this disposition 'a striking example of wretched Panzer tactics and the result of Rommel's orders'.[30]

Was Geyr right to blame Rommel alone for these faults? The real answer is much more complex. 21st Panzer Division's commander, Lieutenant General Edgar Feuchtinger, was in Paris on the night of 5/6 June amusing himself with his girlfriend. Furthermore, he was deemed militarily incompetent and had received the divisional command more because of his political loyalty than previous merit on the battlefield.[31] To make matters worse, the division's operational officer, the able Lieutenant-Colonel von Berlichingen, was also absent when the Allied air landings started. However, upon his return in the early morning he immediately gave the order to launch a counter-attack.[32]

Despite Berlichingen's actions 21st Panzer Division lost crucial hours. Even more problematic was the inactivity of Lieutenant-General

Hans Speidel, Rommel's chief-of-staff in Army Group B. Despite Rommel's absence, Speidel should have been aware that a swift response to the landing was central to his commander's plan.[33] But he let all morning pass by in order to get a clear intelligence picture of the Allied landings before taking any action. The general staff of the Supreme Commander West also viewed the evolving events with relative calm and hoped to identify the enemy's main effort before deploying further troops. After the war the German generals accused Hitler of a slow reaction on D-Day, as he had allegedly not released the armoured divisions. In reality, many senior commanders and their staffs were paralysed by inactivity on this decisive day.

The problems with 21st Panzer Division's counter-attack persisted as its single battle groups were ordered in different directions. Some elements engaged the British 6th Airborne Division east of the River Orne; others pushed towards the sea between the Allied landing sectors Juno and Sword. The latter battle group was even able to reach the beaches in the early afternoon. This was the only successful German counter-attack on D-Day, but it remained short-lived. Allied forces threatened to cut off the battle group and, thus, the Germans had to withdraw again in the late afternoon. The other armoured battle groups to the east of the Orne were unable to seize ground from the British airborne forces.[34]

The sector of the 21st Panzer Division was the only one in which Rommel's defence plan was tested that day. It failed due to a combination of poor communication, leadership problems and lack of manpower in the face of overwhelming Allied superiority in firepower. In the evening of D-Day, the German 7th Army had to admit that it would not be possible to retake the Allied beach for the time being. Some 150,000 Allied soldiers were already ashore at this time.

Re-called from Germany, Rommel finally arrived on the Normandy front in the late afternoon of 6 June, but he could not positively influence the desperate situation. Seventh Army asked for reinforcement by two infantry divisions, but Rommel denied the request. The reasons for his decision remain unknown, but it sharply contradicted his own plans to destroy the enemy on the beaches. Did the field-marshal tacitly concede the failure of his original defence plan? He did at least order a concentrated counter-attack for the following day with three armoured divisions (Panzer Lehr, 21st Panzer, and 12th SS Panzer) under the command of 1st SS Panzer Corps. But all hopes that this force could change the situation soon vanished. During its march to the front Panzer Lehr had already suffered considerable losses to Allied aircraft and for the same reason the divisions could not deploy in the chosen assembly areas. Communication problems aggravated the situation further. The attack was first postponed to 8 June and later to 9 June. When it finally started it was soon abandoned, again due to Allied air and naval supremacy. Instead of being deployed in an offensive and mobile role, all German armoured divisions were now forced into the defence and had to fill gaps in the thin front line under constant Allied pressure.

Three days after D-Day the last remaining hope had gone and it was clear that Rommel's defence plan could not alter the situation; the Germans had been unable to launch a timely counter-attack in order to hit the Allies hard at their weakest moment during the landing phase. So would a new plan, to manoeuvre the battle further inland, as Geyr had advocated, bring about the necessary victory? His Panzergruppe West ordered another big counter-attack for the night of 10 to 11 June, again to be carried out by Panzer Lehr, 21st Panzer and 12th SS Panzer Divisions. But even before this offensive commenced the Germans suffered the next big blow: the British had deciphered communications from the headquarters of Panzergruppe West based at La Caine and the Royal Air Force bombed it on 10 June. The majority of Geyr's staff was killed in this air raid, amongst them his chief-of-staff, Major-General Sigismund-Helmut Edler von Dawans; Geyr himself was wounded. The remnants of the headquarters moved to Paris. As a result, the Germans lost their best command authority capable of dealing with mobile divisions on the operational level. And in Geyr Rommel lost one of his most intractable adversaries – at least for the time being.

These developments did not solve the problem of confusing command structures which paralysed the German actions in Normandy: two Army Groups (Supreme Commander West and Rommel's Army Group B), one Army (7th Army), and one reinforced army corps (Panzergruppe West)[35] were all charged with the same operational objective, the containment of the Allies in the beachhead. To make matters worse the OKW and Hitler himself interfered on numerous occasions. Rommel was caught between a rock and a hard place, and his scope for acting independently, as in North Africa, remained very limited. He and Rundstedt now put aside their pre-invasion debates and understood that they were in the same boat, which was about to sink. Henceforth they mostly acted in concert and sent alarming reports to Hitler and the OKW pointing out the overwhelming Allied superiority in men and materiel. In particular, the Germans had no response to the enemy's dominance in the sky and the powerful naval artillery, which both relentlessly hammered German positions. This made it almost impossible to manoeuvre larger bodies of troops during daytime, just as Rommel had anticipated. At least the German soldiers on the front remained steadfast and 'fought with greatest doggedness and most extreme devotedness', as Rommel described it in one of his few reports.[36] As in North Africa he preferred to give his orders orally and rarely reported to the Führer headquarters, because he was worried about Allied interception.[37]

In mid-June, Hitler ordered the Supreme Commander West to launch a major armoured counter-offensive and promised to send 2nd SS Panzer Corps with 9th SS Panzer Division 'Hohenstaufen' and 10th SS Panzer Division 'Frundsberg' from the Eastern Front to Normandy. Meanwhile, 2nd Panzer Division had arrived at the front, 2nd SS Panzer Division 'Das Reich' was on route and 1st SS Panzer Division 'Leibstandarte SS Adolf Hitler' was also expected soon. Overall, the Germans intended to rely on eight armoured and three infantry divisions for this big operation. Rundstedt charged Rommel to conceive an operational plan. On 19 June his staff presented two options. The first and preferred plan envisaged an initial attack at the boundary between the 1st US and the 2nd British armies towards the Channel coast. Once the breakthrough was achieved with massive artillery support, the German armoured divisions would split up and simultaneously turn westwards and eastwards before finally encircling both Allied armies. The plan was a classic product of German World War Two doctrine: attacking the enemy at his weakest point, quickly exploiting the initial successes and finally defeating the enemy forces in a pocket.[38] The offensive was the test for Geyr's concept of a manoeuvrist battle in the hinterland. Ironically, Rommel and his staff had to conceive the plan in Geyr's absence. On paper the plan looked good, but reality turned out to be completely different. Due to the lack of ammunition and fuel the attack was scheduled for 1 July, before it was finally cancelled for good. Allied airpower and naval bombardments had already disrupted the armoured forces in the assembly area before the offensive started. Throughout the Normandy battle the Germans were nowhere near launching a major counter-offensive. A series of localised tactical attacks did not alter the situation. The initiative remained firmly with the Allies.

Hitler was furious about this situation, but also aware of the fading morale of his senior commanders in Normandy. On 17 June he flew to France, where he met Rommel and Rundstedt in Margival near Soissons. Impatiently he urged them to attack and regain the initiative. This was wishful thinking, as Rundstedt and particularly Rommel pointed out. The latter warned that the Allied naval artillery would instantly disrupt the German armoured forces in any hasty counter-attack. Instead, Rommel suggested that they retreat outside the Allied naval gunfire range. Here German armour could attack the flanks of any Allied penetration.[39] This was partly a late concession to Geyr's initial concept. Hitler declined this proposal, but his physical presence seemed to have boosted Rommel's morale again. He was temporarily more optimistic about the future of the war.[40] For the last time in his life he was swayed by Hitler's persuasive power.

It did not take long for reality to catch up with Rommel once again. In the immediate aftermath of the British major offensive 'Epsom' (26 to 30 June), Rundstedt, the recovered Geyr and Rommel all urged Hitler to clear the frontline bulge north of Caen in order to save manpower and to avoid the exposure of the troops to the deadly heavy naval artillery. However, General Jodl, in the Führer headquarters, responded by saying that Geyr 'does not display the "ice-cold" logic and the clear rational thinking the situation demands and it is likely the senior staffs and commanders have become "infected" by the view of the commander of Panzergruppe West'.[41]

The entire incident eventually gave the Führer the opportunity to identify scapegoats for the overall military failure and it ended in an almost complete replacement of the senior commanders in Normandy. Rundstedt and Geyr were both relieved of their posts in early July. Field-Marshal Günther von Kluge[42] became the new Supreme

Commander West and the skilful and battle-hardened Eastern Front veteran General Heinrich Eberbach relieved Geyr as commander of Panzergruppe West, which now received full army status as 5th Panzer Army. A few days earlier, on 28 June, the commander of 7th Army, General Friedrich Dollmann, had died from a heart attack. Rommel quickly ordered the commander of 1st Army in south-west France, General Kurt von der Chevallerie, to Normandy as Dollmann's successor.[43] However, Hitler intervened personally and appointed SS Oberstgruppenführer Paul Hausser instead. It was a novelty for an SS officer to be given command of an army. All three new commanders – Kluge, Eberbach and Hausser – personified loyalty to Hitler and his regime as well as energetic determination to turn the tide in Normandy.

As the only senior commander, Rommel kept his post, even though he was no longer deemed untouchable and the Nazi leaders considered him a pessimist. This became particularly apparent during a meeting with Hitler in Berchtesgaden on 29 June.[44] On this occasion Goebbels noted in his diary: 'I have come more and more to the conclusion that it was not expedient to entrust Rommel with the command post in a critical area. Rommel is indeed a good Panzer general, but he is very "prone to the air"[45] and, furthermore, the African campaign seems to have taken its toll on him. As a result he does no longer have that flexibility and inner vitality, so crucial for leading responsibly in such a decisive phase of the war.'[46] Indeed, Rommel's optimism had quickly vanished once the invasion had started and developed so badly for the Germans in Normandy.[47] The only reason why he did not share Rundstedt's and Geyr's fate was his continued popularity with the German public, who still saw him as an invincible war hero. Removing Rommel from his post would have been tantamount to the Nazi regime admitting defeat in Normandy.

On 3 July Rommel sent Kluge and Hitler a ten-page long memorandum in which he outlined his own view on the situation in Normandy and the reasons for the series of setbacks. The paper was full of fundamental criticism about the wrong deployment of the armoured forces before D-Day, the overlapping command structures, the constant interferences of the OKW in operational questions, the miserable logistics and the insufficient support from the Luftwaffe and the Kriegsmarine.[48] Unsurprisingly the paper failed to produce any reaction from Hitler, although the OKW did mostly stop interfering. The military situation remained unchanged. The German forces thinned out more and more; substantial reinforcements did not arrive due to the simultaneous large-scale Soviet summer offensive in the East; and there was no antidote to the Allied superiority in men, materiel and firepower. According to German estimates the Allies fired almost twenty times more artillery shells than the Germans.[49]

On 15 July Rommel sent another memorandum to Hitler. This time he took an even more alarming tone and warned of the imminent collapse of the Normandy front. The letter ended with the cryptic paragraph: 'The troops are everywhere fighting heroically, but the unequal struggle is approaching its end. It is urgently necessary for the proper conclusion to be drawn from this situation. As C.-in-C. of the Army Group I feel myself in duty bound to speak plainly on this point.'[50] What Rommel meant about the 'proper conclusion to be drawn' has always been a subject for debate. Did he want to urge Hitler to fight the battle for France further inland? Or did he mean that political steps should be taken to end the war in the West? Evidence rather suggests the latter, for a number of reasons. First, the document makes no mention of a military solution as to how operations in the West could be conducted in future. Second, Rommel considered his long-standing opponent Montgomery as a potential linkman for a truce in the West.[51] Finally, Rommel had been in contact with the military resistance against Hitler for some time – to what extent has remained a matter of debate ever since. Of special interest here are explicit comments General Eberbach made in eavesdropped conversations during his time in British captivity. According to Eberbach, Rommel had personally confessed to him in Normandy that Hitler had to be killed.[52] Whether this was really Rommel's opinion and whether he was willing to take the consequences will never be truly known: on 17 July Rommel was heavily wounded by a British fighter bomber on one of his numerous inspection trips to the front. This meant the end of his time in Normandy.

## A Gallant German Officer? Rommel and War Crimes in Italy and France

The still-current myths that surround Rommel have arisen from various sources. One such is the claim that he had always fought with gallantry and treated his enemies fairly. Was he really as chivalrous an officer as he has often been portrayed? The following paragraphs examine his behaviour in Italy and France in three areas: first, his time in Italy with the disarmament of the Italian army and anti-partisan operations in autumn 1943; second, the application of the infamous Commando Order in his area of responsibility in the West; and third, his attitude towards the local French population during the Normandy battle.

The German disarmament of the Italian army in September 1943 was accompanied by numerous infringements and war crimes against the former allies. The most brutal incident was certainly the mass murder of 1,000 to 2,000 Italian prisoners on the Ionian island of Kefalonia following a direct order from Hitler.[53] In Rommel's area of responsibility in North Italy, however, the disarmament happened without major bloodshed.[54] The Italians were sent to Germany as military internees for forced labour, but Rommel was not aware of their fate at that time.

A few weeks later he happened to hear that elements of 1st SS Panzer Division 'Leibstandarte SS Adolf Hitler' had shot a number of Jews at Lake Garda; units of the same division also burnt down several hundred houses in Boves in the Cuneo province on 19 September 1943 and killed twenty-four inhabitants. Rommel was shocked by these atrocities and initiated an investigation which, however, did not come to a conclusion.[55] After this episode Rommel allegedly forbade his son Manfred to join the Waffen-SS.[56]

However, during his time in Italy he also issued what was probably the most radical order in his career. On 23 September he ordered, in reference to fighting the partisans, that 'sentimental scruples' against 'Badoglio-dependent bandits in uniforms of the once brothers-in-arms' were 'totally inappropriate'. This drastic order could have certainly meant a radicalisation of anti-partisan operations, but in reality it did not lead to a tangible increase in German atrocities in Northern Italy. Overall, the situation remained calm and the Germans did not execute larger reprisals in the area of Rommel's Army Group B.[57]

During his time in North Africa Rommel had already been confronted by Hitler's infamous Commando Order of 18 October 1942, which ordered the execution of captured Allied commandos regardless of whether they had been caught in uniform or not. When Rommel received the order in North Africa, he allegedly burnt it. Even though this fact has not been proven, it seems very likely, as the Commando Order was not executed in Rommel's Army Group B. Before and after the invasion the army group bluntly reported that captured commandos had been treated just like any other prisoners of war.[58] Also, no trace of the order being followed can be found in the files of Army Group B, even after the OKW reissued the Commando Order on 29 June and explicitly demanded written reports on any commandos executed. In fact, the order can be found in the files of 5th Panzer Army dated from early October 1944, i.e. just when the army came under command of Army Group G. This was at a time when Rommel had left the West and had been replaced. So he had very probably withheld the Commando Order when he was still in charge of Army Group B.[59] After the war Speidel and his senior naval advisor Admiral Friedrich Ruge both claimed that Rommel had always urged his soldiers to adhere to the 'laws of humanity' and 'chivalry'.[60] With regard to the Commando Order this was certainly true.

Unlike the war in North Africa, the battle of Normandy took place in a relatively densely populated area and hence the local civilian population was a factor both sides had to take into account in their operational plans before D-Day. On his inspection tours in spring 1944 Rommel insisted again and again that the local population should be recruited as labour to help build the Atlantic Wall. The civilians should be informed that the stronger the defence fortifications were, the less likely it was that the Allies would invade there and hence the horrors of war would not happen in their area.[61] At the same time, Rommel felt pity for the French when he saw their pain and suffering after the Allied aerial bombings.[62]

The fate of the civilian population was not a top priority for the German military once the invasion started; they had to focus primarily on military matters in this hard battle. Initially they had ordered locals to remain in their houses during the fighting, so that they would not become a liability. But after a while the Germans found that dwellings had become a trap for the civilians during the heavy Allied bombardments. Rommel changed the order and permitted the French population to seek cover in the fields. This probably saved the lives of thousands of local Frenchmen during the battle.[63]

## Conclusion

Normandy was Rommel's last battle, even though he did not have to experience the bitter end due to his injury. According to his initial plans, Normandy was a battle that should have been over in a few days. By that time he had hoped to throw the Allies back into the sea. It is tempting to analyse which of the two defence plans had the greater chance of success: Rommel's battle at the coast based on the 'Atlantic Wall', or Geyr's mobile operations further inland based on the armoured divisions.

With the benefit of hindsight Rommel's plan may have been preferential, but it would have relied upon too many variables to have more than a slight chance of success. First, the Germans would have had to identify the exact time and location of the Allied landings at least twenty-four hours before the invasion so that they could push their armoured reserves as close to the coast as possible. At this point it should be stressed that the majority of the German commanders (Rommel included) expected the Allies to attack at the Pas-de-Calais. A redeployment to Normandy at such short notice would have been very difficult, if not impossible. Second, Rommel's plan would have needed a swift and energetic German reaction on 6 June, but he was in Germany on that day and in his absence his chief-of-staff Speidel did not implement the original plan; precious time was lost and the sole local armoured reserve, the 21st Panzer Division, launched its counter-attacks only after midday. Third, command and control was a major German problem. In practice, all commanders of the armoured forces would have had to share Rommel's view and split up their reserves. But instead they received contradictory orders from the top and this finally allowed them to deploy their forces the way they preferred. In most cases this meant they kept their forces concentrated.

On 6 June only very small parts of the battle could be fought in the way Rommel had intended. Yet this was still a better result than Geyr's plan. His battle had ended before it even started. Allied bombardments from the air, sea and ground disrupted the German armoured forces several times to the extent that they could never launch a major counter-attack. The Allies imposed their kind of warfare on the Germans, and that was a war of attrition the Germans were never able to win. Rommel's piecemeal concept was the exact opposite of the German doctrine of the Second World War.[64] Overall, one can argue that he displayed real mental agility and opted for the unorthodox and unexpected solution, even though his plan would have had only a very small chance of success – even in a German best-case scenario.

Once the Allies had gained a firm foothold in Normandy, Rommel could no longer influence the battle in the way he wished to. The only thing he could do was to visit the front-line troops and give them some words of consolation and to report to Hitler the desperate situation on the front. On this point he did not differ from other commanders like Rundstedt, Geyr and later Kluge. But Rommel did it with more vigour, and he probably alluded to the political consequences – a case almost without precedence in the Third Reich.[65]

## Notes

1. The author would like to thank Matthias Strohn, Klaus Schmider and Sean McKnight for their support in producing this article.
2. Elke Fröhlich (ed.), *Die Tagebücher von Joseph Goebbels* vol. 8, (Munich: Saur, 1993), p. 266 (10 May 1943).
3. Ibid.
4. B.H. Liddell Hart (ed.) *The Rommel Papers* (London: Collins, 1953), p. 425.
5. Ibid., pp. 427-28.
6. Ibid., p. 428.
7. Maurice Philip Remy, *Mythos Rommel* (Munich: List, 2002), p. 180.
8. Gerhard Schreiber, *Die italienischen Militärinternierten im deutschen Machtbereich 1943 bis 1945. Verraten-Verachtet-Vergessen* (Munich: Oldenbourg, 1990), pp. 109-20.
9. Fröhlich (ed.), *Tagebücher*, vol. 10, p. 180 (27 October 1943).
10. The Directive Nr. 51 is printed in its German original in Walther Hubatsch (Hrsg.), *Hitlers Weisungen für die Kriegführung 1939-1945. Dokumente des Oberkommandos der Wehrmacht* (Frankfurt/Main: Bernard & Graefe ,1962), pp. 233-41.
11. Andreas Hillgruber, *Der 2. Weltkrieg. Kriegsziele und Strategien der großen Mächte* (Stuttgart: Kohlhammer, 1982), p. 128.
12. Fröhlich (ed.), *Tagebücher*, vol. 12, p. 244 (9 May 1944), and p. 268 (11 May 1944).
13. Geyr held an interpreter diploma in Russian and French, spoke English and Spanish and had reading knowledge in Dutch and Italian.
14. Hans Wegmüller, *Die Abwehr der Invasion. Die Konzeption des Oberbefehlshabers West 1940-1944* (Freiburg: Rombach, 1974), pp. 130-64.
15. Liddell Hart, *Rommel Papers*, p. 467.

16. Samuel W. Mitcham, *The Desert Fox in Normandy. Rommel's Defence of Fortress Europe* (Westport CT: Praeger, 1997). This book deals exactly with the subject of this chapter. Unfortunately, the author did not use any German primary sources for his work.
17. Imperial War Museum (hereafter IWM), AL 1697/3, Letter from Rommel to Jodl, 23 April 1944.
18. Rundstedt's initiative clearly displayed the highly valued traditional freedom of thought in military matters within the German Army. The answers of his army commanders are printed in: Dieter Ose, *Entscheidung im Westen 1944. Der Oberbefehlshaber West und die Abwehr der alliierten Invasion* (Stuttgart: Deutsche Verlags-Anstalt, 1982), pp. 308-18.
19. Quoted from: David Irving, *The Trail of the Fox. The Life of Field-Marshal Erwin Rommel* (London: Weidenfeld & Nicholson, 1977), p. 298.
20. See the conversation between the two captured generals, Erwin Menny (84th Inf Div) and Curt Badinski (276th Inf Div), in: The National Archives (TNA), WO 208/4168. C.S.D.I.C. (U.K.). S.R.G.G. 991. Information received: 24 Aug 44. See also SS General Sepp Dietrich's negative remarks about Rommel according to Goebbels' diary. Fröhlich (ed.), *Tagebücher*, vol. 12, p. 348 (25 May 1944).
21. In the German original Marcks uses the colloquial word *frühstücken*, which literally translates into 'to breakfast'.
22. Quoted and translated from Otto Jacobsen, *Erich Marcks, Soldat und Gelehrter* (Göttingen: Musterschmidt, 1971), p. 160.
23. NOKW-2533. Der Oberbefehlshaber der 15. Armee. Ia Nr. 0176/43 g.Kdos. Chefs., 26/10/1943.
24. Ose, *Entscheidung*, p. 68.
25. Bundesarchiv-Militärarchiv (hereafter BA-MA), RH 24-74/14. Der Kommandierende General des LXXIV. A.K. Abt. Ia Nr. 800/44 g.Kdos. 19 May 1944.
26. Quoted from Irving, *Trail of Fox*, p. 286.
27. Fröhlich (ed.), *Tagebücher*, vol. 12, p. 129 (18 April 1944), p. 162 (22 April 1944), and p. 171 (23 April 1944).
28. A lot of scholarship has been done in past decades on the German perspective of the Normandy battle. The most important works are: Ose, *Entscheidung*; Wegmüller, *Abwehr*; Richard Hargreaves, *The Germans in Normandy: Death Reaped a Terrible Harvest* (Barnsley: Pen & Sword, 2006); Russell Hart, *Clash of Arms. How the Allies Won in Normandy, 1944* (Boulder, CO: Lynne Rienner, 2001; Niklas Zetterling, *Normandy 1944: German Military Organization, Combat Power and Organizational Effectiveness* (Winnipeg: Fedorowicz, 2000); and Peter Lieb, *Konventioneller Krieg oder NS-Weltanschauungskrieg? Kriegführung und Partisanenbekämpfung in Frankreich 1943/44* (Munich: Oldenbourg, 2007). See also the memoirs of Rommel's chief-of-staff and his senior naval advisor: Hans Speidel, *Invasion 1944: Ein Beitrag zu Rommels und des Reiches Schicksal* (Tübingen: Leins, 1949) (English version: *We Defended Normandy* (London: Herbert Jenkins, 1951); Friedrich Ruge, *Rommel und die Invasion. Erinnerungen*

(Stuttgart: Koehler, 1959) (English version: *Rommel in Normandy: Reminiscences* (London: Presidio, 1979).
29. BA-MA, MSg 1/1508. Kriegsaufzeichnungen aus den Jahren 1941/45 von Heinz von Gyldenfeldt, 2nd volume, entry 6 June 1944. See also his entry from 11 June in which he explicitly criticised Rommel's defence concept.
30. David C. Isby (ed.), *Fighting the Invasion: The German Army at D-Day* (London: Greenhill Books, 2000), p. 236.
31. In the 1930s Feuchtinger had organised the Nazi party rallies. A military court sentenced Feuchtinger to death in 1945 because of racketeering with plundered Jewish property. Hitler converted this sentence to probation on the front and hence Feuchtinger fought as an ordinary infantryman at the Battle of Seelow Heights. After the war he was officially recognised as a victim of Nazism and received a full general's pension. According to the memoirs of Hermann Balck, the later commander of Army Group G, Feuchtinger became a Soviet spy in West Germany after the war. See Hermann Balck, *Ordnung im Chaos. Erinnerungen 1893-1948* (Osnabrück: Biblio Verlag 1981), pp. 577-79.
32. 21st Panzer Division stressed this point very clearly in its own after-action report. IWM, AL 1697/3. 21. Panzer-Division. Kommandeur. BrB Nr. 1753/44 g.K. 17 June 1944. An I. SS PzKorps.
33. Feuchtinger claimed after the war that his division had taken the independent decision to attack 6th Airborne Division at 0600hrs. See Isby (ed.), *Fighting the Invasion*, p. 222. In fact it was not him who gave the order, but his operational officer. After the war Geyr blamed Rommel's chief-of-staff Speidel, who did not dare to release the division in the absence of his commander despite the constant request from 7th Army. Archives Institut für Zeitgeschichte (IfZ-Archives), ED 91/12. Letter from Geyr to Wilhelm Bittrich, 9 July 1963.
34. It is debatable whether 21st Panzer Division launched its counter-attacks wholeheartedly. Given the intensity of the battle the casualties were not particularly high during the first ten days after D-Day with fifty-one officers, 334 NCOs and 1,479 other ranks. IWM, AL 1697/3. 21. Panzer-Division. Kommandeur. BrB Nr. 1753/44 g.K. 17 June 1944. An I. SS PzKorps.
35. The defence sectors were defined only in early July: 7th Army took charge of the western part and Panzergruppe West (later 5th Panzer Army) the eastern part of the Normandy front.
36. BA-MA, RH 19 IX/8. OKdo. d. H.Gr.B. Ia Nr. 3356/44, 11 June 1944.
37. BA-MA, RH 19 IV/134. Telephone conversation between Colonel Zimmermann and Lieutenant-Colonel Meyer-Detering from 22 June 1944. Fröhlich (ed.), *Tagebücher*, vol. 12, p. 441 (10 June 1944).
38. For the maps of this plan see Ose, *Entscheidung*, pp. 325-26.
39. IWM, AL 1697/3. Major i.G. v. Ekesparre. Ib HGr B, 17 June 1944. Bericht über den Führervortrag am 17.6.
40. Fröhlich (ed.), *Tagebücher*, vol. 12, p. 492 (18 June 1944) and p. 517 (22 June 1944).

41. BA-MA, RH 19 IX/85. Army Group B. War Diary, entry from 1 July 1944.
42. Kluge had played a double game for years. Though loyal to Hitler he had also been in contact with the members of the military resistance. On 20 July 1944 he did not support the conspiracy after he learnt about Hitler's survival. Yet, he was deemed suspicious and relieved as Supreme Commander West. On his way to Hitler he committed suicide on 19 August 1944.
43. BA-MA, MSg 1/1508. Kriegsaufzeichnungen aus den Jahren 1941/45 von Heinz von Gyldenfeldt. 2. Volume. Entry of 28 June 1944.
44. IWM, AL 1697/3. Wolfram. Major i.G. 1 July 1944. Meldung. Bericht über die Fahrt OB HGrB zur Besprechung im Führer-Hauptquartier am 29.6., 18Uhr
45. The original German word used is the neologism *luftanfällig*. Here, Goebbels referred to Rommel's constant concerns about the strength of Allied airpower.
46. Fröhlich (ed.), *Tagebücher*, vol. 12, p. 567 (29 June 1944). Hitler assessed Rommel in his conference on 31 August 1944 with the following words: 'Unfortunately Field-Marshal Rommel is a very great leader full of drive in times of success, but an absolute pessimist when he meets the slightest problems.' See Helmut Heiber (ed.), *Hitlers Lagebesprechungen. Die Protokollfragmente seiner militärischen Konferenzen, 1942-1945* (Stuttgart: Deutsche Verlags-Anstalt, 1962), p. 612.
47. See the letters to his wife in June 1944, printed in: Liddell Hart, *Rommel Papers*, pp. 491-93.
48. BA-MA, RH 19 IX/4. Der Oberbefehlshaber der Heeresgruppe B. Ia Nr. 4257 /44 g.Kdos.Chefs. 3 July 1944. Betrachtungen. Printed in Liddell Hart, *Rommel Papers*, pp. 481-84.
49. IWM, AL 1697/3. Besprechung OB HGr B mit Chef des GeStabes PzGr West auf Gefechtsstand PzGr West, 10 July 1944, 12.30hrs
50. BA-MA, RH 19 IX/8. Der Oberbefehlshaber der Heeresgruppe B. Betrachtungen zur Lage. 15 July 1944. Printed in Liddell Hart, *Rommel Papers*, pp. 486-87.
51. Ralf-Georg Reuth, *Rommel: The End of a Legend* (London: Haus 2005), p. 49-50.
52. Sönke Neitzel, *Abgehört. Deutsche Generäle in britischer Kriegsgefangenschaft 1942-1945* (Berlin: Ullstein, 2005), pp.61-65, and documents 37, 155 and 157 (English version: *Tapping Hitler's Generals. Transcripts of Secret Conversations, 1942-1945* (London: Greenhill, 2007).
53. Based on a contemporary German document most publications give the number of 4,000 prisoners shot. Recently, however, the first thorough research on the number of victims came to the conclusion that 2,500 Italians died on Cephalonia and it is unclear how many of them were shot after capture. Hermann Frank Meyer, *Blutiges Edelweiß. Die 1. Gebirgs-Division im Zweiten Weltkrieg* (Berlin: Christoph Links Verlag, 2007), pp. 289-462.
54. Schreiber, *Militärinternierte*, pp. 109-20.
55. Remy, *Mythos*, pp.193-97.
56. Liddell Hart, *Rommel Papers*, p. 429.
57. Carlo Gentile, *Wehrmacht, Waffen-SS und Polizei im Kampf gegen Partisanen und Zivilbevölkerung in Italien 1943-1945* (Paderborn: Schöningh, 2013), pp. 80-85.

58. BA-MA, RH 19 IV/134. OB West. Ic. KTB. Tägliche Kurznotizen 6 to 30 June 1944. Conversation with Lieutenant-Colonel Staubwasser from 22 June 1944.
59. Lieb, *Konventioneller Krieg*, pp. 152-53.
60. Hans Speidel, *Aus unserer Zeit. Erinnerungen (Berlin: Propyläen, 1977), p. 167;* Ruge, *Rommel und die Invasion*, p. 147.
61. BA-MA, RH 24-74/14. Der Kommandierende General des LXXIV. A.K. Abt. Ia 800/44 g.K. 19 May 1944. IfZ-Archiv, MA 1783/4. Armeeoberkommando 1. Ia. Nr. 1481/44 g.Kdos. v. 1 May 1944. Bericht über Teilnahme an der Besichtigungsreise Generalfeldmarschall Rommel am 29. und 30.4.1944.
62. Irving, *Trail of Fox*, p. 481.
63. Lieb, *Konventioneller Krieg*, pp. 211-12.
64. For a concise analysis of the basis of German military doctrine in the inter-war years see Matthias Strohn, *The German Army and the Defence of the Reich: Military Doctrine and the Conduct of the Defensive Battles 1918-1939* (Cambridge: Cambridge University Press, 2011).
65. Of all field-marshals only Kluge explicitly urged Hitler to end the war in his farewell letter from 18 August 1944 before he committed suicide. For a print of his letter see: Ose, *Entscheidung*, pp. 339-40.

CHAPTER SIX

# Rommel and the 20 July 1944 Bomb Plot

*Russell A. Hart*

It has become widely accepted that the conspirators who sought to assassinate Adolf Hitler during the failed 20 July 1944 bomb plot had recently won over Erwin Rommel to their cause and – had Rommel not been severely wounded in an air attack on his staff car on 17 July – that he would have led the plotters in the West towards a separate capitulation in France, thereby giving the attempted *coup d'état* a chance to succeed, despite the failure to kill Hitler. The events that unfolded after the failed assassination attempt helped forge such an assessment. Rommel came under suspicion of complicity in the bomb plot during the witch hunt that followed its failure and on direct orders from Hitler was forced to commit suicide on 14 October 1944. In return for taking his own life, he was given a state funeral with full military honours, rather than facing trial by the notorious People's Court established to condemn the guilty. In addition, his family was spared collective arrest and even possible death under the Nazi principle of *Sippenhaft*: shared collective responsibility and punishment. Unfortunately, the true extent of Rommel's involvement in the 20 July bomb plot is very difficult to ascertain. Like many of those ultimately snared in the vicious Nazi backlash that led to almost 5,000 deaths, Rommel's involvement remains ambiguous and unclear, but clearly it was much more minor than both his *Gestapo* inquisitors and many historians have subsequently concluded. In reality, Erwin Rommel was not a member of the 20 July conspiracy, abhorred assassination, was only superficially connected with the anti-

Hitler Resistance and, therefore, it is highly improbable that he would have actively aided the *coup d'état* on 20 July if he had not been incapacitated.

Much of the legend of Rommel's involvement stems from his post-war hagiography, linked to two of his closest staff officers and confidantes: his chief of staff, Colonel Dr. Hans Speidel; and his naval advisor, Vice-Admiral Friedrich Ruge. Speidel was (despite his post-war claims) only peripherally connected to the plot and, through dint of passivity on 20 July, covered his tracks well enough to escape being executed, though he was incarcerated in a concentration camp. He survived the war and then became the primary advocate of Rommel's full participation in the 20 July assassination plot. Both officers developed abiding friendships with the field marshal and, after Rommel's forced suicide, Speidel, more than any other individual, forged the modern view of Rommel as a committed conspirator. Combined, Speidel's and Ruge's post-war efforts significantly created the legend of an apolitical Rommel uncorrupted by the evils of National Socialism. However, both officers had their own agendas to pursue that make their claims regarding Rommel's complicity in the 20 July bomb plot suspect.

In addition, numerous dignitaries and scholars have embraced, elaborated upon and disseminated the Rommel legend to both academic and popular audiences to such an extent that Rommel's central involvement in the conspiracy has become rooted in popular consciousness. Academic interpretations have varied: hagiographic assessments portray a distinguished field commander and resistance martyr, who was forced to commit suicide.[1] Even Peter Hoffmann, the leading chronicler of the German Resistance, has largely embraced this sympathetic assessment of Rommel.[2] Other historians have labelled Rommel as an unthinking collaborator who betrayed the Führer only when the war had turned against the army.[3] Yet even these less flattering portraits have largely failed to re-examine critically Rommel's involvement with the anti-Hitler Resistance. Thus it is fitting in this collective reappraisal of Rommel's life and career to begin such a reevaluation.

A careful sifting and weighing of the limited, fragmentary, problematical and ambiguous extant evidence suggests that Rommel had at best very superficial knowledge of ill-defined efforts by an amorphous group of army officers and others to extricate Germany from impending defeat. Moreover, not only was he only very peripherally involved in the anti-Hitler Resistance, but his supposed commitment to the conspiracy to assassinate Hitler (*à la* Speidel) is highly implausible. Therefore, both the available evidence and logic dictates that had he not been seriously wounded on 17 July, Rommel would have almost certainly sat on the fence on 20 July, as most senior German officers did that day, and once sure that Hitler still lived, Rommel would have done nothing. Thus, his post-war image of being a committed member of the anti-Hitler opposition prepared to overthrow the Führer, ironically, owes much to his having been being incapacitated and removed from any decision-making possibilities three days before the assassination attempt.

Inevitably the reality of any conspiracy is very hard to reconstruct. This is particularly so given that most of those actively involved in the 20 July bomb plot died after its failure. Accurately reconstructing the degree of Rommel's actual involvement is therefore very challenging. Yet it is necessary to posit that the modern image of Rommel the committed conspirator ready and willing to act is overblown. Rommel, like many other senior German officers, remained deeply torn between his fears that Hitler was leading Germany toward catastrophe and his sworn oath of loyalty to Hitler as 'Leader' of the German people, as commander-in-chief of the German armed forces, and as 'providential protector' against the supposed 'Jewish-Bolshevik Menace'. Moreover, Rommel shared the strong anti-Communist sentiments of the German officer corps and no evidence exists that he (like the rest of the 20 July conspirators) ever contemplated ending the war against the Soviet Union. The available evidence, therefore, simply does not support the proposition that Rommel would have acted decisively to aid the coup had he not been severely injured three days earlier.

What follows therefore is a re-examination and reassessment of the degree of Rommel's knowledge of, and involvement in, the 20 July assassination plot. Because of the necessarily secretive and compartmentalized nature of conspiracy in a totalitarian state like Nazi Germany, accurately recreating Rommel's involvement is fraught with difficulty: at best we can partially reconstruct events and make logical inferences from known facts. Moreover, to understand these events and

Rommel's place in them contextualization is required. Obviously the conspirators were deeply desirous to initiate a German war hero of Rommel's stature – the famed 'Desert Fox' – into their ranks. Consequently, in the weeks leading up to the coup attempt the conspirators tried repeatedly to win over Rommel to their cause. They were thus psychologically predisposed to both believe that Rommel had committed to the conspiracy (whether it was true or not), and to disseminate 'knowledge' of this accomplishment to win over dozens of other senior officers who had not decisively committed to the coup. Indeed, Rommel was probably the most popular senior commander, among the German people at least, and he would have been the first active-duty field marshal to lend support to the plot, if he had been won over.[4]

Although it is likely that by summer 1944 Rommel had come to believe that he had to 'come to the rescue of Germany', he remained deeply opposed to killing Hitler because doing so would transform the Führer into a national martyr and the public would refuse to recognize his responsibility for numerous Nazi crimes.[5] Indeed, after the war, his widow maintained that Rommel believed an assassination attempt would spark vicious, brutal civil war in Germany and as a consequence National Socialism would endure.[6] Instead, Rommel supposedly wanted Hitler arrested and brought before a court-martial for his many crimes, an impossible scenario in Nazi Germany in its fifth year of a global racial-ideological struggle for the survival of the Aryan *Volk* (*Vernichtungskrieg*). It is hard to believe that Rommel, the hardened pragmatist, could have entertained much hope for the successful arrest and trial of Hitler without plunging Germany into ruinous civil war. It was, after all, fear that Hitler was leading Germany toward ruin that propelled Rommel to contemplate the arrest of Hitler in the first place.

That a number of senior German generals in Western Europe had become active supporters of the coup certainly subsequently helped to taint Rommel with suspicion of involvement. But their paths to committed conspiracy were independent of Rommel's. The western conspirators included General Carl-Heinrich von Stülpnagel, the Military Governor in France, who was to take control of Paris after Hitler was killed and, it was naively hoped, negotiate an immediate armistice with the western Allies. That fact that von Stülpnagel only had nominal control over occupation forces outside the Normandy combat zone made this highly implausible. Yet von Stülpnagel played an important, if unwitting, role in associating Rommel with the conspiracy, for it was he who under torture first revealed Rommel's name in conjunction with the assassination attempt. Soon afterwards, von Stülpnagel's personal adjutant, Lieutenant-Colonel Caesar von Hofacker, likewise 'confessed' under torture that Rommel was an active member of the conspiracy.

Rommel's first direct interaction with the anti-Hitler Resistance appears to have come only in February 1943 (far later than almost all of the other conspirators) when Dr Karl Strölin, the Mayor of Stuttgart, who had served with Rommel in the Great War, informed him of the so-called 'Lanz Plan', an agreement between several senior German Eastern Front generals that Hitler had to go.[7] Incidentally Speidel was peripherally connected to this plot.[8] Unfortunately, like so many of the other plots against Hitler, it failed to materialize into anything tangible.

To understand Rommel's association with the bomb plot, one has to explore Speidel's connection to it. Because very few conspirators survived the war, understanding of Rommel's involvement with the Resistance has been strongly shaped by Speidel's retrospective recollections. It was on the Eastern Front during 1942-43 that Speidel developed growing antipathy toward the corruption, violence, and inhumanity of Nazism. It was his first-hand experience of Hitler's disastrous interference in military operations that finally persuaded Speidel that Germany's political and military future was grim. He gradually became convinced during 1943 that the war could not be won and that Hitler's leadership would ultimately destroy Germany. During that year he became convinced of the necessity of ousting Hitler.[9] Yet even among his own testimony, significant differences regarding Rommel's involvement appeared over time, particularly between the English language version of his memoirs and the original German work.[10] In addition, there are differences between Ruge's original diary notes and those he subsequently published after the war.[11] Thus, doubt remains regarding the reliability and authenticity of Speidel's and Ruge's retrospective recollections of Rommel's supposed involvement.

Moreover, Speidel was only marginally associated with the assassination plot being forged in Berlin during winter 1943-44 by Carl-

Friedrich Goerdeler, the former Mayor of Leipzig and the conspiracy's real dynamo, Colonel Claus Schenk, Graf von Stauffenberg. Speidel was peripherally connected with Goerdeler but not at all with von Stauffenberg. Speidel's role in the anti-Hitler Resistance was therefore quite separate from the main strands of the conspiracy and, crucially, he only came within the assassination plotters' orbit during late spring 1944 after his appointment to Rommel's staff, when the Resistance saw his value as a go-between with Rommel, who was the far more important prize for the conspirators. In his memoirs Speidel implied that Rommel had chosen him in April 1944 to be his chief-of-staff because the Desert Fox sought to undertake direct action against Hitler.[12] Unfortunately the truth was much more laconic. Rommel apparently chose Speidel for four major reasons: Speidel was by reputation a brilliant staff officer; both were Swabians by birth; they had served together in the same infantry regiment between the wars; and Rommel's 'lead-from the front' style necessitated an independently minded and intuitive chief-of-staff with strength of character. Rommel believed that only Speidel of those staff officers currently available best fitted that bill.[13] Rommel's selection of Speidel therefore had absolutely nothing to do with any intentions to remove Hitler. In fact, it is highly unlikely that Rommel had even the slightest idea of Speidel's conspiratorial credentials when he chose him.

Speidel joined Rommel's headquarters on 15 April 1944, offering him an historic chance to win over the most popular German general to the anti-Hitler Resistance. He immediately initiated political discussions with, and joined the established group of, activists led by von Stülpnagel in Paris. Friendship of sorts quickly developed between Speidel and Rommel. The pair and Vice Admiral Ruge discussed Germany's future. Speidel gave Rommel exceptionally frank appraisals of the war, particularly the disastrous consequences of the racial war of extermination that Nazi Germany was waging on the Eastern Front.[14] The clarity and farsightedness of Speidel's erudition allegedly greatly impacted Rommel, who, having spent most of his time in the Mediterranean theatre, apparently remained unaware of the true extent and ramifications of Nazi racism and terror in the east.[15]

Speidel perceived he found in Rommel a German war hero whom he came to believe shared his doubts and uncertainties. Yet both Rommel and Speidel (despite the latter's post-war claims to the contrary) remained loyal German officers, infused with the Prusso-German martial tradition of political neutrality and absolute obedience, and neither was prepared to act either decisively or on his own.[16] Speidel reintroduced Rommel to von Stülpnagel in May and the three struck up a rapport. Slowly Speidel and von Stülpnagel endeavoured to draw Rommel into the conspiracy. Speidel subsequently claimed Rommel sent him to Germany in May to make contact with other opposition leaders, but we have primarily Speidel's word that he acted at Rommel's behest. However, unlike the dynamic war hero von Stauffenberg leading the emerging bomb plot, Speidel, the calculating intellectual, was temperamentally averse to rash and risky behaviour. He manoeuvred slowly, cautiously and calculatingly; he also assiduously covered his tracks to avoid suspicion. He thus had only peripheral involvement in the 20 July assassination plot; and a lesser role than he portrayed post-war. His successful depiction of himself as an active conspirator, however, helped Speidel to rehabilitate his post-war military career in the 1950s *Bundeswehr*.[17]

Speidel's post-war claims that he had managed to win over an evidently increasingly disillusioned Rommel to the German Resistance remains unsubstantiated and probably will never be satisfactorily clarified. With the death of Rommel and the other conspirators, little credible evidence remained either to corroborate or to refute Speidel's retrospective version of events. The lack of documentary evidence and reliable testimony thus precludes definitive determination of whether Speidel won over Rommel to the conspiracy. A close reading of Speidel's post-war recollections shows them to be at times contradictory and ambiguous. In addition, more recent historical claims that Speidel influenced the deployment of Army Group B's armoured reserves in the Pas de Calais in order to have reliable troops at his disposal for the attempted *coup d'état* are based entirely upon superficial evidence that is not supported by any contemporary official documentary evidence.[18] In fact, the claim is not credible: German deployments were wholly consistent with German perceptions of enemy capabilities and intentions.[19]

Moreover, Speidel in his memoirs clearly had the goal of elevating the fallen Rommel to the status of a German national hero. Thus, he likely exaggerated both his and Rommel's involvement in the 20 July bomb plot. Re-evaluation of the available evidence, however, suggests that Speidel failed to win over Rommel. While Speidel probably succeeded in hardening Rommel's attitude to Hitler, the field marshal remained ambivalent toward either a military coup or the assassination of Hitler. Perhaps Rommel may have superficially toyed with the possibility of arranging a separate capitulation in the west, as he came to realise by late June 1944 that his forces could not in the long run defeat the Allied Normandy invasion. But even this is uncertain: this was a hopelessly unrealistic goal that flies in the face of Rommel's well-documented pragmatism.

In fact, in Rommel's absence after his incapacitation, Speidel remained completely passive on 20 July and did nothing to support the conspiracy after von Stauffenberg's bomb narrowly failed to assassinate Hitler. While von Stulpnägel and other conspirators made frantic, but abortive, last-minute efforts to induce Rommel's superior, Field Marshal Günther von Kluge, to join the conspiracy, Speidel remained utterly neutral, to such an extent that active plotters on that day in the West were unaware of his involvement in the conspiracy. Such was Speidel's passivity that even von Kluge apparently had no suspicions whatsoever about Speidel's loyalty. Thus Speidel continued to serve under von Kluge's successor (von Kluge having committed suicide after coming under suspicion himself) Field Marshal Walther Model, until 7 September when the *Gestapo* suddenly arrested him after von Stulpnägel and von Hofacker had divulged his name.[20] Going against the grain of the contemporary and extremely thorough *Gestapo* witch-hunt, Speidel was cleared of complicity in the plot by an army court of inquiry, which saved him from almost certain execution.[21] This outcome provides the strongest evidence that Speidel exaggerated his involvement in the plot after the war.[22]

Though he was guilty of complicity and Hitler was convinced of it, Speidel had covered his tracks so well and proved so passive on 20 July that it helped save his skin. For his supposed participation in the anti-Hitler Resistance, however, Speidel was able to restore his post-war public image. His personal desire to rehabilitate his 'martyred' friend Rommel motivated Speidel to elevate Rommel into the pantheon of leading members of the conspiracy when he published his recollections of the Normandy campaign in 1949.

Speidel's assertion that Rommel planned independent action in the West reflects the influence of Goerdeler's ideas, rather than those of von Stauffenberg.[23] This again suggests Speidel's very limited knowledge of the actual bomb plot itself. Speidel, indeed, did not have a conversation with von Stülpnagel about the assassination attempt until 20 April and Rommel only first talked privately with the military governor on 15 May.[24] When Speidel first discussed 'revolutionary change', allegedly at Rommel's behest with Goerdeler's confidante, Dr Strölin, on 15 May, they talked about legal means of removing war-making authority from Hitler, not assassination.[25] This meant trying to persuade Hitler to cede his command authority to a cabal of senior military commanders that likely would have included Rommel.[26] In contrast, von Stauffenberg had already initiated abortive efforts to kill Hitler. Speidel's claim that Rommel contemplated using a reliable armoured unit to seize Hitler's person and bring him before a court for trial lacks credibility: Rommel, as a highly experienced military commander and former commander of Hitler's army escort battalion, knew that such a course of action had almost zero chance of success, given how well guarded the Führer was.[27]

Sympathizers among Rommel's entourage encouraged his interaction with the Resistance. General Alexander Freiherr von Falkenhausen, the Military Governor of occupied Belgium and Northern France, for example, apparently urged Rommel to commit, but he would be removed from office a week before the bomb plot.[28] In May Artillery General Eduard Wagner, the German Army's Deputy Chief of Staff and Quartermaster General, arrived in France to coordinate coup preparations and met once with Rommel.[29] While Rommel's headquarters at La Roche Guyon certainly became a hub of conspiratorial discussion with the plot ringleaders in Berlin, it remains unclear to what extent Rommel was aware of these conversations.[30] Rommel certainly met with other leaders who had rebuffed earlier attempts to induce them to support the conspiracy, including Dr Julius Dorpmüller, the Minister of Transport, and Karl Kaufmann, the Nazi Party District Leader of Hamburg, but reliable details of their conversations are virtually non-existent.[31]

Indeed, the Berlin conspirators themselves were unaware of Rommel's supposed support. For when they contacted Allen Dulles, the OSS resident in Berne, Switzerland, on 16 May, they informed the

Allies that Rommel could not be counted on to cooperate with the conspiracy.[32] Here is some of the strongest proof that Rommel never committed to the conspiracy; despite the propaganda campaign to rally support for the coup by claiming Rommel had joined them, their official international communications indicated otherwise.

On 27 May, Speidel met with Dr Strölin and former foreign minister Freiherr von Neurath in Germany, ostensibly on Rommel's behalf. Both apparently tried to induce Rommel to commit. Moreover, they urged opening secret surrender negotiations in the West via a neutral country. At this juncture Strölin first divulged to Speidel that Goerdeler and General Beck were leading the conspiracy. Rommel, according to Speidel, assented to further preparations and discussions and Speidel informed General Günther von Blumentritt, the Chief of Staff to the Commander-in-Chief West, Field Marshal Gerd von Rundstedt, as well.[33] Yet, Blumentritt remained even less cognisant of the evolving conspiracy than Rommel.[34] Speidel claimed that he, Rommel and von Stülpnagel discussed armistice negotiations in the west based upon withdrawal to the German frontier following Hitler's arrest. Unconditional surrender was apparently never discussed, nor was cessation of hostilities in the East, since all three were strongly anti-Communist. This plan allegedly envisaged the arrest of Hitler, the formation of a new government, and the trial of Hitler.[35] No credible evidence exists, however, that Rommel ever committed even to the arrest of Hitler.[36]

This conclusion is reinforced by Rommel's actions during Hitler's visit to Margival, France, on 17 June. Rommel undertook no direct action whatsoever: instead he made impassioned, but utterly ineffectual, personal pleas to Hitler warning him about the inevitability of collapse in the West. But Hitler rebuffed Rommel and instructed him to focus on defensive operations. Hitler subsequently cancelled a follow-up conference scheduled for 19 June. Rommel apparently neither protested the cancellation nor made any further efforts to persuade Hitler to return to the West. All of this suggests he had no plans to try and arrest Hitler. Such a scheme was a Utopian flight of fantasy, as Rommel well knew. Hitler, on his rare excursions to field headquarters, was heavily guarded by his elite SS Escort Commando, the Army's Führer Escort Battalion as well as undercover operatives of the State Security Service (*Reichssicherheitsdienst*), who always travelled on ahead in disguise to reconnoitre Hitler's travel routes and undertake counterespionage.[37] Convoys of vehicles and several planes stood on immediate call in close proximity to whisk the Führer away at the first sign of danger, which is what happened when an errant V1 rocket landed near Margival early on 18 June and spooked the Führer into fleeing to Rastenburg in East Prussia. The reality was that the security surrounding Hitler was extremely tight – as the 'real' conspirators knew all too well, as they had been endeavouring for many months to penetrate Hitler's security cordon. Even if Rommel could have persuaded a group of his most loyal staff officers into mutiny, however implausible that seems, there was no possible way Rommel could have successfully arrested the Führer. As a highly seasoned combat veteran, Rommel must have recognised the near impossibility of such a task, which explains why he made absolutely no moves in that direction, either at Margival or when he met Hitler again at Berchtesgaden on 28 June.

On 25 June the new Deputy Chief of Staff of Army Group B, Colonel Eberhard Finkh, reported to Rommel and informed him that von Stauffenberg was planning to assassinate Hitler.[38] This was Rommel's first knowledge of the intent to kill Hitler and he violently opposed it: such action would martyr Hitler; the German people would never recognise his crimes; and finally, it violated his personal oath of loyalty to Hitler as his sovereign head of state and commander-in-chief of the German armed forces. Rommel thus firmly rebuffed the bomb plotters' latest overture to him.

Clearly, then, Rommel remained unwilling to act independently against Hitler. On 9 July he received another overture from the bomb plotters: a visit from the son of his old Great War divisional commander, Caesar von Hofacker. As a general staff officer on special assignment to General von Stülpnagel's staff, he had a legitimate reason for asking Rommel for an update on the conduct of the war in the West without raising suspicion, so he was the perfect intermediary.[39] Historians differ both on how much von Hofacker confided to Rommel, and also about Rommel's willingness to commit to the conspiracy. Speidel alleged that von Hofacker fully informed Rommel of the conspiracy and that Rommel committed.[40]

According to Friedrich von Tauchert, a civilian armed forces auxiliary on Rommel's staff, Rommel instructed that a letter be drawn up addressed to Field Marshal Bernard Law Montgomery, the commander of the Anglo-Canadian Twenty-First Army Group, offering a separate surrender in the west. However, no such letter has ever been found and it was never sent.[41]

Moreover, this assertion seems very implausible. First, Rommel was only the commander of Army Group B, controlling German forces in northern France, not the commander-in-chief of German forces in the West, which was the newly appointed Günther von Kluge.[42] Rommel and von Kluge did not get along well and von Kluge had only just arrived, a week earlier, from the Eastern Front. In these circumstances it seems improbable that Rommel would have drafted a surrender letter to Montgomery without knowing he had the full support of his new superior, which given their past friction and von Kluge's recent arrival, seems highly unlikely. Moreover, Rommel and von Kluge had immediately clashed over appropriate strategy, deployments, and tactics in France.[43] Therefore, it is highly likely that von Tauchert retrospectively exaggerated whatever Rommel communicated to him. Moreover, as a civilian it is possible that he misunderstood Rommel's statements. As no extant record of this alleged conversation survives, its meaning and import remains problematic. All interpretations have been filtered through von Hofacker and other conspirators, thereby distorting their assessment.[44] Moreover, given Rommel's well-established moral aversion to murder, one must conclude that both von Hofacker at the time, and Speidel subsequently, greatly exaggerated their success in persuading Rommel to join the conspiracy.

It is known that von Hofacker optimistically reported back in Berlin that Rommel had become a supporter of the conspiracy. However, he likely exaggerated Rommel's commitment to keep Resistance momentum building and also possibly to demonstrate his value and utility to his co-conspirators. But it remains unclear whether von Hofacker actually mentioned to Rommel the planned assassination attempt at all. Given the conspirators' previous lack of success with the 'Desert Fox', that they knew that the *Gestapo* was on their tail, and that Rommel was a leader of enormous potential influence, von Hofacker would surely have been cautious in his first sounding, as had been the consistent pattern of conspirator approaches over the previous two years. He summarised his conversation with Rommel to his friend

Freiherr von Falkenhausen that same evening, but Falkenhausen, tellingly, did not write down his recollection of the conversation for over a year, during which time the plot had failed, Rommel had been forced to take poison, Germany had been utterly defeated, and Hitler had committed suicide. Undoubtedly the dramatic and catastrophic events of 1944–45 influenced his subsequent recollections of the conversation. However, even Falkenhausen recalled that von Hofacker claimed that while allegedly interested, Rommel was not prepared to be a party to assassination, but that if Hitler stepped down (utterly improbable as that was), Rommel would be willing to step forward to help lead Germany. If true, this was no greater an opportunistic floating of a possibility than, for example, Heinz Guderian himself made.[45] Thus the reality was a far cry from von Hofacker's triumphant boast that Rommel had committed to support the assassination attempt.

After von Hofacker's visit, the next morning Rommel talked with one of his aides, an old friend from North Africa, Colonel Hans Lattmann. Rommel again allegedly claimed that he was willing to enter into unilateral negotiations with the Western Allies against Hitler's wishes if they would be willing to enter into a military pact against the Soviet Union. This discussion reveals that Rommel remained deeply committed to the National Socialist ideological struggle against Soviet communism. Since Rommel knew that the Allies had demanded unconditional surrender, it would seem improbable that he could seriously entertain successfully concluding a treaty of alliance with the Western Allies for a war of aggression against the Soviet Union under Hitler's nose and get away with it! Such an alleged plan was so quixotic it stood no chance of success and was devoid of the pragmatism Rommel was known for. Consequently it seems highly implausible that this reflected a genuine plan of action that Rommel seriously discussed. At best it was a flight of fantasy born out of his growing frustration.[46]

If we look at the conspirators in general, almost all of them went through a significant period of incremental disillusionment with Hitler and National Socialism that preceded personal commitments to the assassination of Hitler. It is absolutely unrealistic to believe that in the few weeks that he had been courted by the conspirators Rommel could have made such rapid evolution in his opinion. On 15 July Speidel claimed that Rommel drafted a letter to Hitler allegedly giving Hitler a 'last chance' to avoid disaster and, if not, Rommel was prepared to act unilaterally. However the message was never sent because Rommel was severely wounded two days later and Speidel apparently removed the original 'ultimatum' (as it became inaccurately known) from the Army Group B war diary as the *Gestapo* inquisition began.[47] That same day, Rommel allegedly told another old comrade from North Africa, Lieutenant-Colonel Elmar Warning, that both he and von Kluge would present Hitler with this 'ultimatum' regarding their lack of freedom to command the battle in France and that if Hitler refused their ultimatum, he would 'open the doors of the Western Front' so that the western Allies could reach Berlin before the Soviets.[48] These alleged statements were those of an increasingly embittered and disillusioned commander, but they do not prove that Rommel had committed to independent action.

In fact, there is no credible evidence indicating that Rommel took any affirmative action toward removing Hitler. That Rommel publicly spoke to multiple aides about possible 'independent action' is the strongest evidence that he was aware of only the broadest contours of the conspiracy. For, had he been more aware of the impending assassination plot, one can reasonably infer that he would have been more circumspect in his public utterings. It has also been posited that Rommel talked to those around him to assess their loyalty if he took independent action.[49] But again this is merely supposition based upon conjecture. The weight of the available evidence indicates that Rommel was not yet willing to take independent action against Hitler. Second, even if he had endeavoured to do so, it is highly implausible that he could have successfully implemented such a plan: Hitler and the Nazi regime would not have allowed him to do so. Inevitably the regime would have initiated decisively swift countermeasures at the first inkling of Rommel's 'independent action', as the ruthless reaction to the assassination attempt clearly demonstrates. Certainly there is little to suggest that Rommel did or could have trusted his superior, von Kluge, to join such independent action. It was not something that by character, personality, and reputation von Kluge was predisposed towards. Von Kluge, according to von Falkenhausen, told him on 26 July that he was in full agreement with the 'ultimatum's' contents.[50] But von Kluge had not committed to the conspiracy either and when he, too, fell under suspicion and was recalled on 19 August, the original 'ultimatum' disappeared.[51]

Moreover, the conspirators who heard about the 'ultimatum' misunderstood the politico-military context of Rommel's discussion regarding the report that he had written to Hitler. The so-called 'ultimatum' actually dealt exclusively with military matters and demanded more command freedom to make strategic decisions in the West. It predicted that an Allied breakthrough would occur soon and stated that '...the uneven struggle is nearing its end. In my opinion, it is necessary to draw conclusions from this situation'. However, Rommel never articulated precisely what he thought those conclusions were, so we will never know what he really thought.[52] Such a statement reflected his increasing frustration with Hitler's micromanagement of the German response to the invasion and his mounting pessimism regarding the German prospects of forestalling an Allied breakout from Normandy. But it did not reflect an act of insubordination, let alone treasonous conspiracy.

One has to remember that much was a stake for Rommel in mid-July 1944. If he failed to thwart the Allies, his military reputation and career would have been ruined. He had been plucked from North Africa 'sick' in February 1943, therefore preserving his reputation from the taint of the final and utter German defeat in Tunisia that May. There would have seemed to him little prospect that his reputation could have withstood failure in the West. Based on his *modus operandi*, Hitler would never conceivably have granted the discretion Rommel and von Kluge allegedly sought and, if they had pursued further actions of insubordination, Hitler would have relieved either or both of them of command peremptorily, as he had done dozens of times before to other German generals.[53] Moreover, neither Rommel nor von Kluge could have had much confidence that however strongly worded an 'ultimatum' would have had an impact on Hitler. Therefore it seems impossible to imagine Rommel's frustrated ruminations to close confidants reflected commitment either to oust Hitler or to support his assassination.

The notion that Rommel had joined the 20 July assassination plot was actually an erroneous inference by the *Gestapo* during the frantic witch-hunt for those responsible in the aftermath of its failure. In that fevered atmosphere of suspicion no stone was left unturned to identify and eradicate those responsible. Consequently many hundreds of individuals very superficially associated on the outer fringes of the conspiracy inevitably came under suspicion and were rounded up in the *Gestapo* dragnet. It is worth noting that torture is well known to be an erratic and unreliable means of eliciting the truth.[54] Some of those tortured gave their interrogators the names they appeared to want to hear; a few wildly named anyone who came to mind.[55] Von Stülpnagel and von Hofacker, as we have seen, first named Rommel. Additionally, Goerdeler left incriminating documents that identified Rommel as a potential supporter and an acceptable military leader to be placed in a position of responsibility should the coup succeed. Finally, Nazi party officials in France reported that Rommel extensively and scornfully criticized Nazi incompetence and crimes. That a German military commander of Rommel's legendary stature became identified as a possible conspirator should hardly surprise us: in fact, it would be much more remarkable if his name had not surfaced at all during the inquisition that followed.

None of the *Gestapo* 'discovery' provides credible evidence of Rommel's involvement in the assassination plot, however. The secret police's failure to identify and foil the plot seriously embarrassed the *Gestapo* and consequently it reacted with haste and fervent overzealousness to identify anyone and everyone responsible, with little concern for their relative involvement – all were collectively and equally guilty. Therefore there was little subtlety to the *Gestapo* witch-hunt.[56] Yet, ironically, it was the flawed *Gestapo* inquisition more than anything else that created the post-war legend of Rommel as an active supporter of the 20 July assassination plot.[57]

Rommel, again ironically, also came under suspicion because of his connection with von Kluge. When it became clear that von Kluge was associated with the heart of the conspiracy – the general staff in the headquarters of Army Group Centre on the Eastern Front – von Kluge's and Rommel's 'joint action' against Hitler's interference in their command of the war in France took on more sinister connotations. With suspicions aroused (in a prevailing atmosphere of paranoia), the *Gestapo* dismissed the long-standing friction between Rommel and von Kluge. When von Kluge, recognising that he had fallen under suspicion, committed suicide on 20 August, his death reinforced the exaggerated perception of his centrality in the conspiracy and raised more suspicion about his acquaintances. Indeed, his very suicide suggested both his own guilt and that he had killed himself to protect others who were similarly implicated. Von Kluge's suicide, therefore, inadvertently put another nail in Rommel's coffin. It was a bitter and twisted irony, given they disliked each other.

Nor is it reasonable to assume that had Rommel not been wounded on 17 July that he would have responded decisively to push for a unilateral capitulation in the West on his own initiative on 20 July. First, having no direct knowledge of the assassination attempt's timing, it would have come as a tremendous shock to him, particularly given his vehement opposition to the assassination of Hitler. Second, it is logical to infer that prudence would have dictated that Rommel confer with von Kluge before taking any action. Since von Kluge took no direct action himself on 20 July, Rommel, like most other senior German commanders that day, would have almost certainly temporised while the situation clarified itself, dooming any possibility that he might have initiated independent action in the West.

Since Rommel had rebuffed the conspirators he could hardly be expected to have acted decisively when both his superior and his chief staff officer, who were both more complicit, were not prepared to act! Moreover, as a highly experienced combat commander, Rommel must have been seriously concerned about the consequences for the German military. For a putsch would surely have unravelled the German forces in the West, pitting German Army forces in fratricidal strife with elite, fanatical SS troops. Moreover, Rommel acutely understood the limits of his authority – he only commanded German ground combat forces in the invasion theatre in northwest France, not even all of France, let alone the Luftwaffe, naval, Waffen SS, police, and other paramilitary formations, nor even the army garrison forces of the German military governors. The notion that troops outside his control would have automatically adhered to his unilateral actions are impossible to credit: Rommel was not naïve and must have known his ability to pull off a unilateral capitulation in the West and an ordered withdrawal to the West Wall was next to nil. As a pragmatist, it is impossible to believe that Rommel genuinely harboured such expectations. Consequently, both

## 154   Rommel: A Reappraisal

the extant evidence and logic dictate that we have to interpret Speidel's claims as greatly distorted.

This exploration supports the contention that Rommel was one of a large number of German officers on the margins of the 20 July conspiracy (and the outer margins at that), who possessed some very limited, superficial knowledge of the plot but certainly not concrete detail, let alone anything remotely approaching a solid commitment to support it. Rommel sympathised with the basic goals of the anti-Hitler Resistance: that Hitler was leading Germany toward catastrophe. But despite the efforts of his surviving friends post-war, he showed in 1944 no disposition toward extra-legal or extra-judicial action. Field Marshal Erwin Rommel, therefore, cannot be counted among the active participants of the 20 July 1944 assassination plot.

### Notes

1. Patrick Major, '"Our Friend Rommel": The *Wehrmacht* as 'Worthy Enemy' in Postwar British Popular Culture', *German History* 26, 4 (2008), pp. 520-35.
2. Hoffmann calls Rommel naïve due to his unwillingness to support Hitler's assassination. Peter Hoffmann, *The Resistance to Hitler* (Cambridge, MA: MIT Press, 1979), pp. 351-54.
3. Major, 'Our Friend Rommel', p. 520.
4. Field Marshal von Witzleben was a leading conspirator but he had been on the inactive list (*ausser dienst*) since 1942. Robert Wistrich, 'Witzleben, Erwin von (1881–1944) General Field Marshal of the Wehrmacht' in Robert Wistrich (ed.), *Who's Who in Nazi Germany* (New York: Routledge, 2001), pp. 279–80.
5. Hoffmann, *Resistance*, p. 352.
6. Hans Speidel, *Invasion 1944: We Defended Normandy* (Chicago: H. Regnery, 1950), pp. 68, 73.
7. Hoffmann, *Resistance*, p. 280.
8. Ibid, p. 352.
9. Russell Hart, 'Hans Speidel', in David Zabecki (ed.), *Chief of Staff: The Principal Officers Behind History's Great Commanders* (Annapolis, MD: Naval Institute Press, 2008), Vol. II. (WWII to Korea & Vietnam), pp. 52-62.
10. Speidel's original German language memoir titled *Invasion 1944. Ein Beitrag zu Rommels und des Reiches Schicksal* (Tübingen: Wunderlich, 1949) was translated and published in English the next year. A full memoir, *Aus unserer Zeit: Erinnerungen* (Frankfurt: Propyläen, 1977) appeared decades later.
11. Ralph Blank et. al., *Germany and the Second World War: German Society 1939-1945* (New York: Oxford University Press, 2008), fn. 145, pp. 897-98. For a

biographical sketch of Speidel see: Elmar Krautkrämer, 'Generalleutnant Dr. phil. Hans Speidel', in Gerd Überschar (ed.), *Hitlers militärische Elite. 68 Lebensläufe. 2. durchgesehene und bibliographisch aktualisierte Auflage* (Darmstedt, WBG, 2011), pp. 516–26. The best discussion of his military career is Klaus-Jürgen Müller, 'Witzleben, Stuelpnagel and Speidel', in Corelli Barnett (ed.), *Hitler's Generals* (New York: Grove Weidenfeld, 1989), pp. 43-74.

12. Speidel, *Invasion* (1950), pp. 133-85; idem, *Aus unserer Zeit*, pp. 168-69.
13. Hart, 'Speidel', pp. 55-57.
14. Geoffrey Megargee, *War of Annihilation: Combat and Genocide on the Eastern Front, 1941* (Lanham, MD: Rowman & Littlefield, 2006), passim.
15. Hart, 'Speidel', pp. 55-56.
16. Ibid.
17. Speidel, *Invasion* (1949), part IV, chap. 2.
18. Walter Dunn, *Heroes or Traitors: The German Replacement Army, the July Plot, and Adolf Hitler* (New York: Praeger, 2003).
19. Russell Hart, *Clash of Arms: How the Allies Won In Normandy, June-August 1944* (Boulder, CO: Lynne Rienner Publishing, 2001), chap. 10.
20. Hart, 'Speidel', pp. 48-50.
21. Speidel's escape was quite remarkable. One of those most opposed to his dismissal from the army by the honour court was Field Marshal Gerd von Rundstedt. It is possible that von Rundstedt feared that if Speidel was interrogated, the inquisition might encompass him and his Commander-in-Chief West headquarters personnel as well.
22. Nonetheless Speidel remained in custody – clearly the Gestapo considered him suspect – until liberated by French troops on 29 April 1945.
23. Blank, *Germany and Second World War*, p. 898.
24. David Irving, *Trail of the Fox* (London: Focal Point Publisher, 1977 edn.), p. 401; Speidel, *Invasion* (1950), p. 84.
25. Hoffmann, *Resistance*, p. 351.
26. Speidel, *Aus unsere Zeit*, p. 169.
27. Blank, *Germany and Second World War*, p. 348; Speidel, *Invasion* (1950), pp. 84-85; Gerhard Ritter, *The German Resistance: Carl Goerdeler's Struggle Against Tyranny* (New York: Frederick Praeger, 1958), p. 400.
28. Hoffmann, *Resistance*, p. 352.
29. Speidel, *Invasion* (1950), pp. 84-85.
30. Hoffmann, *Resistance*, p. 352.
31. Ibid.
32. Ibid, p. 238.
33. Ibid, p. 352.
34. Ibid, pp. 470-74.
35. Speidel, *Invasion* (1950), pp. 82-91.
36. Speidel tellingly says nothing about this. See ibid., pp. 105-06.
37. Peter Hoffmann, *Hitler's Personal Security* (New York: Da Capo Press, 2000).

38. Hoffmann, *Resistance*, p. 354.
39. Blank, *Germany and Second World War*, p. 899.
40. Speidel, *Invasion 1944* (1949), pp. 122-24; Christian Mueller, *Oberst IG von Stauffenberg: Ein Biographie* (Düsseldorf: Droste, 1970), pp. 433-34.
41. Blank, *Germany and Second World War*, p. 900.
42. Von Kluge replaced von Rundstedt as Commander-in-Chief West on 2 July 1944.
43. Irving, *Trail of the Fox*, pp. 419-20.
44. Blank, *Germany and Second World War*, p. 900
45. Russell Hart, *Guderian: Panzer Pioneer or Mythmaker?* (Washington, DC: Potomac Books, Inc., 2006), pp. 98-102.
46. Blank, *Germany and Second World War*, pp. 900-01.
47. Speidel, *Invasion* (1949), pp. 138-39; Speidel, *Aus unserer Zeit*, pp. 168-89; B.H. Liddell Hart (ed.), *The Rommel Papers*, pp. 486-87. However, a teletype copy of it did survive and it has been published in Peter Hoffmann (ed.), *Behind Valkyrie: German Resistance to Hitler [Documents]* (Montreal: McGill University Press, 2011), pp. 343-45.
48. Blank, *Germany and Second World War*, p. 901
49. Ibid.
50. Hoffmann, *Resistance*, p. 354.
51. Ibid, pp. 354-55. Rommel implied that Speidel had destroyed the original in the Army Group B war diary just prior to his arrest. See Hoffmann, *Behind Valkyrie*, p. 345.
52. Hoffmann, *Behind Valkyrie*, p. 345.
53. See, for example, Richard Lamb, 'Von Kluge', in Barnett (ed.), *Hitler's Generals*, pp. 395-410; Hart, *Guderian*, pp. 77-81; Richard Giziowski, *The Enigma of General Blaskowitz* (New York: Hippocrene, 1996).
54. Jennifer Harbury, *Truth, Torture, and the American Way: the History and Consequences of US Involvement in Torture* (Boston, MA: Beacon Press, 2005).
55. Hoffmann, *Resistance*, pp. 509-23.
56. Ibid, chap. 46.
57. Ibid.

CHAPTER SEVEN

# Rommel as Icon

*Mark Connelly*

Rommel's exploits in the Second World War made him famous not only in Nazi Germany, but also in Britain and the USA as well. The fame he won through his daring leadership, particularly in the North African campaign, was not dented by his defeats, his death, nor the conclusion of the war. Far from fading into historical obscurity like many other generals of the conflict, Rommel's reputation grew after 1945 as numerous books, newspaper articles and films were produced examining his life and achievements. Like many who achieve enduring fame, the difference between reality and image quickly blurred as Rommel was used for the promotion of different ideas and messages. This process started during the conflict and was accelerated after the war as different agencies adopted Rommel for their own ends. The myth-making has had a profound impact on public perceptions not only of Rommel himself, but also of the men he led and the nation he served as a soldier.

Rommel made his first steps towards public fame in the 1940 campaign against France and the Low Countries. The Nazi propaganda minister, Joseph Goebbels, quickly appreciated the publicity value of Rommel's exploits and decided to use him as a symbol of Nazi Germany at war. Goebbels saw in Rommel a commander who reflected National Socialist values – dedicated to duty, mentally and physically agile, modern and therefore able to outwit and out-think the lumbering generals of the decadent British and French democracies. These themes were stressed in the propaganda masterpiece, *Victory in the West*, a film based on the excellent newsreel footage collected by Goebbels's cameramen during the course of the campaign. It was given a gala premiere in February 1941 at the Berlin Ufa Palace and gave the German public the opportunity to see Rommel, who had already been played up in the press as a key component in the Nazi victory.[1]

Of course, Rommel's reputation in Germany was enhanced massively in the North African campaign, in which his actual achievements were given even greater impact by a carefully constructed propaganda programme. Goebbels ensured that Rommel was accompanied by two Ministry of Propaganda officials, Karl Hancke and Alfred Ingemar Berndt, whose tasks were to ensure good photographs and well-polished copy. The campaign proved highly effective, as Rommel found himself the recipient of huge amounts of fan mail, with a large number coming from women who seem to have equated him with the matinee idols of Nazi cinema.[2] Fortunately for his public image in Germany, Rommel's absence from North Africa during the final phase of the campaign meant that his reputation was spared tarnish through defeat, and he retained a high profile until his death. Even Rommel's involvement in the July Plot was not allowed to undermine his reputation. It was kept secret from the German people and Goebbels maintained the image of Rommel as a loyal Nazi by giving him a hero's funeral. No hint of the rift between Rommel, Hitler and the party was allowed to enter the public domain.[3]

Perhaps more surprising is the fact that Rommel came to play such an important role in the British and American media during the war. With the British introspective in the wake of defeat in France, it took until 1941 and the reverses in the Western Desert for the British public to become aware of Rommel. From that moment he quickly achieved a very high profile, with the press repeatedly pointing out that Rommel had great, quasi-mystical strengths: he could parry British assaults with ease, seemed capable of reading British intentions in advance and was always able to surprise the British when he went on the offensive, leaving them flatfooted. It was a feeling encapsulated by the influential journalist William Connor, who wrote under the pseudonym Cassandra. His column appeared in the centre-left populist and essential other rank newspaper, the *Daily Mirror*, which gained fame for its acerbic comments on the British war effort. In a January 1942 article he noted that in the recent fighting 'Rommel was quicker off the mark and once more his Afrika Korps have caught us on the hop'.[4] It was a sentiment reflected in an editorial a few weeks later when readers were told that the

British had once again been caught in reactive mode and never seemed capable of dictating the pace to Rommel. The piece concluded that the mood of the British government and army was 'Beware of Rommel's new offensive towards Egypt'.[5]

The effect of such journalism was to set up a dichotomy between the dynamic Rommel and the leaden British responses. But it was not the British army as a whole that was singled out; rather, the criticisms were heaped on the army's leaders in a campaign which linked the left-wing and establishment press. In February 1942 *The Times* carried a leading article which in content, if not style, was the equivalent of the *Daily Mirror*'s scathing stance. In a piece rolling together all of the recent disasters including the 'Channel Dash' of the *Gneisenau*, *Prinz Eugen* and *Scharnhorst* and the collapse in Malaya, it stated that in the early days of the war unpreparedness was a legitimate excuse for defeat, but now it was inadequate: 'this plea [can] no longer suffice for the miscalculation of Crete, for the failure to match Rommel's mastery of mechanised warfare in the Libyan desert, or the absence of local preparedness, the tragic naval blunder and the total confusion of our defences in Malaya'.[6] Rommel was at the heart of the comparison and his perceived skill, and by contrast its seeming absence in British commanders, was ruthlessly highlighted by the influential war correspondent Richard McMillan when Tobruk fell in June 1942. He summed up the national mood of recrimination and humiliation in a syndicated article which reached the front pages of most of the populist dailies. 'We allowed the enemy in Libya to make every move – it was wait and see again', McMillan stated, before going on to note that: 'Rommel has become a bogy in the desert and the biggest bogy of all to many of the high-ups themselves. More often than I cared for I heard the words, "I wonder where Rommel's going to strike next".'[7] He absolved the ordinary British soldier from blame, stating that the British infantry was always resolute and brave, but was let down continually by poor kit and lack of direction from the higher command. Unsurprisingly, the *Daily Mirror* reinforced this message with an equally bitter editorial in which the government was mocked for predicting the collapse of Rommel. 'We were thenceforward encouraged to believe that adequate reinforcements and new weapons had been assembled and would assuredly do the trick. Rommel's doom, apparently, was sealed. How effectively that elusive

General has broken through we now know.' The reasons behind this disaster were now required: 'the nation demands an answer'.[8]

The ubiquity of Rommel in the British press was gradually making him a mythological figure on the British home and fighting fronts. His symbolic function was to personalise all of the traits required by an effective general in order to be compared and contrasted with his allegedly incompetent foes. Rommel therefore played a central role in the British wartime debate about the extent to which it was hobbled by its class system, symbolised so effectively by David Low's cartoon creation, Colonel Blimp. This process reached its height when two Labour parliamentarians, Aneurin Bevan and Lord Strabolgi, made the same accusation against the British army. Both men stated that had Rommel been in the British army, he would have been promoted to sergeant and no further as such unorthodoxy, such imagination and such genius would have been frowned upon by a hidebound, conservative institution. Somewhat ironically two Labour politicians therefore came to the same conclusion as Goebbels. Bevan made his claim in the Commons during the no confidence debate occasioned by the fall of Tobruk, while Strabolgi published an article in the mass-circulation American magazine, *Collier's Weekly* titled 'What's the matter with the British army?'.[9] The piece provoked a furious response in the Lords from the commando leader, Lord Lovat, who was particularly disgusted by the slurring of the British army in front of the Americans.[10]

The Americans were certainly aware that Rommel had become the British nemesis summed up in a *New York Times* headline of June 1942, 'Rommel lectures British on tactics'.[11] But this gave way to reflections on their own up-coming clash with him and his forces. In an interview with *Time* magazine Patton stated that he wanted to fight 'The Champ', with the heavy implication that Rommel was the man he had in mind.[12] The heaping of such accolades upon Rommel soon caused the US high command as many problems as it did the British. In April 1943 Eisenhower moved to quell the hyperbole surrounding Rommel by telling the *New York Times* that although he was a 'great general' he was 'not a superman'.[13] His comments do not appear to have had much of an effect on the *New York Times*, for in the run-up to the Normandy campaign it still referred to him as 'The man we have to beat'.[14]

Rommel's ubiquity, flexibility and dash earned him the admiration of

Winston Churchill, who told the Commons in January 1942 that in Rommel 'we have a very daring and skilful opponent against us, and may I say across the havoc of war, a great general'.[15] Cassandra was prepared to echo this sentiment, stating that 'Rommel is undoubtedly a brilliant soldier and the way he fights back compels our respect – if not our good wishes.'[16] But this graciousness did not extend far, for a few weeks later the *Daily Mirror*'s editorial rounded on such chivalrous statements, stating that the ascription of great skill to the enemy was a way of avoiding rigorous self-analysis: 'We shall even have to endure once more generous public-school-tie praise for the enemy's daring... For if all else fails, it is always possible to minimise our failures and blunders by exalting the enemy's daring and foresight'.[17] Such responses show that the British press was capable of looking further than Rommel, for although he was the immediate explanation for British defeat, he was not its ultimate cause. This allowed the British press to pursue interlinked concepts about Rommel. Acknowledging him as a military genius and bemoaning the lack of similar men in the British army was not the same thing as bestowing omnipotence upon him. Instead, the British press praised Rommel for his quality while condemning the British army for its inability to find an answer.

Fortunately, the British discovered their own military media miracle in Montgomery. Montgomery was presented as the man who decisively checked and defeated Rommel. This version was given a great deal of emphasis in the key British propaganda interpretation of the desert campaign, *Desert Victory* (1943), a film which culminated in the Second Battle of El Alamein and the drive to the Tunisian frontier. A brilliantly constructed documentary (it won an Oscar for best factual film), which entranced ecstatic British audiences, *Desert Victory* placed a good deal of emphasis on Rommel. By stressing the final stages of the campaign the film celebrated the destruction of 'the myth of Rommel's invincibility'. *Desert Victory* did not deny his skill, but implied that the autocratic, centralised decision-making of Rommel was very different to the teamwork and mutual trust displayed in British forces. Rommel was also condemned for being indifferent to the fate of his men, especially his Italian allies, and was thus seen to be as egotistical and arrogant as Hitler.

The myth of Rommel's invincibility may have been shattered by El Alamein, but it did not mean his disappearance from the British public stage. Instead, the press gleefully grasped the opportunity of presenting the rest of the war as a grand pitting of wits between Montgomery and Rommel. The run-up to the Normandy campaign unfolded according to this narrative framework and reached its culmination in July 1944 when the *Daily Mirror* proudly announced on its front page that 'Monty has outfought Rommel'.[18] Thus, by 1944 the tables had turned. The master of warfare had been humbled and his weaknesses exposed by the brilliance of Montgomery and the dogged skill of the British army.

Rommel's death was given cursory coverage by the British and American press, more intent on following the unfolding campaign in France than an ancillary detail, but he left the Anglo-American consciousness only briefly. The end of the war in Europe and the emergence of two Germanys caused major concerns for the Americans and British. On the one hand there was the need to ensure that German military power was decisively destroyed, but on the other there was the desire to maximise western military strength against a rapidly forming communist bloc. The East-West German border became the focus point of European affairs from 1945 and there was a desperate need for West Germans to accept the Anglo-American presence as friendly and beneficial rather than one intent on extracting revenge or tribute. This required a delicate balancing act between forcing West Germans to admit their role in Nazism, and to accept political re-education as a safeguard against its repetition, while ensuring that no one in the new state felt dangerously alienated through too heavy-handed a demonisation campaign.[19] West Germans had to be given a sense of national pride and they had to be given heroes. Rommel seemed the natural answer. Here was a bold, brave and brilliant German who had been lauded by his enemies, as well as his own compatriots.

It was the British who led the Anglophone rehabilitation of Rommel in two crucial texts, Desmond Young's best-selling biography in 1950 and Basil Liddell Hart's edition of *The Rommel Papers* (1953). Brigadier Desmond Young had served on the British staff during the desert campaign and so had direct experience of Rommel's impact. In the post-war years he rekindled his interest in writing and was a professional journalist and author by the late forties. By using friends and connections, he was introduced to Rommel's widow and son, Manfred, as well as many of Rommel's surviving intimates, for whom he sketched plans for a biography. Finding them and Collins, his publisher, very enthusiastic he set about the task of researching and writing. Collins' publicity department was convinced it had a winner on its hands and wanted an initial print run of 50,000, believing total sales of 200,000 were possible. In the event, 86,000 copies were pre-ordered and it quickly proved a publishing phenomenon. It outstripped 200,000 UK sales, going through eight editions in 1950 alone, and was also a huge success in the Dominions and the USA. The *Sunday Express* bought the British newspaper serialisation rights, which resulted in the addition of 92,223 new readers to its existing circulation.[20] The *Daily Mail* made it book of the month in January 1950 and praised Rommel as a 'brave, resolute, intelligent and honest' man.[21]

The incredible success of Young's book is hard to explain, but it clearly revealed that Rommel's wartime image, which had so intrigued and interested the wartime English-speaking world, could easily be reignited, especially when told by a skilful story-teller who added to the human interest of the tale by playing up the role of Rommel's family. Three years later Liddell Hart boosted the Rommel renaissance with his collection, which built upon an original German publication revealingly titled *Krieg ohne Hass* (*War Without Hate*), put together by his widow with the assistance of his former comrade, Fritz Bayerlein. These publications set the agenda for all post-war interpretations of Rommel, ensuring that they would be built around the following three themes: Rommel's lukewarm commitment to Nazism, his genius as a military leader, and the lack of animosity shown by all combatants in the North African campaign. All three were crucial to the rehabilitation of West Germans. Rommel was to become the expression of the real Germany, hidden, hijacked and perverted by the Nazis.

In setting the ground for all future biographers, Young stressed that Rommel paid lip-service to Nazism like most Germans in the 1930s and that he was never an intimate of Hitler. Instead, Rommel went along with Hitler solely because he thought it was good for Germany and the army, but he certainly had no real devotion to his wider vision. Rommel's involvement in the July Plot was then presented as the culmination of his long-standing doubts about Nazism.[22] Sir John Squire picked up on this aspect in his review for the *Illustrated London News*. He asked how an intelligent man like Rommel could have got involved in Nazism in any way, but then absolved him from blame by implying that he was politically naïve. Somewhat ironically, given this statement, he then averred that had he lived Rommel would have made an ideal president for the new West Germany. Squire's review therefore buttressed the idea of the good German and told British readers that Germans could be trusted as they were essentially decent, normal people.[23] This interpretation has been followed by the overwhelming majority of English language biographies and commentaries on Rommel. When John Terraine reviewed Ronald Lewin's *Rommel as Military Commander* (1968) he noted that Rommel ensured that the Afrika Korps was a formidable military instrument, but that its 'tang was untainted' by fervent Nazism.[24] Unsurprisingly, David Irving took much the same line in his 1977 work, *The Trail of the Fox: the Life of Field-Marshal Erwin Rommel*. 'Rommel was virtually non-political', stated Irving, offering that as an excuse for involvement with Nazism. He 'tolerated' the party 'to put it no higher'.[25] At the other end of the political spectrum Bernard Levin praised Rommel's lack of commitment to Nazism in an article for *The Times* and called him one of 'the wartime Germans we should salute'.[26] One of the most extreme statements of Rommel's political virtue was provided by David Fraser in *Knight's Cross: a Life of Field Marshal Erwin Rommel* (1993). Fraser goes to great lengths to argue that Rommel only made the odd anti-Semitic comment and can in no way be regarded as a great supporter of Nazi campaigns against European Jewry. This interpretation is then emphasised by a chapter titled 'Soldier without Politics'.[27] By contrast, German-language biographies such as that by Wolf Heckmann, *Rommels Krieg in Afrika* (1976) have been far less sympathetic on this point and imply a much more ambiguous relationship between Rommel, Hitler and the Nazi party.

Intimately connected with Rommel's alleged distasted for Nazism is the stress many biographers place on his equal disgust for cheap propaganda. Rommel is therefore portrayed as a man uninterested in any concept of personal fame and public honour. Young stated that Rommel was contemptuous of the media entourage Goebbels attached to his headquarters and the only interest he had in their work was to ensure its accuracy.[28] Irving made a similar argument, claiming that Rommel's sole interest in propaganda was the psychological impression it made on his enemies and not for any sense of personal aggrandisement.[29] However, this seems slightly disingenuous, as one of Rommel's close associates, Heinz W. Schmidt, stated in his highly successful *With Rommel in the Desert*, published in 1951 and clearly inspired by the success of the German version of *The Rommel Papers* and Young's biography, that Rommel was happy to be photographed and was very good at striking dramatic poses.[30]

The second major theme of the popular biographies is the undoubted military genius of Rommel. Young set the benchmark in 1950. According to Young, Rommel was a military 'phenomenon, a nonpareil' who had, in battle, 'a sixth sense'.[31] Basil Liddell Hart argued that Rommel was a very rare commander imbued with a genius for both strategy and tactics.[32] Although a little more circumspect in terms of the range of Rommel's skills, General Sir John Hackett was also prepared to be fulsome in his praise, stating that 'there was no better commander of armoured troops in a fluid battle'.[33] David Fraser took this further, arguing that no general had a better intuitive understanding of a battle, which gave Rommel the confidence to take risks at precisely the right moment.[34] Closely associated with Rommel's brilliant grasp of battle is the argument that he was an equally inspired leader of men. Once again Young set the standard and few have deviated from it. 'He was a natural leader, and he relied, both instinctively and deliberately upon his personal leadership'.[35] The appeal of this image is so potent that authors writing since have found it almost impossible to stray from this concept. Hackett noted of Rommel: 'His method of command was forceful, direct and personal. If he wanted something done, he was there to get it done... no one was more willingly followed by troops. They understood him as thoroughly as he understood them. He led, as all good leaders do, from the inside.'[36]

Historians who have tried to contextualise Rommel's military skills by stressing the weaknesses inherent in his overly personalised form of command, which led to inefficient staff work, his eccentric understanding of logistics and the fact that his successes provided British and American generals and politicians with convenient excuses for defeat, have been overridden by his many supporters.[37] Most manage either to absolve him entirely of these defects, or imply that they were, in fact, strengths. Hackett's introduction to the English language version of

Heckmann's critical study creates a near schizophrenic preface to the text, for he appears to deny the validity of the claims made by Heckmann. Commenting on Heckmann's assertion that Rommel had a much closer relationship with Hitler than many have allowed, which was resented by other generals, Hackett explained it away by stating: 'It is worth recording that the detractors of that brilliant, wayward young British general, James Wolfe, gave their opinion to King George III that he, too, was mad'.[38] Fraser takes a similar path, claiming that Rommel was always aware of logistics and only ever outstripped them when his brilliant instincts told him a gamble was likely to be successful. Such explanations of Rommel's supposed defects led him to the conclusion that victory is not the best indicator of military genius:

> Of course Rommel, ultimately, was beaten. He lost. But, although what must matter in war is to win, that truism cannot provide the sole criterion for judgement of military talent. War may be considered as a business, open to audit, but its conduct is also an art. Ultimately Napoleon was beaten. So was Montrose. So was Lee. Few could deny their genius. With all his imperfections, as a leader of men in battle Erwin Rommel stands in their company.[39]

The final element in the list of Rommel's military strengths is the insistence on his gallantry and chivalry. Field Marshal Sir Claude Auchinleck paid tribute to this aspect of Rommel's character in his preface to Young's biography and expressed the hope that this was not a defunct concept. Remarking on Rommel's gracious attitude towards prisoners, he stated 'this used to be called chivalry: many will now call it nonsense and say that the days when such sentiments could survive a war are past. If they are, then I, for one, am sorry.'[40] Here Auchinleck used the image of Rommel to make an important subliminal point. This was that the war in the desert was an 'old fashioned', clean contest in which the two combatants faced each other free from hatred and in a spirit of professional, rather than ideological, rivalry. Such an implication could be used to buttress the idea that by no means all Germans were devout Nazis and they, too, understood codes of honour and decency. David Irving took up the issue of Rommel's chivalry to make an equally stark political point, but his implied the hypocrisy of Allied claims to moral superiority and thus Irving used Rommel to equate concentration camps with the strategic bombing of Germany: 'He was said to have revived a long-forgotten style of chivalrous warfare. In a war brutalized by Nazi extermination camps and the Allied strategic bomber, Rommel's soldiers were ordered to fight clean.'[41]

Promoting the concept of the special conditions of the desert war and Rommel's leading role in ensuring that honourable standards were maintained became a significant factor in ensuring a good reputation for West Germans and their active participation in the Cold War. Fought between small armies, the British and Commonwealth on one side and the Germans and Italians on the other, and far from any other campaign of war, the desert became a private contest of skill and mutual respect. The German General Johann Cramer told *The Times* that 'the war in North Africa was a gentleman's war'.[42] Another German veteran confirmed this in an anecdote told in Thames Television's highly influential 1972 documentary series, *The World at War*, which revealed the chivalry of the campaign: 'Sportsmanship showed on both sides. Football games were not interrupted by artillery fire during certain periods'. Laurence Olivier's narration asserted, 'The peculiar conditions of the desert bred a comradeship that was unique in the whole war. For many, the desert war was a private war, the last to retain any pretence of chivalry'.[43] When Airfix launched a new series of models at the National Army Museum in 1975, Afrika Korps veterans were invited and one told *The Times* 'both sides in that battle were elitist troops, so they treated each other with great respect, like gentlemen'. The story was run under the headline, 'Oh, what a gentlemanly war!'[44]

The accepted concept that the desert war was a campaign apart fought by two unique sets of soldiers meant that Afrika Korps veterans could hold reunions much more freely than those from other German units. Commencing in the 1950s these reunions were often attended by Australian, British and Italian veterans, which reinforced the idea of the new alliance of free states opposing the communist bloc. In 1953 around 10,000 veterans from all sides gathered in Lower Saxony. The celebrations included a football match between representatives of the DAK and Eighth Army and the veterans were addressed by Dr Lehr, Minister of the Interior, who told them that Rommel 'stood as the paragon of the true and, in the best sense, heroic and chivalrous German profession of arms'.[45] Three years later an even bigger event was staged which attracted some 20,000 veterans, including a significant British and Australian contingent. The gathering culminated in community singing in which the famous Afrika Korps anthem, *Lili Marlene*, was sung.[46] *Lili Marlene* was, of course, adopted by British and Commonwealth troops in North Africa and became a phenomenon on the home front, too, encapsulated in the Humphrey Jennings documentary film, *The True Story of Lili Marlene*, in 1944.[47]

The idea of mutual respect was then linked to the fact that, like its famous commander, the Afrika Korps was far from a hotbed of Nazism. Schmidt emphasised this in his book. Recalling his first dinner in the staff officers' mess he commented on a debate about the 1938 Crystal Night, and like a good West German was prepared to admit that though not entirely free of taint, he was by no means an anti-Semitic fanatic. 'Though no friend of the Jews, I said that the anti-Semitic policy was disgraceful. A middle-aged Reservist officer, a land-owner from Mecklenburg, seemed pleased at my forthright utterance and said: "I am glad to hear that from a young officer, but turn to your neighbour – he thinks differently."' Of course, the officer who thought differently is identified as a representative of Goebbels's propaganda ministry.[48]

Of great significance in creating the idea of the gentlemanly, 'pure' desert war was the landscape, which denuded combat of its disquieting twentieth-century elements. There were no towns or villages to provide refuges and obstacles for defenders, which would in turn demand that an attacker flatten them, and there were no centres of civilian populations which removed all fear of causing death and destruction to non-combatants. The vast and empty spaces gave battle and manoeuvre a seemingly textbook quality, which turned the campaign into a clash of professional wits devoid of ideology. Correlli Barnett wrote in his highly successful history of the campaign, *The Desert Generals* (1960), that 'The desert war of 1940–43 is unique in history... The desert campaign was... war in its purest form'.[49] 'This land was made for war,' as Laurence Olivier put it in *The World at War*; 'Here is no nubile, girlish land, no great, virginal countryside for war to violate', he concluded.[50] Such conditions allowed it to be remembered with fondness as a clean war, regardless of the actual nature of the fighting. But, significantly, this strips it of ideological and xenophobic overtones, a rare quality in British popular perceptions of the conflict.

The denuding of time and politically-specific concepts to Rommel and the desert war is part of the presentation of Rommel as a 'great captain', a military genius who transcends history. Unsurprisingly given his great belief in this concept, Liddell Hart was keen to emphasise Rommel's status as a true original, comparing him with Hannibal, Napoleon, Lee and Lawrence of Arabia.[51] Irving also made the parallel with Hannibal and the similarity between Cannae and Rommel's concept of battle.[52] This romanticising of Rommel has been pushed furthest by David Fraser, in a piece of dramatic, swirling prose which encapsulates the post-1945 hagiographic approach:

> Erwin Rommel's name stands as one of the great masters of manoeuvre in war, one of that select company whose personalities transcend time and whose energy still communicates. The victories of these men once depended on their ability to signal their intention, impose their will, and act with alarming speed amidst the confused conditions and across variable distances of the battlefield. In a comparable way their personalities cut like sabres through the curtains of history, penetrating to successive generations with an immediacy which quickens the blood. Living legends, they project, each in his way, the classic image of the warrior: brave, vigorous, sharp of eye and mind, rapid in decision, alert in danger, faster and bolder in the fight than his enemies. Of this extraordinary brotherhood is Rommel – the brotherhood of Hector, of Rupert of the Rhine, of those who can only be described as heroes; and it is curious that so determinedly practical a modernist as Rommel – the least fanciful of men – should have joined a company so bonded by myth.[53]

Fraser's purple description has the cinematic quality Goebbels brought to Rommel in *Victory in the West*. Rommel's exploits lent themselves to the cinema screen, as was shown in *Victory in the West* and *Desert Victory*. In 1943 Hollywood produced its first interpretation in Billy Wilder's *Five Graves to Cairo*. The German émigré director and actor Erich von Stroheim was cast as Rommel in a thriller involving the identification of five secret supply dumps the Afrika Korps had prepared to ensure victory in the desert. Von Stroheim played Rommel as a flamboyant, ruthless and maniacal general utterly intent on securing a crushing victory. It is a menacing and highly theatrical portrayal, reminiscent of the mannered style of silent cinema, and is thus a long way from the post-war image of the gallant, chivalrous adversary.

Rommel returned to the big screen in 1951 in a film version of Young's biography. Impressed by the book's sales figures, Twentieth Century Fox quickly approached Young for the film rights, for which it was prepared to pay £15,000.[54] Despite the success of the book and the implication that the Anglophone public was prepared to accept a positive interpretation of Rommel, Twentieth Century Fox was sensitive enough to announce that it did not intend to produce a filmic hagiography. A spokesman for the company stated that 'we will try to present Rommel realistically without suggesting that he was either a hero or a villain'.[55] During production the film gained much publicity, partly due to the casting of the popular British actor James Mason in the lead role, and partly because of the close interest Rommel's widow and son were alleged to have in the film. As has been noted, Young had stressed his gratitude to Lucie and Manfred, and Liddell Hart had done much the same in the introduction to *The Rommel Papers*. Indeed, *The Times* review of *The Rommel Papers* had even suggested that the editorial team lacked objectivity, a hint the hypersensitive Liddell Hart denied in a waspish letter to the editor.[56] The impact of the Rommel family on biographers and commentators appears to have been considerable over the years and may well have influenced the interpretations. Hackett was clearly impressed by them and wrote that 'to meet Frau Rommel more than once and enjoyed the society of this good, simple, intelligent woman who absolutely declined to be a hero's widow' was something he 'rejoiced in', as was the opportunity to meet 'more than once the admirable public servant, her son Manfred'.[57] The *Illustrated London News* published a lavish range of stills in the run-up to the premiere as well as a photograph of Lucie and Manfred Rommel under the headline, 'People who made this film possible'. The stills were carefully captioned to draw a distinction between good and evil Germans with Rommel and the Afrika Korps clearly in the former camp: '[Rommel] gained the respect of Allied soldiers on account of his military genius and because he upheld the traditions of honourable warfare ignored by the SS troops.'[58]

The film, given the evocative title *Desert Fox*, was released in October 1951 and proved to be very popular at the box office.[59] James Mason played the general as an honourable man, deeply concerned by the actions of the Nazi party, who then endangers himself and his family for the greater good of Germany by taking part in the July Plot. By making Rommel's wife and son victims of Hitler, the film expertly played upon audience sympathies. Press comment was on the whole highly favourable, highlighting not only the quality of the production, but also its moral. The populist cinema magazine *Picturegoer* noted that Rommel was an officer who upheld his professional code to obey orders, but that 'doesn't make him a sinister Nazi'.[60] However, there were those who were aware that others might not be so impressed. C.A. Lejeune, the influential film critic of the *Observer*, stated that 'there will inevitably be voices raised in protest against the sympathetic, even heroic portrait of the German Field Marshal', while *The Times* reminded its readers than anyone unimpressed by such a positive interpretation should remember 'that the process [of praising Rommel] was in full swing while our troops were actually fighting him'.[61] Stronger resistance to the film came from the Jewish communities of Britain and America. In the Commons David Weitzman, Labour MP for the Jewish-dominated constituency of Stoke Newington, asked the Home Secretary why he was allowing exhibition of a film 'which glorifies a general who upheld the Nazi creed'. He reflected the feelings of many other East London Jews: the Association of Jewish Ex-Servicemen saw the film as a celebration of a 'ruthless enemy of Britain' and a system that had brought ruin and misery to East London through bombing, while the Stepney Peace Council condemned the film as 'the most bitter and humiliating insult which could be offered to the people of Stepney'.[62] The Communist newspaper, the *Daily Worker*, encouraged these opinions by urging ex-servicemen to protest against the film and linked it to the issue of West German rearmament.[63] Similar sentiments were expressed in the USA. The association of Jewish war veterans joined other Jewish groups in sending a letter of complaint in which they condemned the film as a 'glorification of Rommel and a virtual whitewash of Nazism'. Subsequently, a New York woman was jailed for demonstrating too violently outside a cinema. Twentieth Century Fox responded by stating that 'Rommel had never been implicated in the crimes of the Nazis, that his military conduct was above reproach [and] that he had broken with Hitler during the war'.[64] The centre-left, high-brow British film magazine *Sight and Sound* was unimpressed by the argument that Rommel's role in the July Plot proved his credentials, noting that he became involved in the conspiracy not because he opposed Nazism, but because he feared a German defeat, echoing a point originally made by Malcolm Muggeridge in his review of Young's biography.[65]

Further proof that Rommel and his immediate associates were not fully accepted by former enemies came in 1953 when it was announced that General Hans Speidel, formerly on Rommel's staff, was scheduled to visit Britain in order to inspect armaments as a member of the European Defence Community. Emmanuel Shinwell, a firebrand Jewish Labour MP, raised objections in the Commons, asking whether it was wise 'that this ex-Nazi should be permitted an inspection of modern British arms'. Churchill responded by stating that 'there are many people in Germany who were Nazis to support their country, but who did not associate themselves with the crimes of the Nazi regime… And here is a man who was the intimate friend and supporter of General Rommel, who gave his life in resisting one of the wickedest regimes that has ever brought misery on the human race'.[66] The *Daily Mirror* covered the story the next day under the headline, 'Let hatred die call by premier'.[67] Churchill's stance did not go unnoticed in West Germany and earned him a special vote of thanks from the Afrika Korps' veterans association.[68] For Churchill this was merely the latest stage in an ongoing rehabilitation of West Germany with Rommel and the Afrika Korps the vehicle. In 1951, when excitement about Young's biography and the imminent film version was at its greatest, volume four of his war history was published, which included the period when Rommel's desert campaign was at its peak. With one eye very firmly on the present he wrote:

> I could not resist paying my tribute to Rommel [in his 27 January 1942 address to the Commons]… My reference to Rommel passed off quite well at the moment. Later on I heard that some people had been offended. They could not feel that any virtue should be recognised in an enemy leader. This churlishness is a well-known streak in human nature, but contrary to the spirit in which a war is won, or a lasting peace established.[69]

It is an example of Churchill at his most disingenuous brilliant best, for it deliberately ignored the cogent and penetrating arguments made as a result of his original comment by belittling them as nothing but churlishness. It also allowed him to make a subliminal reference to the 'moral' of his history, *In Victory: Magnanimity*, while implying his great foresight and good sense about the post-war world, for in reminding his readers about his tribute to Rommel, he was also making a comment about the contemporary role of West Germany.

As has been seen, the new West German government and Afrika Korps veterans were not slow to make capital out of Rommel. Encouraged by the thaw brought about by Young's biography and subsequent film version, by October 1951 veterans were able to hold a formal ceremony to honour Rommel at his grave.[70] Other memorials and monuments followed. Two barracks were named in his honour, as were two ships of the German navy, a plaque has been placed on his house, and his death mask is housed in a military museum. The high regard in which Rommel was held allowed his former colleague, General Crüwell, to use an Afrika Korps reunion to make an impassioned plea for the total rehabilitation of West Germany. Speaking a fortnight before the release of *Desert Fox* in September 1951, he told veterans that West Germany should be rearmed fully, but reassured outside audiences that it was in order to allow the nation to play its role in the protection of peace in co-operation with its allies. More controversially, he received generous applause for openly questioning the legality and morality of continuing Field Marshal Kesselring's imprisonment without trial before a neutral court.[71] The presence of large numbers of British and Commonwealth servicemen at these gatherings throughout the fifties and sixties created an atmosphere of political neutrality and thus provided safe conditions for West Germans to express sentiments that might cause disquiet if aired elsewhere.

Unsurprisingly, *Desert Fox* proved a great success in both West Germany and Austria. As with the 1956 *Battle of the River Plate*, Germans flocked to see sympathetic portrayals of their uniformed countrymen.[72] The film also helped the new West German film industry find a method of dealing with the conundrum of maintaining an anti-communist position while dealing with the Nazi past. *Desert Fox* and *The Battle of the River Plate* therefore became the model for early West

German war films such as *The Devil's General* (1955) and *The Jackboot Mutiny* (1955). The former was based on an air-force general (the character is a mix of Kesselring and Rommel) who eventually becomes disillusioned with Nazism, while the latter was directed by the celebrated G.W. Pabst. The film explores the July 1944 plot to assassinate Hitler and concentrates on General von Beck's leadership of the plotters. Both films therefore depicted the German officer class coming to its senses and rediscovering true honour and dignity. This opened the way for other celebrations of German heroics in *The Star of Africa* (1957) and *Lieutenant Commander Prien* (1958).[73] However, not all were prepared to accept these interpretations. The East German and Russian Communist parties encouraged West Germans and Austrians to protest against *Desert Fox*, ostensibly as a glorification of Nazism, but implicitly as an attempt to destabilise the two states and befog the issue of rearmament. The British *Daily Worker* referred to the screenings in West Berlin as 'the latest American move to prepare the minds of West German people for war'.[74] In Vienna, where the victorious powers existed in uneasy condominium, the Russians deployed officers in uniform outside the cinema screening *Desert Fox*. Passers-by were stopped and questioned as to whether they intended to see the film. It was a clear act of intimidation, which was supplemented by the transporting of communist sympathisers who demonstrated against the film for three consecutive nights and clashed with Austrian police trying to ensure free access to the cinema.[75] The disturbances in Vienna represent a significant illustration of Rommel's importance as a political symbol in the new Europe.

It is a significance that has not yet disappeared. In the 1970s Manfred Rommel rose to fame as a local politician in Hamburg and in 1982 became the city's mayor on behalf of the Christian Democratic Party. The British and American press commented on his essential decency and integrity and implied that he shared such attributes with his illustrious father.[76] Success in Hamburg then led most to speculate as to whether he would make the step into national politics, and once again it was felt that his family traits might assist him if he adopted such a path. *The Times* noted that 'he has been widely praised for his modesty, realism and willingness to listen to all points of view, which, together with the reputation at home and abroad of his father, would place him in a strong position'.[77] According to this view, like his father, Manfred was the ideal (West) German.

The fall of the Berlin Wall in 1989, the reunification process in the 1990s and the opening up of more archival sources have allowed Germans to re-examine the role of Rommel in the Second World War. Works that have appeared since the 1990s have tended to emphasise his propaganda value to the Nazi state, his relationship with Hitler and to examine more closely his attitudes towards Nazism. This approach was summed up most fully in works such as Maurice Philip Remy's *The Rommel Myth* (2002) and Ralf Georg Reuth's article, 'Erwin Rommel: propaganda creation' in Enrico Syring's edited collection, *The Military Elite of the Third Reich* (1997). However, the extent to which these works will ever overcome the image so deeply entrenched in the American, British and German popular imagination is highly debatable.

Rommel therefore continues to be an icon: he is presented as the paragon of military skill and its concomitant sense of military honour and chivalry. The image of Rommel created by the Nazis has been eclipsed by that created by the Americans and British. It was a process which commenced during the war and was subtly altered in the post-war years. During the years of conflict, Rommel became a by-word for German military efficiency for the British and Americans, but it was not an uncritical admiration. Certain British journalists and MPs used him as a stick with which to beat the government and army. They saw in Rommel not an invincible foe, but one who showed the British army the qualities it was missing. In the post-war years elements of the original Anglo-American image were reshaped in order to make him a role model for West Germans. Rommel's life was recast as a parable which could be used to comfort and energise West Germans. It was comforting in that it presented a decent, honourable man who did what he thought was right for his country, but remained aloof from the dark side of Nazism. It was energising in its promise that the Americans and British accepted this tale as an explanation of most Germans' behaviour and were prepared to view them as equals in the new struggle for freedom in Europe. Rommel, his men and their campaigns have been depoliticised, removed from their context and presented instead as praiseworthy models of warfare. In a post-war world haunted by the death camps, insurgency and counter-insurgency campaigns, and the shadow of indiscriminate nuclear warfare, such a vision was (and is) romantic and attractive. Rommel's myth has proved remarkably resilient; it resists all academic attempts to contextualise and explain his

## 176  Rommel: A Reappraisal

strengths and weaknesses. His entire career can be portrayed as a triumph of myth-making by both Nazis and the western Allies, but the power and popularity of that image cannot be denied.

### Notes

1. See Ralf Georg Reuth, *Goebbels: The life of the Mephistophelean genius of Nazi propaganda* (London: Constable, 1995), pp. 285-86, 302-09, 320.
2. Ward Rutherford, *The Biography of Field Marshal Erwin Rommel* (Greenwich, CT: Bison Books, 1981), p. 97.
3. Rutherford, *Rommel*, p.161.
4. *Daily Mirror*, 28 January 1942.
5. *Daily Mirror*, 28 February 1942.
6. *The Times*, 21 February 1942.
7. *Daily Mirror*, 22 June 1942.
8. *Daily Mirror*, 22 June 1942.
9. House of Commons debates, 2 July 1942, vol. 381, cc. 527 – 611; *Collier's Weekly*, 22 August 1942.
10. House of Lords debates, 1 October 1942, vol. 124, cc. 461 – 511. See also the rather arch comments made about this episode in the *New Yorker* magazine, 10 October 1942.
11. *New York Times*, 4 June 1942.
12. *Time*, 12 April 1943.
13. *New York Times*, 15 April 1943.
14. *New York Times*, 6 February 1944.
15. House of Commons debates, 27 January 1942, vol. 377, cc. 569 – 690.
16. *Daily Mirror*, 28 January 1942.
17. *Daily Mirror*, 14 February 1942.
18. *Daily Mirror*, 3 July 1944.
19. For a study of this process see, Arthur L. Smith, *The War for the German Mind. Re-educating Hitler's Soldiers* (Providence, RI: Berghahn, 1996).
20. Desmond Young, *Try Anything Twice* (London: Hamish Hamilton, 1963), pp. 343-59.
21. Quoted in Myra Cross, 'The Depiction of Germans in British Films: how it changes, how far such changes reflect government policy and public opinion' (Unpublished PhD thesis, Open University, 2009).
22. Desmond Young, *Rommel* (London: Collins, 1950), pp. 52-53, 58-61, 219-41.
23. *Illustrated London News*, 4 February 1950.
24. Churchill College Cambridge, Lewin Mss, RLEW 1/5, *Daily Telegraph* clipping, 1968.
25. David Irving, *The Trail of the Fox: The Life of Field Marshal Erwin Rommel* (London: Weidenfeld and Nicolson, 1977), pp. 22-23.

26. *The Times*, 14 March 1985.
27. David Fraser, *Knight's Cross. A Life of Field Marshal Erwin Rommel* (London: HarperCollins, 1993), pp. 131-32, Chapter 5 'Soldier without Politics', pp. 81-99. It could be argued that the interest in Rommel's political beliefs in the populist historiography has its academic parallel in the debate over what Michael Geyer has called the 'idealist' and 'technician' schools of German military thought in the inter-war period. See Michael Geyer, 'German Strategy in the age of machine warfare, 1914-1945' in Peter Paret (ed.), *Makers of Modern Strategy from Machiavelli to the Nuclear Age* (Princeton, N.J.: Princeton University Press, 1986), pp. 527-97; and Azar Gat, *A History of Military Thought. From the Enlightenment to the Cold War* (Oxford: Oxford University Press, 2001), pp. 608-21.
28. Young, *Rommel*, pp. 26-27.
29. Irving, *Trail*, p. 6..
30. Heinz W. Schmidt, *With Rommel in the Desert* (London: George C. Harrap and Co, 1951), p. 71.
31. Young, *Rommel*, pp. 24-25, 141.
32. B.H. Liddell Hart (ed. With Lucie-Marie Rommel, Manfred Rommel and General Fritz Bayerlein), *The Rommel Papers* (London: Collins, 1953), p. xv.
33. Wolf Heckmann, *Rommel's War in Africa* (London: Granada, 1981), p. 19.
34. Fraser, *Knight's Cross*, p. 240.
35. Young, *Rommel*, p. 135.
36. Heckmann, *Rommel's War*, p. 19.
37. For critics, see Douglas Porch, *Hitler's Mediterranean Gamble. The North African and the Mediterranean Campaigns in World War II* (London: Weidenfeld and Nicolson, 2004); and Martin Kitchen, *Rommel's Desert War: Waging World War II in North Africa, 1940-1943* (Cambridge: Cambridge University Press, 2009).
38. Heckmann, *Rommel's War*, p. 17.
39. Fraser, *Knight's Cross*, pp. 237-38, 562.
40. Young, *Rommel*, p. 10.
41. Irving, *Trail*, p. 4.
42. Quoted in Young, *Rommel*, p 148.
43. *The World at War*, Episode Eight, 'The Desert: North Africa, 1940-1943'.
44. *The Times*, 23 October 1975.
45. *The Times*, 19 September 1953.
46. *The Times*, 1 October 1956.
47. See James Chapman, *The British at War. Cinema, State and Propaganda, 1939-1945* (London: I.B. Tauris, 1998), pp. 164, 166.
48. Schmidt, *With Rommel*, p. 21.
49. Correlli Barnett, *The Desert Generals* (London: William Kimber, 1960), p. 21.
50. *The World at War*, Episode Eight.
51. Liddell Hart, *Rommel Papers*, pp. xiv-xv.
52. Irving, *Trail*, pp. 410-11.
53. Fraser, *Knight's Cross*, p. 3.

54. Young, *Try Anything*, pp. 343-59.
55. *Daily Mirror*, 19 February 1951.
56. *The Times*, 22, 25 April 1953.
57. Heckmann, *Rommel's War*, p. 17.
58. *Illustrated London News*, 8 September 1951.
59. Young, *Try Anything*, p. 356; Cross, 'Depiction of Germans', p. 269.
60. *Picturegoer*, 17 November 1951.
61. *Observer*, 14 October 1951; *The Times*, 10 October 1951.
62. House of Commons debates, 29 November 1951, vol. 494, cc. 169; *East London Advertiser*, 30 November 1951.
63. *Daily Worker*, 26 November 1951.
64. *The Times*, 17 November 1951; *New York Times*, 4 November 1951.
65. *Sight and Sound*, 1 January 1952; *Daily Telegraph*, 23 January 1950.
66. House of Commons debates, 29 April 1953, vol. 514 cc. 2153 – 2157.
67. *Daily Mirror*, 30 April 1953.
68. See John Ramsden, *Don't Mention the War: the British and the Germans since 1890* (London: Little Brown, 2006), pp. 266-67.
69. Winston S. Churchill, *The Second World War*, Vol. IV, 'The Hinge of Fate' (London: Cassell, 1951), p. 59.
70. *New York Times*, 19 October 1951.
71. *The Times, Daily Mirror*, 17 September 1951. Doubts about the trials of German alleged war criminals were by no means confined to West Germans. American and British legal experts were often sensitive over the proceedings at Nuremburg and elsewhere. In 1957 the British jurist, M.R.T. Paget, published *Manstein: His Campaigns and His Trial* (London: Collins). Paget had defended Manstein at his trial and his book expressed his severe doubts over the robustness of the proceedings. The publication of such works reveals how open British society was to the issue of West German rehabilitation in the 1950s, even if significant minorities held qualms.
72. For the success of *Desert Fox* in West Germany see *New York Times*, 23 August 1952. Michael Powell's and Emeric Pressburger's *The Battle of the River Plate* contained a highly sympathetic portrayal of the *Admiral Graf Spee*'s commander, Captain Hans Langsdorff, played by Peter Finch. See John Ramsden 'Refocusing "The People's War"': British War Films of the 1950s', *Journal of Contemporary History*, vol. 33, no. 1, 1998, pp. 35-64.
73. See James Chapman, *War and Film* (London: Reaktion, 2008), pp. 145-49.
74. *Daily Worker*, 19 January 1952.
75. *The Times*, 20 September 1952.
76. See *New York Times*, 3 February 1978; *Daily Mirror*, 31 January 1975, 1 August 1978.
77. *The Times*, 10 November 1982.

# Select Bibliography

Fraser, David, *Knight's Cross: A Life of Field Marshal Erwin Rommel* (London: Harper Collins, 1994).
Heckmann, Wolf, *Rommel's War in Africa* (London: Granada, 1981).
Irving, David, *The Trail of the Fox: The Life of Field-Marshal Erwin Rommel* (London: Weidenfeld & Nicolson, 1966).
Kitchen, Martin, *Rommel's Desert War: Waging World War Two in North Africa, 1940-43* (Cambridge: Cambridge University Press, 2009).
Lewin, Ronald, *Rommel as Military Commander* (London: Batsford, 1968).
Liddell Hart, B.H., *The Rommel Papers* (London: Collins, 1953).
Major, Patrick, '"Our Friend Rommel": The Wehrmacht as "Worthy Enemy" in Post-war British Popular Culture', *German History* 26 (2008), pp. 520-35.
Marshall, Charles, *Discovering the Rommel Murder: The Life and Death of the Desert Fox* (Mechanicsburg, PA: Stackpole Books, 1994).
Mitcham, Samuel, *The Desert Fox in Normandy: Rommel's Defence of Fortress Europe* (Westport, CT: Praeger, 1997).
Remy, Maurice, *Mythos Rommel* (Berlin: List, 2007) 2nd Edition.
Reuth, Ralf Georg, *Rommel: The End of a Legend* (London: Haus Books, 2005).
Rommel, Erwin, *Infantry Attacks* (London: Greenhill Books, 2006).
Ruge, Friedrich, *Rommel in Normandy: Reminiscences* (San Rafael, CA: Presidio Press, 1979).
Speidel, Hans, *Invasion 1944: Rommel and the Normandy Campaign* (Chicago: Henry Regnery, 1950).
Watson, Bruce Allen, *Exit Rommel: The Tunisian Campaign, 1942-43* (Westport, CT: Praeger, 1999).
Wilks, John, and Wilks, Eileen, *Rommel and Caporetto* (Barnsley: Leo Cooper, 2001).
Young, Desmond, *Rommel* (London: Collins, 1950).

# Index

Africa  4, 60, 62–4, 66–8, 70–1, 73–5, 79, 83, 88, 109–10, 113, 115, 118, 121, 125, 129–30, 149–51, 158, 167–8, 174, 177, 179
Afrika Korps  4, 7, 64–5, 68–71, 73–80, 84–5, 90, 92–3, 95–6, 99–101, 104, 106, 108, 158, 164, 167–70, 172–3
Alam el Halfa  99–100, 104, 111
Alamein  1, 4, 6, 90–7, 101, 104–7, 109, 112, 161
Allies  5, 31, 41, 115–16, 118, 121–2, 124, 126, 128, 130–3, 146, 149, 151, 155
Army Group A  31, 37, 42, 57
Army Group B  37, 41, 115–18, 121, 123, 130, 135, 143, 147–8, 150, 156
Army Group G  122, 130, 134
Arras  3, 37–40, 49–51, 53, 55
Atlantic Wall  119–22, 130–1
Auchinleck, Field Marshal  1, 4, 8, 73–5, 77, 83, 90, 94–5, 110, 166
Australian Division  69, 94, 105
Avesnes  34, 36
Avesnes Raid  37, 47, 49, 53, 55
Balkans  5, 115
Barbarossa, operation  73
Bastico, General  74, 88
Belgium  31
Berlin  4, 6, 13, 24, 28–9, 55, 58, 64, 99, 105, 113, 135–6, 141, 145, 148, 150, 179
Bir Hacheim  84–6

bomb plot  1, 6, 9, 137, 139, 141, 143–5, 147, 149, 151, 153, 155
Britain  1, 7–8, 60, 70, 157, 171–2
British forces  4–5, 66, 69, 77, 81, 86, 89, 109, 125, 159–62, 175
Cerfontaine  34, 56
Channel Ports  40, 57–8
Cherbourg  3, 46–7, 51–2, 54
Churchill, Winston  73–4, 83, 172–3
Cotentin Peninsula  46
Crüwell, General  74–8, 173
Cunningham, Lieut Gen  74, 76–7
Cyrenaica  66, 68, 71, 73, 78–9, 81, 83
D-Day  120–1, 123–4, 127, 130, 134
Dresden  3, 15, 28
Eastern Front  60, 117, 119, 141–2, 148, 152, 155
Egypt  60, 67, 70, 83, 89–94, 96–8, 104, 107, 109, 159
Eighth Army  4, 74–5, 78, 81, 83–96, 99–102, 104–5, 107–9
  advancing  109
  exhausted  94
  Headquarters  85
  positions  90, 92
El Agheila  65, 79, 83
El Alamein  90, 92, 94, 96–7, 101, 106–7, 161
France  3, 5, 30, 56–8, 60, 65, 67, 117, 119, 126, 128–9, 137, 140,

145–6, 148, 150, 152–3, 157–8, 162
Gazala  78, 83, 90–1, 94, 99
German Army  19, 27, 47, 62–3, 70, 133–4, 136
  forces  4, 65, 86, 94, 108, 128, 148, 153
  High Command  79
  officers  7–8, 11, 14, 16, 60, 77, 123, 139, 143, 151, 154
  Sixth Army  5
Germany  4, 9, 12–14, 22, 26, 28, 60, 62, 65, 69, 73, 79, 101–2, 115, 117, 121, 123, 129, 131, 139–41, 143, 146, 149, 154, 158, 163, 167, 171–2
Givenchy  48
Goebbels, Joseph  9, 18, 20, 60, 72–3, 101, 109, 113, 117–18, 127, 132–3, 135, 157–8, 160, 164, 168–9, 176
Guderian, General  7, 34, 51, 56, 58, 78, 99, 156
Halder, General  4, 37, 57, 62–3, 70–1, 80
Halfaya Pass  71–2
Hamburg  8, 29, 145, 174
Hilsen Ridge  11
Himmler, Heinrich  9, 20
Hitler, Adolf  1, 3–6, 9–11, 13–29, 31, 34, 37, 40, 54–5, 59–60, 62–4, 73, 78, 80, 88, 94, 99, 101–2, 104, 107–9, 112–13, 115–17, 119, 121, 123–9, 132, 134–42, 144–7, 149–56, 158, 161, 163–4, 166, 171–2, 174–7
Italian forces  2, 62, 76, 108, 115–16, 129

Italy  6, 62, 113, 115–17, 129
Jodl, General  109, 115, 126, 133
Kesselring, Field Marshal  5, 27, 81, 83, 88, 91, 100, 115–17, 173–4
Kolovrat Ridge  2
Le Cateau  36–7, 51, 53
Le Havre  43, 45
Leipzig  29
Libya  4, 60, 62–3, 66–8, 109–10, 159
Light Division  30, 62–3, 65–9, 93, 105–6
London  6, 26–7, 29, 55–9, 79–80, 110–12, 118, 132–5, 155, 176–9
Luftwaffe  31, 54, 62, 81, 91–3, 97–8, 115, 119, 127, 153
Maginot Line  31, 34, 36–7, 41–2, 50
Malaya  81, 159
Malta  75, 81, 83, 88, 91–2, 97–8
Mediterranean  62, 64, 73, 79–80, 97
Mersa Matruh  90, 92
Middle East  1, 4, 65, 70, 111
Monte Matajur  3
Montgomery, General  4–5, 99, 101, 105, 111, 128, 148, 161–2
Munich  15, 25, 27–8, 55, 132–3
Mussolini, Benito  60–2, 79, 88, 115
National Socialists  9, 15, 17–19, 26, 149
Nazi Germany  139–40, 142, 154, 157
Nazis  1, 3, 7, 9, 11, 13, 15–17,

19–21, 23, 25, 27–9, 163, 171–3, 175–6
Nazism 7–8, 10, 134, 141, 162–4, 168, 171, 174–5
Normandy campaign 5, 7–8, 121, 123, 126–8, 129–34, 144, 151, 155, 160, 162, 179
North Africa 4, 60, 63, 70–1, 75, 79, 83, 88, 109–10, 113, 115, 118, 121, 125, 130, 149–51, 158, 167, 177
NSDAP (Nazi Party) 10–11, 15–16, 20, 26, 164, 171
panzers 4, 25, 30–4, 36–43, 45–52, 54–6, 59, 63, 67–9, 72, 76–8, 83–9, 91–102, 104–9, 111, 116, 122–5, 131, 134
Paris 6, 41, 43, 56–8, 122, 124, 140, 142
Polish campaign 23–5, 30–1
Potsdam 18, 29
prisoners 36–7, 47, 87, 130, 166
River Plate 173, 178
Romania 2, 11
Rome 5, 64, 116–17
Rouen 43
Ruge, Vice Admiral 8, 130, 133, 136, 138, 141–2, 179
Second World War 1, 7, 11, 14, 19, 23, 27, 58, 60, 79, 81, 111, 121, 132, 154, 157, 175, 178
Sidi Barrani 61
Sidi Rezegh 76–8
Somme 37, 41–2, 52
Speidel, Hans 6, 8–9, 27, 123, 133, 136, 138–9, 141–8, 150, 154–6, 179

St Valéry 45–6, 53–4
Stosslinie 51
Strölin, Dr 145–6
Stuttgart 3, 13, 57, 132–5
tanks 7, 25, 31, 36, 38–41, 47, 64–5, 72, 74, 83–5, 89, 91, 93, 98–9, 104, 106–7
Third Reich 8–9, 16, 19, 26, 62, 117, 132, 175
Tobruk 4, 62, 69–72, 75–6, 78, 83, 85, 87, 90–2, 97, 104, 159–60
Totenkopf Division 38–9, 53
Tripoli 4, 62–5, 67, 75, 81
Vernon 46
Versailles Treaty 12, 15, 18, 26
Vienna 174
von Kluge, Field Marshal 6, 32, 37, 54, 127, 132, 135–6, 144, 148, 150–3, 156
von Rundstedt, Field Marshal 5–6, 31, 34, 40, 78, 118–19, 125–7, 132–3, 146, 155–6
von Schweppenburg, Leo Geyr 5, 7, 9, 27–8, 118–19, 122, 124–7, 131–2
von Shirach, Baldur 18, 20–1, 29
von Stülpnagel, General 6, 140–7, 152
Washington 88–9, 110, 156
Wavell, Field Marshal 8, 65, 71, 73
Wehrmacht 18–20, 24, 29, 102, 121–2, 132, 135, 154, 179
West Germany 172–3
Wiener Neustadt 22–3, 113
Württemberg 2, 10, 15